INTRODUCTION TO PHILOSOPHY

INTRODUCTION TO PHILOSOPHY

Dirk H. T. Vollenhoven

Edited by
John H. Kok and Anthony Tol

Dordt College Press

Published with permission of the D.H.Th. Vollenhoven Foundation

Translated from the Dutch by John H. Kok.
See *Isagoge Philosophiae: Introduction to Philosophy* (Dordt College Press, 2005) for the text in its original language. ISBN 978-0-932914-63-7

Copyright © 2005 by John H. Kok
Fragmentary portions of this book may be freely used by those who are interested in sharing the author's insights and observations, so long as the material is not pirated for monetary gain and so long as proper credit is visibly given to the publisher and the author. Others, and those who wish to use larger sections of text, must seek written permission from the publisher.

Printed in the United States of America.

Dordt College Press www.dordt.edu/dordt_press
498 Fourth Avenue NE
Sioux Center, Iowa 51250
United States of America

ISBN: 978-0-932914-65-1

The Library of Congress Cataloging-in-Publication Data is on file with the Library of Congress, Washington, D.C.
Library of Congress Control Number: **2005931478**

Editors' note

The editors brought together work for which each has primary responsibility.

J.K. provided the translation. Extensive use of his draft versions over the years provided opportunity to experiment with variant formulations of Vollenhoven's distinct use of the Dutch language. He wishes to thank Al Wolters for his translating help early on—it was the early 1980s—and numerous Dordt College students who helped him know better where the translation continued to lack clarity.

A.T. was able to provide a definitive version of the Dutch text through his research on the genealogy of Vollenhoven's text. He wishes to thank Kornelis A. Bril for his continuous interest in the project and his unfailing encouragement and support. And a special thanks to Jan de Koning, who shared with me his notes and his experiences as a classroom user of the *Isagoge* in 1942–1943, more than half a century later, thereby contributing to our knowledge of the effect the Vollenhoven text had in the classroom setting.

Through email contact, the editors were able to undo the divide of continents. In close cooperation they worked together to ensure that the text and the translation would have optimal agreement.

The layout of these pages is identical to that of *Isagoge Philosophiae: Introduction to Philosophy* (Dordt College Press, 2005), which includes the full Dutch text.

Finally, we wish to thank the Vollenhoven Foundation for permission to publish *Isagôgè Philosophiae*.

John H. Kok
Anthony Tol

Contents

Preface i
    Calvin Seerveld

Foreword iii
    Anthony Tol

Isagôgè Philosophiae / Introduction to Philosophy 1

  Introduction: The Place of Philosophy in the Cosmos
                     and its Task... 9
  Part I   The Diversity and Connection of the
               Determinants of the Heavenly Subject 19
  Part II   The Diversity and Connection of the
               Determinants of the Earthly Subject 21
  Part III   The Connection between Heaven and Earth 103

APPENDIX 107
A Number of the More Complicated Questions of Philosophy
  Part I   Human Knowing 108
  Part II   The Theory about Know-how and Technology 139
  Part III   The Theory about Art and Aesthetics 142

Index of Terms 147

Index of Names 163

Preface

This good English translation, based on a researched critical Dutch edition, of Vollenhoven's text, *Introduction to Philosophy*, presents a cornerstone of theory in philosophical reflection germinated at the Free University of Amsterdam during the past three generations. All those foreigners like myself who spent years in doctoral study there with Vollenhoven, Zuidema, Dooyeweerd, Mekkes, K.J. Popma and Van Riessen, cut our Dutch teeth on this primordial, skeletal text. It had a confusing simplicity, a lingual scrupulosity, and quiet biblical earnestness that both captivated and frustrated us early North Americans who were in a hurry to become christian philosophical thinkers. Vollenhoven takes time to be understood.

The fact that Dirk H. Th. Vollenhoven was a pastor of a congregation and wrote a Ph.D. dissertation on the philosophy of mathematics gives an indication of the range and stature of the man who began to teach **systematic philosophy** at the university in the faith-thought tradition of Abraham Kuyper. Vollenhoven's *Introduction to Philosophy* is a **philosophical** text; it is not worldviewy. Vollenhoven has a chaste love to be exact in word precision when he writes philosophy. His meticulous prose is not colorful. A good teacher of this introductory text will fill out its terse distinctions with concrete life examples. And if one makes the effort to follow slowly and plumb the visionary wisdom in Vollenhoven's conceptual leadership, the result is a humbled redemptive orientation in the philosophical task.

Other building blocks Vollenhoven, with colleagues, offered toward construction of an on-going Scripturally directed christian philosophy are now also available in the English language. They are mentioned in the fine introduction to this volume by Anthony Tol. My hope is that many christian college instructors, who may be looking for a radically Bible-true (but not biblicistic) effort to give a new generation of students good direction for thinking through matters in their varied disciplines, will examine this basic introductory text. For those who are able to be patient to do justice to Vollenhoven's slowly unfolding analysis of the creatural world we inhabit, which belongs to

God revealed in Jesus Christ, there is a surprise coming: the blessing which makes one thankful that our local stories and philosophical reflections can share in the certain, enduring, worldwide promise of the Lord's Rule acoming in God's historically troubled but well-ordered creation.

    Calvin Seerveld, emeritus
    Institute for Christian Studies, Toronto
    July 2005

Foreword

The publication of Vollenhoven's *Introduction to Philosophy* is an important step forward in making the work of the Protestant-Christian Dutch philosopher, Dirk H. Th. Vollenhoven (1892–1978), more generally available. While the text does not fully summarize his whole thought at the time it was written nor adequately represent his later thought, it nevertheless touches on the central themes of his thought. It has a unique place in his *oeuvre*, both in its content and its style. No serious study in Vollenhoven can afford to ignore this text.

Besides illuminating the thought of its author, the text also reflects in many ways the context in which it arose. Vollenhoven worked at the Free University of Amsterdam, and at that university he, along with his brother-in-law, Herman Dooyeweerd (1894–1977), initiated a development in philosophy usually referred to as *Reformational philosophy*. The text portrays something of the atmosphere of the Free University in the 1930s and 1940s. Thus, this publication will also help the reader gain a better view of Dutch (Neo-)Calvinism in the twentieth century, particularly as this concerns the Free University in the *interbellum* period. In this introduction, we shall concentrate on the context in which the text arose and the goals that Vollenhoven hoped to achieve with it. It is through the context of this work that the peculiarities of its content and style find their explanation. We shall end with a discussion of some select features of the text.

Philosophy at the Free University of Amsterdam

The text of this *Introduction to Philosophy* arose in the context of Vollenhoven's teaching duties. When he was appointed professor of philosophy at the Free University of Amsterdam in the fall of 1926—the first full-time appointment in philosophy since the university's founding in 1880—Vollenhoven's duties included teaching a course on the main contours of philosophy and a survey course in the history of philosophy. Both courses were required courses for all first-year students. The present text is the syllabus, in its most developed form, of the first of these two courses.[1]

The requirement of philosophy had everything to do with the distinct character of the Free University. When founded, the university committed itself to the pursuit of academic goals in the light of a Reformed understanding of humankind, the world, and history. To secure an academic counterweight to humanism, scientistic worldviews, and speculative history, the university expressed its explicit commitment to "Reformed-Calvinist principles." The university hoped that, in time, both its own community and academia at large would be served as the example of an academic pursuit of knowledge based on Reformed-Calvinist principles took on more explicit form.

By disposition and training, Vollenhoven was an ideal candidate to develop a program of philosophy that would comply with the university's general aim. Before he accepted the university appointment, Vollenhoven had been a minister in the Reformed churches (Gereformeerde Kerken). This attests to his firm allegiance to the Reformed cause. But of more specific significance was that Vollenhoven had written a remarkable dissertation on the philosophy of mathematics from what he then called "a theistic point of view."[2] This work gave evidence of an impressive knowledge of the whole history of Western philosophy as well as a distinct ability to discern philosophical problems that lie buried in the foundations of mathematics. The courage and resolve shown by the young Vollenhoven in executing a *principled* investigation in this area, where the relevance of a *faith commitment* is not immediately evident, became exemplary of the kind of standards, regarding both personal qualities and the work

---

1. The syllabus offering an overview of the history of philosophy, entitled (in translation) "Short Survey of the History of Philosophy," is now available in English, in D. H. Th. Vollenhoven, *The Problem-Historical Method and the History of Philosophy*, ed. Kornelis A. Bril (Amsterdam: De Zaak Haes, 2005).
2. D. H. Th. Vollenhoven, *De Wijsbegeerte der Wiskunde van Theïstisch Standpunt* (Amsterdam: Van Soest, 1918). Vollenhoven soon regretted the use of the adjective *theistic*, because he found this in practice to be ambiguous. The last chapter of this dissertation, titled *The thetical part*, has been translated by John H. Kok; cf. his *Vollenhoven: His Early Development* (Sioux Center: Dordt College Press, 1992), 308–53. Kok's work contains a detailed discussion of Vollenhoven's dissertation.

achieved, that the Free University wished to promote.³

When Vollenhoven accepted the chair of philosophy, there was no existing philosophy program at the Free University.⁴ Various professors, such as Abraham Kuyper, Jan Woltjer, Wilhelm Geesink, Herman Bavinck, and (especially) Hendrik J. Pos,⁵ interspersed their lectures with philosophical themes of their own choosing. Vollenhoven had to set up a program from scratch; hence, it took a few years before he had developed his first-year courses to the point of meeting his specific goals. By 1930, his notes on the main contours of his philosophical position were sufficiently rounded out to enable them to be mimeographed as syllabi for student use. He gave it the title *Isagôgè Philosophiae,* which means "Introduction to Philosophy." From that time on, a syllabus has been available, even up to the present time, though the text underwent many revisions in the subsequent years until 1945, when Vollenhoven ceased working on it.

Isagôgè Philosophiae and the university's goals

The text of the *Isagoge*—Vollenhoven's preferred working title of this syllabus—attempts to meet different goals. There is, to start with, the context of the university, in particular its distinct "Reformed-Calvinist foundation."

The Free University was founded by the multitalented and influential Abraham Kuyper (1837–1920). Calvinism had taken firm root in the Netherlands, and Kuyper gave Calvinism in the Netherlands a

---

3. Vollenhoven's thesis played a prominent role in the early years of the Faculty of Mathematics and Natural Science of the Free University, when this faculty opened its doors in 1930. Cf. H. Blauwendraad, *Worsteling naar waarheid. De opkomst van Wiskunde en Informatica aan de VU* [*Wrestling for Truth: The Rise of Mathematics and Information Science at the Free University*] (Zoetermeer: Meinema, 2004); cf. especially Chapter 2.
4. In 1926, the Free University had only three faculties, a Faculty of Theology, a Faculty of Law, and a Faculty of Classical Languages. Philosophy was a section of the latter faculty. Philosophy became an independent faculty only in 1964—a year after Vollenhoven's retirement—when a change, in 1963, in the legislation regarding higher education made this possible.
5. Vollenhoven mentions the first four names in his article on "Calvinistic philosophy" in the *Oosthoek Encyclopedie*, 4th edition, 1953. H. J. Pos, a linguist, also had definite philosophical interests. In 1932, he left the Free University for the University of Amsterdam, where he accepted an appointment in philosophy.

new *élan* in terms of what he called "sphere sovereignty." This was a religiously motivated view of society, in which the social "spheres" of family, business, school, jurisprudence, state, church, and so on are each seen as divinely endowed with the responsibility of regulating its own affairs, without one sphere encroaching upon another. This multiple responsibility implies division of power. This fits in with the Christian confession of *divine* sovereignty having authority over all of life and calling for human responsibility in all of its walks. But as Dutch national life became increasingly influenced by Enlightenment ideals and modernistic humanism—and the dominance of the state that these developments brought with it—the acknowledgment of divine sovereignty in national life eroded. Accordingly, the Calvinist sector felt the need to counter this effect in the social spheres in terms of a more principled view of responsibility, which Kuyper formulated as "sphere sovereignty." As applied to education, Calvinist forebears had fought hard for the right to establish Christian schools that were free of state control. The establishment of a "free" university was the last step in this educational emancipation.[6]

The establishment of the Free University was, therefore, part of a movement in which Calvinism did not accept a limitation to an ecclesiastical identity, but became aware of itself as implying a broader and distinct "worldview." In practice, Calvinism found its main support among "Calvinist believers," in other words, those who belonged to Calvinist churches, though in theory it could be supported by all who were attracted to the pluralistic form of societal governance that this worldview upheld. Kuyper worked hard to effect this worldview of sphere sovereignty in Dutch national life. He initiated and ran a Christian-Calvinist press, formed a Christian labor union, and established an "antirevolutionary" political party. The founding of the Free University also brought academia within the sphere of influence of this Calvinist worldview.

Kuyper was fully aware that the Free University could only legitimate its existence in terms of a "foundation" that clarified where the

---

6. Sociologically, the implementation of sphere sovereignty resulted in an emancipation of the *kleine luyden* (simple folk of Calvinistic conviction). While there is certainly something to say for this, the more important factor is the freedom from state and ecclesiastical tutelage. The word *free* in "Free University" was chosen to indicate the freedom from both state and ecclesiastical domination that this university enjoys.

university stood in the world of learning. While this foundation would be consonant with the "Reformed confession" and openly affirm the Scriptures as having leading authority, it had also to contain (or imply) such principles as are relevant to academic learning and scientific research, and as are applicable to meeting the responsibilities of academic affairs with a view to their own nature and needs. This foundation was referred to as "the Reformed foundation" (*de Gereformeerde grondslag*). While most members of the Free University community had an intuitive awareness of the kind of principles involved, these principles were never actually spelled out. There was always a certain haze of uncertainty about them. There was a tendency, after Kuyper's death, to give theological pronouncements pride of place. Kuyper himself probably came the closest to explicating the intuitively felt principles in his Stone Lectures, six "Lectures on Calvinism," delivered at Princeton University in 1898.[7] There he presents Calvinism explicitly as a worldview, and in the fourth lecture he discusses "Calvinism and science." But while he forcefully argues that science always involves a faith commitment, of whatever signature, he does not settle the question as to the nature of the "Reformed foundation."

In developing his philosophy program for the Free University, Vollenhoven was expected to throw light on this matter; at least, philosophy at the Free University would have to rest on the foundation of Reformed principles and be a "Calvinistic philosophy." Vollenhoven openly chose the latter term as label for his philosophical endeavor, even though it invited misunderstandings. But anyone acquainted with the Kuyperian context of the Free University would understand that the adjective *Calvinistic* is not used here in reference to the sixteenth-century reformer personally, nor to suggest that philosophy is ancillary to Calvinistic theology, but rather—as will be argued below—to emphasize the relation, and hence also an implied

---

7. A. Kuyper, *Lectures on Calvinism* (Grand Rapids: Eerdmans, 1931). In the course of time, various reports were drafted, attempting to clarify the nature of the principles involved, but none proved to be satisfactory. In practice, in the 1930s to the 1950s, the work of Vollenhoven and Dooyeweerd was accepted by many as an application of the intended principles. But this never became official. In about 1970, a broadly formulated ecumenical "mission statement" replaced the "Reformed Foundation." A detailed description of the history of this discussion is in J. Roelink, *Een blinkend spoor* [*A Glittering Trail*] *1879–1979* (Kampen: Kok, 1979), 9–46.

difference, between philosophy and worldview.[8] Philosophy is here taken as *comporting with* the Calvinian-Kuyperian worldview, an acknowledgment of its "Sitz im Leben" (situation in life), without sacrificing genuine philosophical demands.

The philosophy program that Vollenhoven developed sought to effectuate a "reformation of philosophy." The term *reformation* is intentionally ambiguous. Vollenhoven wanted on the one hand to point to the tradition of the Reformation as forming the worldview context of his philosophical thought, and on the other hand to signal the internal difference in philosophy itself that would accrue when philosophy is informed by the Calvinian-Kuyperian tradition. In appealing to the Reformed tradition, in its Calvinian-Kuyperian strand,[9] Vollenhoven was able to put "Reformed principles" to work, not by assigning philosophy the task of routing them up and coming to their defense, but by showing how the historical tradition of the Reformation itself places *limitations* on philosophy. When one's "Sitz im Leben" is duly recognized, there is a sounding board for specifying what may and what may not be expected or demanded of philosophy when the context of the Reformed tradition functions as a presupposed context. It was in appealing to the living Reformed tradition

---

8. The term *Calvinistic philosophy* occurs only once in the *Isagoge*, but Vollenhoven wrote a major work under this flag, published as "Calvinism and the Reformation of Philosophy" in 1933. In its opening pages, he defends the choice of the term *Calvinistic* in connection with philosophy. The term *worldview*, or, as the Dutch prefer, *world and life view*, doesn't even occur in the *Isagoge* and is hardly encountered in Vollenhoven's earlier work. But in later publications, it becomes more than clear that Vollenhoven looks on Calvinism as a worldview. As to "Calvinistic philosophy," cf. D. H. Th. Vollenhoven, *Het Calvinism en de Reformatie van de Wijsbegeerte* (Amsterdam: Paris, 1933), 14–21; regarding "Calvinistic worldview," cf. "Schriftgebruik en wijsbegeerte" in A. Tol and K. A. Bril, *Vollenhoven als Wijsgeer* (Amsterdam: Buijten en Schipperheijn, 1992), 97–106. Both texts are translated in *A Vollenhoven Reader*, edited by John H. Kok (Dordt College Press, 2005).

9. N. Wolterstorff distinguishes, quite correctly, "two perspectives that have been prominent in the Calvinist tradition": the common-sense philosophy stemming from Thomas Reid in Scotland and neo-Calvinism in the Netherlands. Needless to say, Vollenhoven is a distinct representative of the latter. Cf. N. Wolterstorff, "Introduction," *Rationality and the Calvinian Tradition*, ed. H. Hart, J. van der Hoeven, and N. Wolterstorff (Lanham: University Press of America, 1983), vii.

that Vollenhoven put the Free University's identity to work.

To start with, philosophy is not a panacea for all human ills. Much traditional philosophy has overt, but also covert, redemptive aims, not least of all in such down-to-earth philosophies as Marxism and positivism. Such philosophies evince not only an alliance of philosophy with worldview matters, such as social struggle or technological innovation, but also bring secular religious motives into play. In the Calvinian-Kuyperian context of the Free University, religion is taken as standing on its own feet in the heartfelt acknowledgment of divine sovereignty in covenant relation with humankind. Philosophy is not to be a redemptive surrogate, either in covering over a religious lack or in being a secular substitute. The opening paragraphs of the *Isagoge* discuss the religious context as *prior* to philosophy.

In the second place, Vollenhoven did not assign to his program specifically apologetic or constructive aims. The defense of the faith is the direct responsibility of ecclesiastical institutions. There may be meaning in calling upon philosophy to give argumentative support to (or critique specific) statements of faith and forms of faith experience. But clearly, any subject matter that calls for defense or critique needs to be understood in terms of its own context before philosophy has anything to perform. (A translation in "secular" terms often amounts to setting up a "straw man.") The "life of faith" is one example, indeed an important one, of a sphere or "form of life" (to use Wittgenstein's phrase) that philosophy takes cognizance of. Philosophy builds no world except that of its own concepts and statements. It needs to be able to appeal to—namely, name, describe, explain, affirm, criticize, or deny—a world of activity and experience that we acknowledge as being our societal, cultural, and natural world. A worldview calls attention to this reality and elicits from it a primary interpretation.[10] It is at this level that Kuyper's "sphere sovereignty" is of importance. Philosophy may criticize, affirm, or suggest reform as to what goes on in the "life-world" of these spheres. But philosophy would overstep the bounds of credulity if it turned to dictating what ought and what ought not to take place there. Philosophy interacts with this concrete reality and, while it can discuss reflectively the

---

10. In "Levens-eenheid" [The Unity of Life] (1955), Vollenhoven speaks of "circumspective concepts" (*omramingsbegrippen*) in this regard; cf. A. Tol and K.A. Bril, *Vollenhoven als Wijsgeer*, 131; also *A Vollenhoven Reader*.

internal boundaries of the spheres of which concrete reality is composed, it does not take over the prime responsibility of a sphere nor legitimate its governance.[11]

There is a third delimiting factor that devolves upon philosophy. This factor is only indirectly related to the Reformed tradition; at least its direct motivation is less clear in Vollenhoven's work. It is the view that philosophy is for the most part concerned with the theory of knowing and its ontological underpinnings (cf. §6 of the *Isagoge*), so that, accordingly, the proper treatment of the problems of philosophy ought to be scientific in a general sense. In other words, philosophy, in the strict sense of the term, is a general science. It shares with the special sciences the characteristics of a science, and, together with the special sciences, philosophy is distinct from nonscientific matters, among which are religion and worldview matters (cf. §§9 and 10 of the *Isagoge*). Though philosophy is distinct from the latter, it still needs to reflect upon the matters of religion and worldview so as to be in proper comportment with them. That reflection would appear to be a reflection on the foundations of philosophy as general science.

An influential factor promoting this point of view would appear to stem from the factual historical context of the "current philosophy" of Vollenhoven's student days, namely the context of late nineteenth- and early twentieth-century philosophy. At that time, philosophy began to be "pulled apart" (decentralized) in three directions: (i) philosophy as a "strict science" (as in phenomenology [Edmund Husserl] and analytical philosophy [Bertrand Russell]), (ii) philosophy as a form of "social engagement" (as in socialist thought [Marx and Lenin]), and (iii) philosophy as "worldview interpretation" (as in hermeneutical historicism [Wilhelm Dilthey]). It is easy to imagine that for someone who reflects on this situation and takes his or her cue from the Reformed tradition, philosophy as social engagement would not be an option—the practice of sphere sovereignty needs no direct guidance from philosophy—and that philosophy as "worldview interpretation" could be taken as confusing the religious moment,

---

11. In the opening paragraphs of the *Isagoge*, Vollenhoven discusses this matter in the terminology of "non-scientific knowing" (within a sphere) and the "scientific knowing" of philosophy; cf. especially §§9–11.

which is determinative for interpreting a worldview,¹² with the broad scope of philosophical thought. Only philosophy as a "strict science"—in other words, as concerned with questions pertaining to the (encyclopedia of the) sciences—remains a viable option.¹³ Vollenhoven's early philosophical preference for Henri Bergson and Henri Poincaré is in line with this alternative.¹⁴

These three delimiting influences on Vollenhoven's view and understanding of philosophy were consonant with the Free University's general position, at least as Vollenhoven understood this. The difference this was to make in the practice of philosophy will be touched on after we first indicate the impression that Vollenhoven's work has had on his public.

Isagôgè Philosophiae and its initial readers

The text of Vollenhoven's *Isagoge* also had to answer to the specific needs of the first-year students, who were required to study its content. Every teacher of "introductions" knows how challenging introductory courses can be. There is the constant dilemma of either speaking over the hearer's heads or simplifying the material to the point of falsifying it. Vollenhoven certainly did not want to be open to

---

12. The Dutch tend to see all worldviews as basically implying a religious or faith stance, which is probably why they prefer to speak of "world and life view." Dilthey's basic division of worldviews into artistic, religious, and philosophical types is not persuasive in the Dutch setting.
13. In this light, we can understand why Vollenhoven, early in his career, was open to the influence, as he later admitted, of the Marburg school of neo-Kantianism and Husserlian phenomenology. Both schools take philosophy as primarily serving a basic scientific-cognitive interest. Cf. D. H. Th. Vollenhoven, "Divergentierapport I" in A. Tol and K. A. Bril, *Vollenhoven als Wijsgeer*, 112. A statement from the opening discussion in Vollenhoven's dissertation is also telling in this regard: "Every topic in philosophy derives its importance from questions as to values, boundaries, and relations of the distinct sciences mutually" (*De Wijsbegeerte der Wiskunde van Theïstisch Standpunt*, 2).
14. Vollenhoven admits to "many points of agreement" with Bergson in his dissertation, in particular the various kinds of intuition (=intuitive knowing) in Bergson, as interpreted by H. Höffding. The chapter on Poincaré is basically affirmative, except for the latter's leaning towards conventionalism and pragmatism. Cf. *De Wijsbegeerte der Wiskunde van Theïstisch Standpunt*, 348–51 and 352–84.

the latter accusation. The constant reworking of the text is sufficient indication of his wanting to get it "just right." The opposite danger of being too difficult Vollenhoven tried to assuage in his own way.

Vollenhoven no doubt thought that by being brief and succinct, he would increase his chance of being clear and understood. At least he explains in the text that he in no way tries to be complete—indeed, that would have called for a major volume of philosophy. His self-expressed aim is "to indicate with words, as clearly as I can, the most important determinants and diversity that I discern in the cosmos, so that others may also see them" (§18).

It is a known fact that, despite Vollenhoven's efforts to be clear, only a small percentage of the students could grasp what he was teaching. A larger percentage could appreciate his effort, especially upon realizing that Vollenhoven's thought comported with the ideals of the university. The remaining students were left puzzled and perplexed—but also impressed! There is but slight evidence that the difficult work of Vollenhoven engendered disrespect. Indeed, Vollenhoven's reputation rose quickly. For many years, he was greatly honored for his insight and knowledge. And while his rhetorical and pedagogical skills were never strong, these were more than compensated for by his unassuming and ingenuous personality and by his general openness towards students and their circumstances. The fact that he cared for his hearers and their intellectual development itself stimulated the study of his work.

Vollenhoven's effort to be clear dictates the style of the *Isagoge*. The text develops at two levels. The first level is its organization, with its division into main parts and the progressively refined subdivisions of these parts. This organization tells its own story, for in fact the organization delineates the main features of Vollenhoven's "philosophical conception." One must be constantly aware as to "where one is" as reader, not only to stay on track, but also to be conscious of which part of the conception is under discussion.[15]

---

15. It is something of an enigma why almost every version of this text that was printed over the years lacked the visual aid of a table of contents. The re-typed version of 1967 did finally include such an overview, but by then the text no longer served as syllabus for a course. Without such an aid, the understanding of the text is greatly impaired.

The second level is that of the textual content. This "fills in" the architectonic framework. This content unfolds in a sequence of consecutively numbered paragraphs, each with its own section head that briefly indicates the content. The length of these paragraphs varies greatly, from a simple statement of six words to a disquisition of over 1,700 words. The text on the whole is marked by brevity and clarity, and, as one progresses, one cannot help noticing Vollenhoven's talent for combining beguiling simplicity with deep subtlety, sweeping generalization with careful distinction. However, there is no attempt to achieve a balance in the treatment of topics that are placed at the same level of distinction. For example, in treating the main distinction of the work, that between things heavenly and things earthly, the discussion of the first topic is confined to two pages (§§19–21), while the discussion of the second comprises the bulk of the work (§§22–136). This main text is rounded off with a discussion of the relation between things heavenly and things earthly, which, though it caps the entire discussion, is limited to what strictly needs to be said (§§137–140).

Many a reader today may feel, and not without reason, that Vollenhoven's way of "indicating what he saw" is marked by his time and place. The Free University of the 1930s and 1940s was a Reformed bastion. The vast majority of its students came from Reformed homes. Not only could Vollenhoven assume an affinity with the Reformed tradition—indeed, the students themselves would not have expected less—there was no need to specifically defend or explain it. Vollenhoven could suffice with a mere mention of its relevance as backdrop for the philosophical distinctions he wished to make. Readers who are not acquainted with this background—such as the growing population of students at the Free University after World War II—or those preferring a more ecumenical engagement could feel some estrangement with the "flavor" of this text.

Vollenhoven himself was aware of the theological climate he had to work in, in particular the element of scholastic intellectualism concerning matters of faith. (This, too, is a feature of the Reformed tradition, a feature that Vollenhoven much regretted.) This led him to be more reticent in his discussions of themes that touched on matters of scholastic dispute, such as the nature of the soul (cf. §§92–93) and Christology (§140), than he would perhaps otherwise have been.¹⁶ He placed more emphasis on religion, which he saw as man's living, practical, and intellectual dependence on God, and the implied acceptance of divine revelation. Vollenhoven's appeal to the Scriptures is very direct. No doubt this reflects genuine piety on his part. But it was also meant as antidote to the attitude of scholasticism.¹⁷ On the other hand, this appeal could give the impression of an almost positivistic reading of Scripture, lacking hermeneutical sensitivity within Vollenhoven's overall covenant understanding of the Christian religion. However, other sources indicate that Vollenhoven was definitely aware of—indeed he emphasized—the relevance of the social and historical context of biblical revelation.¹⁸ If there were less occasion to be cautious, Vollenhoven would in all likelihood have been more explicit in the *Isagoge*.

What marks the text perhaps more than anything else is the way philosophy is presented. The reader sees the unfolding of the contours of a "philosophical conception." A reader today might expect more explicit argument in defense of the thoughts expressed or to be given more leeway to help make up his or her own mind. Again, the situation reinforced Vollenhoven's concern to show how philosophy is able—indeed, in his view, ought—to comport with Scripture and accord with a Calvinian-Kuyperian worldview. But one must not thereby overlook the genuine philosophical concern Vollenhoven invests in this text.

When all of the circumstances of time and place have been taken into account, the bottom line is still that the *Isagoge* is distinctly challenging. Thoughts of great complexity are expressed in sentences of disproportionate brevity, involving a terminology that is honed for its use. The philosophical conception unfolds only slowly, and it takes

---

16. Vollenhoven's caution was realistic. In 1939, he had to defend his formulations of both topics before the curators of the Free University, as the result of an official complaint lodged against him by the theological faculty. Cf. Chapter 9, "Vollenhoven beschuldigd" [Vollenhoven accused] in J. Stellingwerff, *Vollenhoven (1892–1978) Reformator der Wijsbegeerte* (Baarn: Ten Have, 1992).
17. A core element of scholasticism is its view of a direct concord, however conceived, between human intelligence and the divine mind. This view requires that faith be intellectualized (or theologized) and that religion and life practice be subsumed under it.
18. Cf. A. Tol and K. A. Bril, *Vollenhoven als Wijsgeer*, 185–87, 207–10.

some effort to let its elements fall into place. But even when one grasps "the whole," distinct statements still call for prolonged reflection. There are but few works of this genre, if indeed it is a genre, but in the austerity of its style and structure there is some analogy with the *Tractatus Logico-Philosophicus* (1921/1922) of Ludwig Wittgenstein.

Isagôgè Philosophiae and Vollenhoven's own aim

From the beginning of his career, Vollenhoven had his own aim with regard to philosophy. The *Isagoge* itself does not express this aim distinctly, at least with regard to its motivation, but the important volume of 1933 does, even in the terms of its title: *Calvinism and the Reformation of Philosophy*. In that work, Vollenhoven states that a "synthesis between the Christian faith on the one hand and the current philosophy on the other is impossible."[19] The upshot of this conviction is the clash between the normative heart of Christianity and the humanistic pretensions of current philosophy. Here lie both the positive and the critical aspects of Vollenhoven's program. The *Isagoge* develops the positive side of this program.

The negative side of "current philosophy"—to touch on this briefly—focuses on its humanism in its religious meaning. Vollenhoven's criticism should not be read as "anti-human," but as referring to the role that the doctrine of humanism ascribes to human beings. Throughout the history of philosophy, there is a strong tradition of seeking consolation or edification in philosophy. Human beings are thought of being capable of gratifying this desire by means of a self-gained, or self-constructed, access to a higher wisdom or a better life. This lacks, in Vollenhoven's view, a sense of assignment or charge, for its purpose is fed by the sense of need, lack, or even evil in current experience, which it wishes to contain, avoid, or transcend. This makes one vulnerable to ignoring or being insensitive to human limitations. Such a project all too readily overreaches itself, turning its promises into illusions as one discovers that the need, lack, or evil itself is not fundamentally challenged. There is a dialectic here, a "religious dialectic" with respect to the world, as Vollenhoven once

---

19. *Het Calvinisme en de Reformatie van de Wijsbegeerte*, 16. On the same page, Vollenhoven specifies that philosophy's terminology is "so drenched with humanism" as to be unserviceable for use in Christian thought.

called it,[20] which (we might add) is in its effects not unlike tragedy. In Vollenhoven's view, a Christian approach ought to proceed from a sense of being addressed—there is a law or delimiting norm for philosophical knowing (cf. §14)—in response to which there is a task at hand, namely to work towards *reforming* the situation in which the need or lack manifests itself as relevant to philosophy.[21]

In line with what has been said about the factors that limit the meaning of philosophy, it ought to be clear that Vollenhoven's own program of philosophy does not advocate a religious philosophy as such, nor even a worldview philosophy. Philosophy does presuppose the context of the life-world and its historical setting. But rather than taking the life-world, as is commonly done, as the prereflective and naively understood context of concrete life and subsequently subjecting it to reason's reconstruction and legitimation, Vollenhoven takes concrete life as itself involving its own challenge. The Reformed tradition formulates this in terms of the "(partial) offices" of a human being: prophet, priest, and king. A person speaks, celebrates, and regulates, all with due regard to the complexity of his or her experience of creaturely life. Philosophy is not called upon to lord over this creaturely life. Its main task is to inquire what this entails for the cognitive enterprise of philosophy, or—more in Vollenhoven's terminology—the possibility of thinking and knowing reality to the extent that this falls within human reach. Religious and worldview matters are prior to philosophy, but not without implications for philosophy.

Vollenhoven formulates two notions that belong to the foundation of philosophy.[22] The first is the notion of *subjectivity*. This notion differs from the more common, modern meaning on two counts. In the first place, before a human being can initiate activity, he needs to

---

20. D. H. Th. Vollenhoven, "Divergentierapport I," in A. Tol and K. A. Bril, *Vollenhoven als Wijsgeer*, p. 114.
21. The last sentence of §12 of the *Isagoge* is apposite in this regard: "And the deepest motive for our making this demand [of philosophy being consonant with Scripture and thus accepting the divine charge] is not the desire to avoid the sorrow that any division of life brings with it, but respect for God, who forbids fragmenting life in any way."
22. For a more thorough discussion of the foundation of philosophy in Vollenhoven, in particular in its relation to religion and worldview, cf. John H. Kok, "Vollenhoven and 'Scriptural Philosophy,'" *Philosophia Reformata* 53 (1988), 101–42.

acknowledge that he "stands in subjection." It is as creature, situated in the concrete, created world, that a human being finds him- or herself called to be responsible. This "standing in subjection" is prior to judgment and spontaneous response. In modern thought, the subject is usually taken to be the source or principle of its own activity, as grounded in the *Cogito* ("I think") and expressed as dominance over an object in the aim of pursuing one's (enlightened) self-interest. Vollenhoven's meaning comes close to Emmanuel Levinas's more recent use of *subject*, when Levinas characterizes the subject as "responsibility" and the human being's primary situation as that of being addressed by the Other. (For Levinas, this situation is also the beginning of philosophy.) Vollenhoven is perhaps less reticent than Levinas in attributing the authority of the "Other" to the divine will.

But Vollenhoven gives the term *subjectivity* a second, or rather a broader, meaning that is not readily found elsewhere. Not only is humanity addressed, but the whole of cosmic reality is addressed in having been creatively "called forth" and in being sustained by the same divine will. If the human awareness of "standing in subjection" is elicited by his concrete life situation (the sense of responsibility in light of one's vulnerability, finitude, dependence, and the like), then there is nothing "illogical" in holding that the whole cosmos, as created reality, similarly stands in subjection, namely in being subject to, and sustained by, the Sovereign will, who takes fundamental responsibility for it. In its cosmic or universal breadth, Vollenhoven takes this "standing in subjection" to be the *point of orientation* of philosophy (cf. §17). It characterizes everything creaturely in relation to divine Sovereignty, whose expressed will Vollenhoven calls "law." Whatever stands in subjection has the passivity of possibility and is sustained by a will that can activate it. Standing in subjection is possibility for activity and actualization. Human knowledge is a species of actualization, requiring submission to a determining law. While human knowledge can be retraced as to its own actualization—at least that is an element in "the problem of knowledge"—this presupposes the depth of the creation's (and thus a human being's) possibilities. Possibilities deploy in the process of development (cf. §189, comment 4), but their source is the mystery of creation that man cannot plumb.[23]

---

23. Cf. §17. We might add that this "point of orientation" of philosophy characterizes the being of created reality not as a (theoretical-intellectual) *is*, nor a

The second notion that Vollenhoven formulates is that of "law-sphere." Here, too, we are at the founding edge of philosophy. If the notion of subjectivity has a religious provenance, that of law-sphere has a worldview background.

The worldview background in question is that of Kuyper's doctrine of sphere sovereignty. However, that doctrine is adjusted to make it serviceable for philosophy.[24] To start with, Kuyper had limited this doctrine to societal realms. He assumed that there is a diversity of divine ordinances relevant to the pluralistic governance of society. Vollenhoven expanded the application of this doctrine. With his cosmically broad view of subjection, he felt that the notion of realms for which ordinances hold need not be limited to society. Hence, his worldview formulation of the spheres came to include the whole of created reality as standing in subjection to a diversity of ordinances.

Vollenhoven also emphasized another difference with Kuyper's view. Kuyper certainly maintained that sovereignty is a divine prerogative. But his understanding of sovereignty in the doctrine of sphere sovereignty included the idea that those who are responsible for the governance of the societal spheres have a delegate sovereignty to act on God's behalf.[25] They are delegated to enforce divine ordinances. Vollenhoven, on the contrary, holds that what is delegated is responsibility and a task, not sovereignty. It is completely improper to speak of human sovereignty (except in a guarded and limited way). The relation of man to God's law is always one involving subservience, never substitution. The very awareness of law (as ordinances) takes place in an intuition that calls for compliance. (It is in this sense

---

(practical-moral) *ought*, but, in emphasizing address and response, a (poetical-religious) *can*. In his lectures of 1926–1927, Vollenhoven called the cosmos a divine "work of art."

24. For Vollenhoven's discussion of Kuyper's thought, cf. "De soevereiniteit in eigen kring bij Kuyper en ons" and "De visie op de Middelaar bij Kuyper en ons," in A. Tol and K. A. Bril. *Vollenhoven als Wijsgeer*, 36–46, 66–92. The first of these is translated in *A Vollenhoven Reader*.

25. Kuyper gave this doctrine a Christological setting in maintaining that the divine sovereignty is channeled as "messianic sovereignty." Thus, the office bearers in societal spheres act on behalf of Christ. It is in this context that Kuyper exclaims: "there is not a square inch in the whole domain of human existence over which Christ, who is Sovereign over *all*, does not cry: 'Mine!'" Cf. *Abraham Kuyper: A Centennial Reader*, edited by James D. Bratt (Grand Rapids: Eerdmans, 1998), 488.

that law activates or motivates, resulting in meaningful activity when ordinances are followed.) When law is merely described or, worse yet, used as means of repression, its normative essence is fundamentally denatured.[26] This is of particular importance for the way in which Vollenhoven puts the idea of a cosmically broad range of spheres to use in his doctrine of law-spheres.

A law-sphere, contrary to the *prima facie* impression, is not a sphere of laws (ordinances), but a specific mode of standing in subjection (cf. §40). In its plural form, the term emphasizes intrinsic differences in subjection, differences that equally characterize fundamentally distinct responses. In being a mode of *subjection,* a law-sphere is *correlated* to the law (or ordinances) that holds for that which stands in subjection to it. But in being a *mode* of subjection, a law-sphere is a distinct sphere differing from other law-spheres. Possibility of response is graded modally, each fundamental modality of which is warranted by its distinct law or rule.

There is no explicit account as to the "how" and the "why" of the diversity of modes of subjection given in the *Isagoge.* In lecture notes prior to the first edition of the *Isagoge,* Vollenhoven argues that one cannot deduce the diversity of laws, to which the law-spheres are correlated, from the general notion of law to which subjectivity, as point of orientation of philosophy, appeals. The worldview assumption of a diversity of spheres can only be turned into a philosophical principle if we are enabled, within the orientation point of subjectivity, to argue for the required distinctions. The drift of the argument is that if we deny modes of subjection, we will do violence to our understanding of subjectivity. For example, if we take it to be one, we cannot account for plurality; if we look on it as mind, we cannot

---

26. This is not to deny the importance and relevance of positive law, or laws enacted and enforced by human beings. In the *Isagoge,* Vollenhoven holds that those who enact laws must be in touch with the people for whom the laws are to hold (cf. §111). Thus, there must not be autocratic rule. Vollenhoven's later formulations are more explicit. From 1953 on, he held that positive laws must always respect the "central law of love,"—hence, serve to encourage good life and not promote evil, and address historical and geographical situations of need, the latter being discerned when norms are vitiated in concrete life. Thus, those who enact laws always remain subject to the love command and to norms (ordinances) that hold in virtue of creation. Cf. A. Tol and K. A. Bril, *Vollenhoven als Wijsgeer,* 105, 127–28, 188.

account for matter, and so on. But also if we acknowledge modes of subjection, we need to be sufficiently aware of their diversity, if antinomies in our understanding are to be avoided. If physical reality is extension, as Descartes held, can geometry account for all physical forces? If logic is basically psychological, is logical validity no more than felt compulsion? If social structures are determined by economic relations, are family relations in some sense commodities of goods? Vollenhoven looks on questions such as these as formulating antinomies. And the correlate of the acceptance of law is the exclusion of antinomies! This is his guiding principle in distinguishing the modes of subjection (cf. §§33, 201, 202). Once law-spheres are distinguished according to the principle of the exclusion of antinomies, we can confirm the distinctions of the modes of subjection involved by seeking to intuit the rules that are applicable to the phenomena of the law-spheres in question. These rules or laws stand in correlation to the law-spheres they govern.

Since antinomies can arise in our understanding of the natural world as well as our understanding of the societal world, we may include the natural world in this dimension of law-spheres along with the law-spheres of human interaction. It is probably Vollenhoven's most basic *philosophical* postulate that the law-spheres constitute a sequential order of modes of subjection that is basic for any understanding of the structure of created reality.[27]

The notion of a law-sphere refers to the domain of an obtaining law (or rules of a distinct modality). Law and domain are correlated, and in speaking of correlation Vollenhoven emphasizes their mutual difference. The domain of a law-sphere stands in subjection to its law, so clearly that law cannot be subject to itself. Accordingly, Vollenhoven needs to say how the things of a domain (the states of affairs) evince their subjection to law. Such subjection is evidenced in the lawfulness of activity; namely, activity that is law-bound has a positive

---

27. One might object that the occurrence of "created reality" still contains, direct or indirect, a religious or worldview component that, in view of Vollenhoven's insistence that philosophy is to be distinguished from worldview, is not properly philosophical. We can then say that any thing's being created means that it is not self-sufficient—whether as abstract possibility, mindful necessity, or concrete actuality—its insufficiency stemming not only from its "standing in subjection" but also its standing in some relation or connection to other beings.

and orderly outcome, while activity that takes place in disrespect of law results in brokenness and failure. The lawfulness is discerned in a domain, but its possibility calls for a law's obtaining or impingement in order to elicit law-bound activity. Activity takes on definiteness and determination only to the degree that it is law-bound.

Vollenhoven uses the term "subject function" to characterize activity in relation to law. This term is ambiguous, because the term *subject* has gained two meanings in modern thought. The older meaning of "being subject to" (*subjectum*) catches the passivity of subjection to law that brings about definitiveness. But this meaning has had to make room for the more active "subjecting," as something brought about by activity, usually in opposition to an object. Vollenhoven avails himself of a difference in Dutch pronunciation to distinguish these meanings, a distinction not preserved (except indirectly) in translation. He speaks of *subjèctsfunctie*, literally "function of subjection," in the context of the first meaning, and when referring to the second, the more active meaning, he speaks of *súbjectsfunctie*, i.e. "subjecting function." To avoid clumsiness of expression in English, it seems best to simply use "subject function" and to let the context decide which meaning is intended. The important point for Vollenhoven is that the active meaning of subjecting itself calls for determinateness, hence subjection is prior.

When speaking of individual things, Vollenhoven keeps the priority of subjection in mind. He refers generically to things as "unities of subjection" or "subject units" (*subjèctseenheden*), thus characterizing individual things in their multiple but simultaneous participation in modes of subjection. To explicate the lawfulness of this participation that individual things display, Vollenhoven appeals to two "cosmic determinants." The first is a vast network of the *relational* connections between things, namely, such relations as pertain to one and the same mode of subjection of the things relationally connected. The second determinant pertains to the "structure" of things. Multiple participation in different modes of subjection simultaneously calls for structured connections between the functions within one and the same thing. Things are more than mere conjunctions of functions. Accordingly, there are what Vollenhoven calls "analogical" connections between subject functions of an individual thing. Such analogical connections account, on the one hand, for the intrinsic *properties* of things—whereby things actively influence other things (their "subject[ing]-functions")—and, on the other hand, for the *qualities* of things—those features of things (their "object-functions") that call for the subject(ing) functions of other things to be realized.

So, in summary, (i) from out of the religious background of his thought, Vollenhoven broaches the notion of the *point of orientation* of philosophy, which he specifies to be that of "standing in subjection," or "being-subject." When such a notion is ignored, or insufficiently accounted for, philosophy will, practically speaking, find itself confronted with sovereignty-subjection tensions, usually formulated in any of many alternative ways, such as domination and subservience, good and evil, substance and phenomenon, determining and determined, and the like, without being able to account for this distinction in a way that avoids blatant injustices. (ii) The worldview affect upon his thought, in turn, provides the springboard for his ontological generalization of the sequence of the *law-spheres* and their implicit intuition of fundamental characterization. The awareness that a plurality of law-spheres is called for, but without forfeiting systematic connectedness, relieves one of the supposed need to reduce complexity for the sake of adequate explanation and at the cost of harboring antinomies. (iii) Finally, the cosmological grandeur of the diversity of things calls for the recognition of a thing's *unity of subjection* as it participates in the *diversity of law-spheres*. Individuality in relationships and functionality in lawful actualization together delineate a vast scope of cosmic possibilities. There is more between heaven and earth than is dreamed of in many a philosophy.[28]

About *Isagôgè Philosophiae*

There are a number of features of the text that is reproduced here that call for commentary. In the first place, there is the matter of the provenance of the "definitive" edition. Secondly, something needs to be clarified as to Vollenhoven's choice of method adopted in this text. Then, thirdly, the notions of "structure" and "direction" call for some comment. Finally, there are a number of features that we feel

---

28. Needless to say, we do not wish to suggest that Vollenhoven has watertight means of avoiding all vicious splits, debilitating antinomies, or realities debunked. The point is that his prephilosophical orientation enjoins the reader, as belonging to the *task* of philosophy, to seriously analyze a problem situation, as required of responsible philosophy that responds to the norm of being just and fair to created things, as opposed to silencing (with a view to a chosen rational strategy?) the conscience that calls to account.

would not have been included in a final edition, had Vollenhoven himself been able to prepare the text for publication.

1. *The "definitive" edition.* The current text, translated here, is based on the syllabus edition of 1941, which Vollenhoven corrected and dated "1945." We interpret this dating to mean that Vollenhoven worked on the text until (and into) 1945. There is evidence that Vollenhoven hoped eventually to publish the text. But it is also clear that he wished the thoughts expressed in the text to "ripen" further, and so—perfectionist that he was—he set the text aside for further consideration later.

Ever since the first "complete" version of the *Isagoge* appeared in 1930, the text underwent many revisions. Initially, it counted 145 paragraphs, which is about two-thirds of its final count of 224 paragraphs. The version of 1932 incorporated changes that affected the structure of the main text. Here, he introduced the three-part division of first discussing things heavenly, then things earthly, and concluding with a discussion of the connection between heaven and earth. He also rewrote the account of knowledge, which he now placed in the appendix. This may give the impression that the theme of knowledge is somewhat additional. But in the introduction of the *Isagoge,* Vollenhoven states that the kind of distinctions one needs in an introduction to philosophy pertains, in the main, to the theory of knowledge (cf. §6). While these distinctions belong, generally speaking, to ontology, they are such as to warrant the resorting of knowing within or under being. The text on the theory of knowledge demonstrates this "resorting."

Other revisions were introduced in the version of 1939. At this point, Vollenhoven definitely drops the terminology of the "biblical dualism" of God and the world. The account of good and evil is given more prominence, and—not unrelated to this—the law is said to be distinctly knowable. Of course, ever since 1926 (if not 1922), Vollenhoven made specific mention of the law in its role as "boundary" between God and the world. But its account had remained within the religious awareness and the general "biblical dualism" (or difference) of God and the world. Now, in 1939, the law is interpreted as being basic for the relation between God and the world (which, of course, in no way cancels their difference).[29] In the 1941 version, Vollenhoven brings the account of religion up to par. The difference of God and the world is mediated by the law, which is expressed in God's covenant relation with regard to the world, as centered in man, and man's response to God is religiously evident in man's attitude to the law (as God's will), as compliance or rebellion. The pursuit of good and evil is linked to these religious attitudes. Along with this revision, Vollenhoven now adds the account of society. Society had not been discussed explicitly in prior versions.

The version of 1941 was the last major revision of the text. But now new confusion is evident in the copies of the 1941 version, which was probably occasioned by the situation of war.[30] In replenishing the stock of this text, new stencils were needed to replace ones that were worn or torn. In the retyping, several hundred errors arose. Many, but not all, of these were noted in a correction notification. The *Isagoge* of 1943 tried to incorporate these corrections, but this did

---

29. Vollenhoven never held to a monistic view of relations (the view that a relation is but a property of the whole of the related terms, a view favored by Idealism), but this does not prevent him from speaking of "wholes," for example, the natural kingdoms, organic species, and the like. In his dissertation of 1918, he had committed himself exclusively to a monadistic view (the view that relations hold between two and only two terms, and that relations are based on two [inherent] properties of the terms said to be related). The felt need to reform his thought in the early 1920s, leading to the first published statement of his "Calvinistic philosophy" in 1926, has much to do with freeing himself of monadism and its implications. In the *Isagoge*, the view of what may be called "external" relations is required (the view that relations have a status that is not reducible either to properties of the terms said to be related nor to the whole of these terms), though this requirement is not exclusive. At least in speaking of the relational connections between individual things, the relational factor is here irreducible.
30. In the Spring of 1942, the University of Leiden ceased to operate to avoid compromising itself to German occupational demands. As a result, many students came to the Free University, who accordingly had to take the required introduction to philosophy. This called for extra copies of the (1941) *Isagoge*. In April of 1943, the Free University, in turn, closed its doors but Vollenhoven continued to teach at his home until the end of the war. Cf. G. Zondergeld, *Geen duimbreed?! De Vrije Universiteit tijdens de Duitse bezetting* ["Not an inch?! The Free University during the German Occupation"] (Zoetermeer: Meinema, 2002), 111; also J. Stellingwerff, *D. H. Th. Vollenhoven (1892–1978) Reformator der Wijsbegeerte*, 153, 179.

not completely succeed. In addition, the errors that had not been listed, some of which are quite serious, remained undetected. The stencils of the 1943 version were used to make a large backlog of copies, which lasted into the 1960s. To keep the text available, Vollenhoven agreed to a new edition of the *Isagoge* in 1966, which was typed anew and appeared in 1967. This version was based on the 1943 version.

Vollenhoven's own copy of the *Isagoge*, on which he based his lectures, is one of the earlier copies of 1941. His copy, which contains the original typing errors of the initial 1941 stock, did not contain the errors that arose in the retyping of the text. It seems he did not check the text that was used to type the 1943 version, for he does not seem to have been aware of the later errors. Also, he evidently did not check the text used for the 1967 version. What Vollenhoven had done is read his own copy of 1941 carefully. He added all the corrections that had been listed, but, in the process, he introduced new changes in the text, which he added in the margins of his copy along with the corrections. It would seem he completed this in 1945. After the war, others took over the teaching of the required course in philosophy. So Vollenhoven stored his own copy away. The fact that it played no role in the production of the version of 1967 means either that he forgot he had his own corrected version or that he was under the assumption that his version did not disagree with the version of 1943. In any case, his private copy of 1941, as corrected and dated 1945, is the most definitive version of the text. This text has now been edited and forms the basis of the current publication.[31]

2. *The Isagoge's method*. Vollenhoven views philosophy as an enterprise of a general scientific nature. That means that method must be explicit. After the discussion of preliminaries, which sets the stage for the actual discussion of philosophy, Vollenhoven applied a method of "resolution and composition," as required in a scientific approach. The method's two components specify its "two routes": (i) when *resolving*, one analyzes, beginning with concrete reality and ending where the material itself resists further analysis; (ii) when *(re)composing* (or proceeding "in the direction of ever-greater complexity"; cf. §23),

---

31. This history of the text of the *Isagoge* is carefully documented in the Dutch critical edition. That edition includes all the versions prior to Vollenhoven's 1945 copy, from 1930 on.

one retraces the steps taken on the first route, proceeding now from where the analysis had ended toward the concrete.

Now in the *Isagoge,* Vollenhoven limits his discussion to the "second route" of his method, the way of composition (cf. §§23 and 24). Because this route proceeds from what is structurally "abstract" towards the concrete, the impression might be gained of the concrete being constructed via abstractions of thought, with relations being the work of thought. In emphasizing that there is a prior route of analysis, the said impression is at least partially dispelled. But some discussion of the whole method is in order.

In beginning with concrete reality, Vollenhoven emphasizes the context in which philosophy—or scientific work in general—takes place. This has been discussed above. The actual work of analysis is not so much a process of abstraction as a way of discovering what is present in all the subject-matter of thought and which, in the end, resists analysis. One applies, if you will, a "scheme of difference" so as to discover the most discernible identities of thought. Then, in retracing the way back to concrete reality, one comes to explicit knowledge as to how that which had resisted analysis is determinative (like a framework) for the details that progressively accrue as one approaches the concrete again.

So Vollenhoven avails himself of a systematic scheme of thought, roughly put: of pulling apart and of putting together. This follows from the methodological principle he appeals to throughout his thought: "In every case where two things are different, we can ask about the relationship between the two" (§10). Analysis (resolution) seeks to make the difference explicit to the extent that this is discernible. Thus, analysis is applied to what is in some sense a complex whole. Synthesis (or composition) seeks to account for the initial togetherness of the complex whole in terms of structural relations that secure the connectedness. Vollenhoven speaks of a "determinant" when the analysis and the synthesis are of a type, such as "modal difference and connection," "individual difference and connection," "genetic difference and connection." The differentia*ting* and the connec*ting* are here the "work of thought." But the discerned differences are not themselves "merely conceptual," nor are the connecting relations "the product of thought." Vollenhoven holds to a "realism of terms" in this regard. (In 1926, he spoke of "*Gegenstände,*" later replaced by "states of affairs.") But the realism is interpreted as being part and parcel of a "created" structure, a product of divine activity and subject to the divine will. A "platonic realism," namely of terms subsisting in an absolute sense, undercuts the biblical understanding of *creatio ex nihilo*.

The deepest application of the method is in connection with "being." The way of resolution ends in the discovery of the complete generality of "being-subject" or "standing in subjection." This discovery serves as the "point of orientation" of all subsequent philosophy both as to things heavenly and things earthly (§§17 and 18). The point of orientation of things earthly displays two kinds of being: being thus-or-so and being this-or-that. This sets the stage for the discussion of the *modal* (thus-or-so) determination and the *individual* (this-or-that) determination.

3. *Structure and direction.* We call attention to these terms because the editorial hand has had to finalize their occurrence in the text. In Vollenhoven's own copy, at the point where he introduces the distinction between "the structure of things and humans" on the one hand and "the structure of the kingdoms and of humankind" on the other (cf. §26), he changed the wording in both cases to read "structure and direction." Because these topics are discussed in their respective "subparts," the phraseology recurs in the headings of these subparts. The heading of the first subpart is duly changed to read "Structure and direction of things and humans" (§27). But Vollenhoven failed to change the reading of the heading of the second subpart, which starts at paragraph 95. To be consistent, this ought to read "Structure and direction of the kingdoms and of humankind," replacing the unchanged "The structure of the kingdoms and mankind." Assuming this to be a mere lapse on Vollenhoven's part, the expected reading has been incorporated here.

Now each of these subparts consists of two divisions. In the introduction of the two divisions of the first subpart (cf. §27), Vollenhoven adds, in brackets, the term *structure* to the first division and *direction* to the second. In the heading of the first division, at the place where this topic starts (§28), Vollenhoven also adds, as is to be expected, the term *structure* to the heading of this division. But in the heading of the second division, which starts at paragraph 85, the term *direction* has not been added, contrary to expectation. Taking this, too, to be a lapse, the term has been added in the text at this point.

We note that the addition of the term *direction* here is appropriate in the light of the contents of this division. Vollenhoven discusses the antithesis of good and evil, and, linked to this, the direction of the functions as determined by the human hart.

But now what about the second subpart? If we accept the changed reading of its heading, can the distinction of "structure" and "direction" be apportioned over the two divisions of this subpart? The topic of the first division, the discussion of which begins at paragraph 96, is about the genetic connections within the kingdoms and the general relations between the kingdoms. The heading "The structure of the kingdoms" could be deemed appropriate here. The second division, which starts at paragraph 109, treats the main structures of society and the topic of religion. The latter includes the contrary responses to the "fundamental law of love." Thus, the most appropriate heading of this (second) division would appear to be "Structure and direction of humankind." The headings of each of these divisions of this second subpart now read as indicated.

We wish to note that an alternative reading of the first division of the second subpart is possible. Something can be said for the reading "Structure and direction of the kingdoms." The term *direction* would then have to pertain to the genetic connections within humankind. Now Vollenhoven does hold that human procreation involves "man as living soul, in other words man as whole, including the soul in the meaning of heart." Here, the theme of direction is at least implicit, though the term *direction* does not occur. Vollenhoven adds a remark here about the conception of Christ our Mediator. Because the role of Christ is also central to the topic of religion, this is an added point supporting the possible alternative reading of the heading.

Now while the general subpart heading "Structure and direction of the kingdoms and of humankind" does not rule out the alternative reading of the division as pertaining to the kingdoms, we feel that the inclusion of "direction" here would be strained. In the light of the whole division, the evidence is too circumstantial and too limited to warrant the alternative reading. So apart from noting its possibility, we leave the reading of this division heading as Vollenhoven had it.

The theme of structure and direction is an important one in Vollenhoven's thought. Structure is intrinsic to created reality. It is expressed in what Vollenhoven calls the modal and the individual determinations. There is the modal order of distinct modes of being, connected, so to speak, analogically. And there is the network of individual differences, mediated in turn by relational connections. But to account more adequately for human life, we need a factor that pertains to the whole of an individual's concrete being. Here the determination of good and evil—a third determinant besides the modal and the individual determinants—comes into play, which is direction determining for the whole of one's individual living. The criterion for differentiating good from evil is the (religious) love command. Good and evil are not "essences" but pertain to fundamental attitudes of obedience and disobedience, respectively, in light of the law of love.

Because individual things are genetically situated in kingdoms, there is at the human level a comparable matter of direction as pertaining to the whole of mankind. Here Vollenhoven places the Christ in his office of representing humankind in the work of redemption. Through his work of obedience to the will of God, which was a work of love, those "in Christ" are enabled to act for the good, being motivated by love in bearing responsibility in representing others, in the "partial offices" of human society.

Thus, direction is specified neither modally—it is more than a matter of faith belief or morality in a modally ethical sense—nor individually as goal of individual pursuit apart from humankind. It is a holistic determination of a religious nature, affecting a human being's concrete redemptive living. For philosophy, it is a prerequisite that cannot be decided or determined merely in structural terms.

4. *Some infelicities*. Vollenhoven's checking of the text of the *Isagoge* in 1945 must not be seen as the definitive preparation for its publication, though he did initiate plans in that direction with an Amsterdam publisher. It is likely that Vollenhoven wished to give the text a final working over when his new method of historical research was more settled. Because that method—the so-called "consequential problem-historical method"—proved to be much more challenging than Vollenhoven had initially expected, he never found the time to bring the *Isagoge* up-to-date, which was why he agreed to the reprint of the 1943 version that appeared in 1967. The current text (Vollenhoven's own copy of 1945) has numerous features that would, in all likelihood, not have survived in a published version. The following are possible candidates for revision.

a. Vollenhoven speaks of a "main part" ("Hoofddeel") of the *Isagoge* (cf. §6). This is a remnant of the earlier setup, whereby the first main part of the *Isagoge* is, in fact, the text as we have it, said to be the positive results of what Vollenhoven considers to be "scripturally responsible" reflection. The second "main part" was a discussion of prominent nonscriptural features of traditional philosophy. This second part has only been found in a 1932 edition of the *Isagoge*. This text—the second main part—was subsequently published, with some alterations, as Chapter 3 of Part I of Vollenhoven's *Het Calvinisme en de Reformatie van de Wijsbegeerte* (Amsterdam: Paris, 1933, 49–67), and it was no longer included in the *Isagoge* after 1933. The content of this whole "second main part" became definitely dated when Vollenhoven began to develop his problem-historical method for the study of the history of philosophy in the early 1940s. It is probably an oversight that there are still some references to this setup (e.g., cf. §§6 and 141).

b. In paragraph 61, Vollenhoven gives the impression that one can count with irrational numbers and that this constitutes an anticipation of spatial continuity. This impression is unfortunate. A mathematician never counts with irrational numbers, and the sequence of the square roots of the natural numbers in no way approaches continuity. A first degree of continuity is found in connection with the set of rational numbers (numbers that can be written as fractions) when ordered according to magnitude. Between any two fractions, there is always another fraction. This implies that the number of fractions between any two fractions is unending, and accordingly the set of rational numbers is said to be "compact." If the rational numbers are ordered according to the increasing sums of the numerators and denominators—in other words, 1/1 [sum of 2], 1/2, 2/1 [sum of 3], 1/3, 2/2, 3/1 [sum of 4], 1/4, 2/3, 3/2, 4/1 [sum of 5], and so on—then this sequence of rational numbers includes every rational number, and it constitutes a countable sequence (though one would not use it to actually count). But what mathematicians think of as continuity in the full sense is found in connection with the set of "real numbers," ordered according to magnitude. The set of real numbers consists of the rational numbers and the irrational numbers, the latter being numbers that cannot be written as a fraction, for example, $\sqrt{2}$, $\sqrt{5}$, or π, and so on. Now, because irrational numbers, such as the given examples, mark distinct positions on a line, as do the rational numbers, the rational and the irrational numbers together form a sequence reflecting the one-dimensionality of the line. The irrational numbers "fill-in," so to speak, the interstices between the rational numbers, on account of which the set of real numbers is said to be "dense." However, this set is not denumerable (countable). The set of real numbers reflects the continuity of the line. It is in this sense that the set of real numbers displays a "spatial anticipation." One may ask whether the "compactness" of the set of rational numbers does not reflect (or anticipate?) the more primitive spatial relation of "part and whole," as suggested by the numerator and denominator of fractions.

c. In the course of the 1950s, Vollenhoven agreed with Dooyeweerd in splitting the physical law-sphere into two spheres, one concerned with motion and the other with energy forms or interactions.[32] In fact, this constituted a reintroduction on Vollenhoven's part. Vollenhoven had distinguished these two law-spheres in the 1930 version of the *Isagoge*, but he subsequently dropped the distinction. The history of the "modal sequence" is not without its own interest, for it took time to settle. In 1926, Vollenhoven enumerated the lower spheres (in order of increasing complexity) as being: the logical, number, space, time, motion, energy, biotic, psychic, and so on (there is no complete listing in 1926 of the remaining law-spheres).[33] In (early) 1927 (in the lecture notes of 1926–1927), the logical sphere is moved to its "canonical position," namely, between the psychical and the technical-formative ("historical") spheres. In the lecture notes of 1929–1930, Vollenhoven gives a provisional listing of the law-spheres as: arithmetical, spatial, mechanical ("including energy, chemistry"), organic, psychical, logical (analysis and synthesis), social, historical, linguistic, economical, juridical, ethical, and pistical. Vollenhoven notes that the position of the aesthetic remains uncertain. We, in turn, note that time is now no longer viewed as a law-sphere, and that motion and energy are merged, only to be split again in the 1930 *Isagoge* and reunited in subsequent editions. In addition, the position of the social law-sphere is not yet in its "canonical position," namely, between the linguistic and the economic (as of 1930). In the *Isagoge* of 1931 and later versions, the listing is "standard" (apart from the later resplitting of the physical sphere in the 1950s).

---

32. Cf. A. Tol and K. A. Bril, *Vollenhoven als wijsgeer*, 175, 204.
33. Cf. "Kentheorie en natuurwetenschap" [Epistemology and Natural Science], *Orgaan van de Christelijke Vereeniging van Natuur- en Geneeskunde in Nederland*, No. 2 & 4, 53–64, 147–97—esp. page 154; also *Logos en Ratio* (Kampen: Kok, 1926), 55.

d. The chapter on scientific knowing (§198 ff.) is very brief and in part incomplete. It consists of two "chapters," the first on scientific knowing in the special sciences, and the second purportedly on scientific knowing in the general sciences. However, the content of this second chapter is deferred with the remark that more needs to be said than can justly be included there. (It is not certain what Vollenhoven meant here.) Vollenhoven refers to pedagogy as one "general science" that would have to be discussed. Philosophy, too, is considered by Vollenhoven to be a "general science." However, he does not mention philosophy here. But, given what Vollenhoven said in paragraph 5 about the "precise determination" of the place of philosophy and the "complete circumscription" of its task, the discussion of these points could be expected here.

The first chapter is brief for the likely reason that Vollenhoven had given its topic a broad discussion in 1926, namely in "Kentheorie en natuurwetenschap," although there is no reference to this long article in the *Isagoge*. In the subsequent editions, the text of this part of the *Isagoge* was only superficially revised; hence, there is little difference here between the original text of 1930 and the text of 1945. It seems one needs to approach this topic through the work of 1926.[34]

In conclusion

Vollenhoven was aware, especially in later life, that the *Isagoge* had its faults and that it did not represent fully numerous features of his later thought. In the brief foreword for the 1967 reprint, he writes: "For my initial plan, to adjust the whole of the text here and there, would in fact have resulted in a reworking." He explains that he could no longer afford the time—he was seventy-five years old at the time—for such a major undertaking, preferring to invest his remaining energy in continuing to develop the "problem-historical method" for the study of the history of philosophy. He ends by expressing the hope that the work will nonetheless serve the purpose that its title indicates. We can do no better than repeat the hope that this text will continue to stimulate philosophical thought.

Anthony Tol

---

34. To that end, cf. Chapter 7 on "Logos, states of affairs, and knowledge" of John H. Kok, *Vollenhoven: His Early Development*, 233–90, for a discussion of Vollenhoven's work of 1926.

INTRODUCTION TO PHILOSOPHY

Preface 3

Introduction: The Place of Philosophy in the Cosmos
 and its Task 9

Part I The Diversity and Connection of the
 Determinants of the Heavenly Subject 19

Part II The Diversity and Connection of the
 Determinants of the Earthly Subject 21
Introduction

> **Division I Structure and Direction of Things and Humans**
> Chapter 1: The Two Simplest Determinants and
> Their Basic Relations (the Structure) 24
> *Section 1 The Two Simplest Determinants, The Diversity in Them,
> and Their Combined Occurrence* 24
>   A. The First Most Simple Determinant and Its Diversity
>   B. The Second (This–that) Determinant and Its Diversity
>   C. The Combined Occurrence of Diversities in Both
>   Determinants
> *Section 2 The Two Fundamental Connections in Both Distinctions
> and Their Occurrence in Combination* 34
>   A. The Connection between Entities that Differ Individually
>   B. The Connection between Subject Functions
>   C. The Combined Occurrence of Both Connections
> Chapter 2: The Third Determinant, Its Diversity, and the
> Combined Occurrence of This Determinant with
> Both of the Others (the Direction) 56

> **Division II The Structure [and Direction]
> of the Kingdoms and of Humankind** 62
> Chapter 1: The Structure of the Kingdoms 62
> *Section 1 The Variety of the Kingdoms* 63
> *Section 2 The Connection between the Different Kingdoms* 67
> Chapter 2: The Structure [and Direction] of Humankind 69
> *Section 1 The Societal Connections* 69
> *Section 2 Religion* 77
>   A. Introduction 77
>   B. The Covenant of Creation 80

C. The Covenant of Re-Creation 85
      1. Introduction
      2. Before the Incarnation of the Word
         a. The period of the nondifferentiated Logos revelation
         b. The period of the differentiated Logos revelation
      3. After the Incarnation of the Logos

Part III The Connection between Heaven and Earth 103

APPENDIX 107
A Number of the More Complicated Questions of Philosophy

Part I Human Knowing 108
Introduction

   Division I Nonscientific Knowing 110
      Chapter 1: The Structure of Nonscientific Knowing 110
         A. The Activity of Coming to Know 111
            1. The role of the interrelation in analytic coming to know
               a. The synchronic interrelations in the analytic law-sphere
               b. The successive interrelations in that which is analytic
            2. The role of the vertical connection in analytic coming to know
         B. The Knowable 122
         C. The Result 124
      Chapter 2: The Development of Nonscientific Knowing ... 125

   Division II Scientific Knowing 136
      Chapter 1: Special Scientific Knowing
      Chapter 2: Nonspecial-Scientific Scientific Knowing

Part II The Theory about Know-how and Technology ... 139
   Division I Know-How
   Division II Know-How and Science

Part III The Theory about Art and Aesthetics 142
   Division I Art
   Division II Art and Science

Introduction to Philosophy

Preface

First a few words concerning the name, purpose, and method of this course and the division of this syllabus.

1. Name

The name of this course consists of two parts: The first is *isagôgè*, to which is added the specification *philosophiae*. We deal briefly with the meaning of each of these words and then with the meaning of their combination.

a. *Isagôgè* is the transcription (rendering of a foreign word in the characters of another language) of the Greek word *eisagôgè*. This word is a compound of *eis-*, meaning "into," and *agôgè* (from *agein*), meaning "a leading." Hence, *isagôgè* means *introduction*.

b. *Philosophiae* is an inflected form of *philosophia*. This word is also a compound, the constituent parts of which are *philos*, or "friendly," and *sophia*, meaning "wisdom." Hence, *philosophy* means *love of wisdom*.

Now this circumscription is very old; if we can believe tradition, it stems from Pythagoras, a Greek philosopher from the sixth century B.C. However, he combined it with a serious misconception. Pythagoras is reputed to have said that he, being a man, did not possess wisdom as did the gods, but strove toward wisdom. He assumed that human thinking can aspire to the possession of divine wisdom. To eradicate this misconception, it is good to note at the outset that in the circumscription of "philosophy" as "love of wisdom," we are concerned exclusively with what human beings can attain—hence, with human wisdom.

As for the relationship of the term *philosophy* to this human wisdom, note that though it first of all denotes this human striving, it also means something else, namely, the complex of statements that express the knowledge men obtained through this striving. Philosophy, therefore, signifies both a *deed* and a *result*.

c. Hence, *isagôgè philosophiae* means firstly, an introduction to philosophizing, and secondly, an introduction to an understanding of the result thereby obtained by others.

Isagôgè, therefore, in whichever sense we use the term, is always an introduction—that is to say, an auxiliary activity—and not a book or syllabus, though we occasionally refer to the latter in passing with the same name. Such a syllabus must not be "cased" but be used. For the sentences denote thoughts that are meant to teach the reader to tackle the questions in different fields philosophically.

2. Purpose

In an introduction in the sense of activity, we should distinguish, in addition to the person to be introduced and the person doing the introducing, also that into which the latter introduces the other. The image evoked is that of a building. However, we must be careful with this image; if we press it too far, we lose sight of the *first* meaning of the word *philosophy*, namely, philosophizing, and see only the second, namely, that of a result.

Now an introduction to philosophy in the second meaning of this term undoubtedly also makes good sense. This holds especially when we have to acquaint ourselves with the many results of numerous philosophers to be found in bygone centuries. A good study of the history of philosophy is simply not possible without an introduction like the one offered in the *Conspectus Historiae* ["Overview of the History"]. An introduction to the work of contemporaries may also be necessary, for example, when what a given thinker has found presents difficulties for a particular group of people. It is with this in mind that A. Drews wrote an introduction to the philosophy of E. van Hartmann (1902), H. A. van Andel one to the work of H. Bavinck, and W. Reyer one to the thought of E. Husserl and his school (1926). The author of such an introduction is usually of the opinion that his or her teacher has a correct view of various problems. Yet such an introduction remains an adduction specifically of the thoughts and books of another and only indirectly of the problems, namely, to the extent that they were seen and solved by this other person.

The important thing in both cases is the following: Has the person in question seen the difficulties sufficiently and has he posed the problems correctly? These questions cannot be answered unless one also grapples with the state of affairs that the thinker being discussed, if he did his work well, thought about as well.

That is why a grappling with the state of affairs should have priority in a philosophical introduction. In other words, if in some investigation one cannot find clarity, the first question may well be: "What did this or that person say about it?" The answer to this question may never be taken as final: What someone else says can help us, but it can also set us back. This happens, for example, when the thinker in question did not have an eye for the difficulties that we discern, and we thereupon ignore them as well. Therefore, after reading a scientific work, the question should always be asked, at least by those who want to work scientifically: "Is what the author asserts correct—that is to say, does it comport well with the state of affairs?" And only if we are of the opinion that this question may be answered in the affirmative, can we uninhibitedly turn to writing, even though this affirmative answer will be far from acceptable to many. In like manner, J. G. Walch gave an introduction to philosophy (1727)—I mention it here because it is the oldest under that name since the time of the Renaissance—from a purely rationalistic standpoint. He maintained that what he and those who thought like him—the rationalists—had to say was built on the state of affairs.

A third group of introductions is prompted by the thought that the problems with which philosophy was concerned hitherto were posed incorrectly, be it completely or in part. Such authors often begin with negations, in other words, with the rejection of other theories, or at least integrate the same in their exposition of what they claim to have found. J. G. Fichte (1797 and 1801) and J. F. Herbert (1813) are examples of older writers, while the Frenchman Charles Renouvier (1895); the Dutchmen J. P. N. Land (1889, $_2$1900) and J. G. Wattjes (1926); the Germans F. Paulsen (1892, $_{40}$1924), O. Külpe (1895, $_{12}$1929), Erich Becher (1926), Wilhelm Wundt (1901, $_8$1920), and W. Windelband (1914, $_3$1923); the Englishmen G. S. Fullerton (1906) and B. Russell (1912, $_3$1918); and the Belgian L. de Raeymacker (1938, $_2$1944) are more recent examples. Their works* (which are to be used with the greatest of caution given that none stand on the scriptural standpoint) not only acquaint us with what these writers positively claim but also with what they challenge.

> Comment: That some of these books were reprinted so often demonstrates how great the need is for introduction, a need that has also been recently expressed in the cry for a "unity in style" in academic forming.

To the extent that their standpoint allows, these authors also deal with the matters at issue. And everyone who does that can help us; everyone, that is, to the extent that they keep the limits of philosophy in mind and, therefore, to the extent that they philosophize well.

3. Method

a. The method of this course must in the first place be *thetical*, for the point is to learn to approach the difficulties faced by thinking from one's own point of view.

> Comment 1: This thetical approach can never be *replaced* by historical expositions: After all, the history of philosophy is something other than philosophy. For that reason, science about this history (*historica*) is something other than introduction.
>
> A *combination* of these two methods, such as has recently been attempted by F. Heinemann (1929), does not foster clarity and is, therefore, not to be recommended.

b. In the second place, however, the method ought also to be *critical*. We who philosophize may not act as though our predecessors and contemporaries lacked philosophic interest. On the contrary, we must seriously consider their expositions. However, we also may not swear by the words of a human master or seek a solution in a patchwork, in which simply out of awe for people of authority we borrow something from each of them. We must always ask ourselves: "Did they sufficiently appreciate the difficulties and did they pose the problem correctly?" And we must also, and repeatedly, ask the same question of the result that we ourselves have arrived at. This kind of fresh consideration of old answers and questions can lead to two kinds of results; the solution being examined can be satisfactory or

---

* *Editor's note*. The titles of these works are listed under "References" on pages 144–45 below.

not, either because it answers wrongly a correctly formulated question or because it proceeded from a wrong formulation of the problem.

Criticism does not necessarily mean that the answer found earlier and now subjected to a reevaluation is found to be unsatisfactory: Critical examination can just as well result in cordially recommending theses obtained by others or maintaining a thesis of one's own that others have contested. "Criticism" is, therefore, certainly not equivalent to "negation." To be sure, criticism can lead to a negative result. But such a negative result has great value: Tenaciously maintaining thoughts that constantly clash with the main lines of a system undermines its power and prevents good questions from being asked and new results from being obtained.

c. The *thetical* and the *critical* approaches in the method are not isolated from one another. Therefore, we must add a word about their relationship, which, in my opinion, is as follows: Every critical activity implies that one takes a thetical position. It is quite possible that this position will later prove to be untenable, but all that means is that one has modified one's position somewhat; one has drawn back a bit or has adopted a thesis that one thought earlier had to be opposed. But whatever the case may be, all criticism presupposes, if it is worthy of the name, that one is confident in maintaining certain thoughts.

> Comment 2: If this is forgotten, then the extreme consequence could be that the person adopts a position hypothetically, one moment accepting the thoughts of P to criticize those of Q, the next minute adopting the position of Q to investigate the thoughts of P. If, however, this kind of hypothetic reasoning is the only thing that a person does, it leads to nothing but *philosophic nihilism.*
>
> Usually a person stops before that. But even then, she does not always take sufficient account of her own standpoint. This has the further consequence that the formulation of a particular problem is accepted as correct but both the negative and the positive answer to it are considered unsatisfactory. Hence, she combines the two, warning others of the one-sidedness of each of the two parties separately. However, this kind of *combination*, if the question is indeed one that can be answered by a clear-cut yes or no, must be rejected. For if both parties are right—if this is not the case, there would be no question of combination—then the formulation of the problem is incorrect and must be replaced by another one and must not be cloaked by a combination.
>
> A phenomenon that is even less desirable is *eclecticism.* It usually does not even penetrate as far as the problem, correctly formulated or not,

but simply supports a number of thoughts encountered here or there, without even bothering to inquire whether they are compatible.

It is by maintaining that which is tenable in one's own position, by critically examining not only the result acquired by others but also the result of one's own thinking at an earlier time, and by having the courage to accept the implications of one's position, that one can make progress through struggle and attain a double profit: a reinforced *position* and a more definite *rejection* of whatever is inconsistent with it.

4. Division

The division of the material is correlate with the distinction within the provisional result, that is to say, the distinction between *positive* and *negative*.

The positive must have precedence. If this is not the case, the anything-but-imaginary danger looms that a person will never be done with his negation. Also the advocate of an opinion that is rejected has the right to know what is behind the criticism that led to this rejection.

One way of proceeding is to take one particular question and deal with it in a positive and then a negative manner and consequently to turn to another problem, and so on. This procedure, however, meets the objection that to clarify the diversity in the formulations of the question and answers, it would be necessary in the case of every problem to outline the schools of thought that have concerned themselves with this question, therefore necessarily leading to repetition. Hence, preference must be given, if only for reasons of economy of time, to the procedure whereby the positive result is given in a coherent whole.

This is, of course, not to say that whatever has implicitly been rejected may also be ignored. On the contrary, it must be precisely presented so that people may also know and understand the conceptions and terminology of others. This, however, should not be done in the present context, but in the survey of the history of philosophy; for it is there that the different schools of thought are outlined within the framework of their basic thoughts and in the context of their historic period.

For these reasons, the *Isagoge* can do no better than to limit itself to a connected account of my own positive result. In the few instances where a negative comment has been made, the only purpose has been to clarify the implications of the position spelled out in the text.

INTRODUCTION

THE PLACE OF PHILOSOPHY IN THE COSMOS AND ITS TASK

5. A preliminary question
Usually people are active in philosophy for some time before considering the question as to the place of philosophy in the cosmos and its task. But those who want to help others should certainly be able to shed some light on this point. Even when this is the case, they are still confronted with a difficult decision: Should they, in their attempt to help others, present their view of the task and place of philosophy at the beginning or can they better save that for later? An argument in favor of the latter solution is that the *precise* determination of that place and the *complete* circumscription of this task always requires the use of distinctions that are related to the conception as a whole and whose tenor becomes fully clear only after numerous expositions. On the other hand, many failures and disappointments in the field of philosophy can be blamed on precisely the fact that people have failed to face this preliminary question. Therefore, an early warning is behooving.

It is for this reason that I, although I am ready enough to acknowledge the objections against dealing with this question first, nevertheless begin with a brief discussion of this point.

6. The nature of this question
The distinctions alluded to above, that we cannot dispense with in an introduction, belong for the most part to the theory about knowing. I believe that the import of most of these distinctions can clearly be grasped only at the end of our discussion. That is why I simply use them here as clearly as possible and refer the reader for further clarification to the Appendix of this main part.

7. Being philosophically engaged is more than thinking
It is well known how Descartes sought to build his philosophic system on the basis of the proposition "Cogito ergo sum," "I think, therefore I am."

So as not to deal with entirely different matters at the same time, I will not consider the second part of this proposition at this point. Nor do I want to raise the question of whether the whole thought experiment upon which this assertion is said to rest, namely, the attempt to isolate thought from its foundation and its past, is even possible. The only question I want to raise here is whether, supposing the reasoning of Descartes was correct, the term *thinking* (*cogitare*) is the right term for being philosophically active. In other words, I am asking only this: Is "philosophizing" indeed the same thing as "thinking"?

In searching for an answer to this question, we take into consideration that the word *philosophy* has two meanings, namely, striving after and the possession of philosophic knowledge and therefore, in both cases, points toward knowing. Now the word *knowing* in the sense intended here denotes something as a constituent and not the whole of which, in one way or another, is "thinking."

It is for this reason that the answer to the stated question must be negative. In other words, being philosophically active and philosophic knowing is more than thinking.

8. *Knowing and being*

Let us now look at the second part of Descartes' proposition, namely at "therefore I am" (*ergo sum*). Is this "therefore" (*ergo*) tenable if we replace—in conformity with §7—the expression "I think" with "I know" (replacing *cogito* by *cognovi*)?

To decide this, we must, of course, first know what Descartes meant by this "therefore." In other words, the question that arises is in the first place a matter of historical interpretation.

Some are of the opinion that this "therefore" denotes a connection of identity. However this cannot be correct, for Descartes does not identify being and thinking: Besides thinking, he also presupposes extension. Therefore, in his opinion, thinking is only a component of being.

Now Descartes meant this in a rationalistic way, that is, in the sense that thinking is the essence of being; an opinion that we, of course, reject, as much as we reject the division of being indicated here.

However, it is not rationalistic but correct to subsume thinking and knowing under being, for it makes good sense to speak of a nonthinking and a nonknowing being. There are clearly many things—for example, minerals, plants, and animals—that are but that do not know.

We conclude, therefore:
    a. Negatively, that knowing is not the same as being
    b. Positively, that knowing is a component of being

> Comment: Therefore, propositions such as "knowing is parallel with or reflects being," "knowing is the agreement of thinking and being," and "knowing precedes being and constitutes it" are incorrect.

9. Not all knowing is philosophic knowing

One remaining question is whether all knowing is philosophic knowing. Even if we restrict ourselves to the basics needed to answer this question, it is not difficult to demonstrate that people do not always understand the same thing by the term *knowing* (or by the term for the correlate of knowing, namely, "knowledge").

The insight with which a businessperson serves his or her firm is, to be sure, the result of more than just thinking. It is the result of knowing. But experience teaches that this knowledge can and often is present in cases where the person concerned has no scientific knowledge. We must, therefore, first distinguish between scientific and nonscientific knowing. Philosophic knowing does not fall under the latter.

Therefore, the question must now be discussed whether language correctly distinguishes scientific and philosophic knowing. First of all, the question arises: Are both identical? In other words, can we say, "All scientific knowing is of a philosophic character"? That is certainly not the case, as many men and women are engaged in the special sciences with great competence without evincing much interest in philosophical questions. This by itself is sufficient to distinguish within science between special science and philosophy.

In summary, I come to the following conclusion: Philosophic knowing is not identical with scientific knowing but is subsumed as nonspecial-scientific knowing, together with the knowing of the special sciences, under scientific knowing. More concisely, philosophic knowing is scientific, but not special scientific, knowing.

10. The relationship of philosophic knowing and nonphilosophic knowing

In every case where two things are different, we can ask about the relationship between the two. That is why we now come to the relationship between philosophic and nonphilosophic knowing.

This relationship, too, cannot yet be extensively discussed. Nevertheless, a few things can be said about it at this point, not only negatively but also positively.

On the negative side, we must hold fast to the insight that philosophic knowing, although itself of a different nature, may not ignore nonscientific and special scientific knowing.

On the positive side, the relationship between the two is a double one:

a. Philosophy presupposes and builds on both kinds of knowing.

b. Philosophy must reflect also on the place and the task of both kinds of knowing and must treat these points at greater length in the theory of knowledge.

11. Philosophic knowing and the knowing in (sacred) believing

In nonscientific knowing, we find included also the knowing that is implicit in (sacred) believing. First, a word to clarify both parts of this term.

"Believing" is often understood to mean a knowing that is concerned exclusively with the outside world: The knowledge that is its correlate is said to be less certain than that concerning one's own existence. This knowing is often seen then as the first step toward approximating sacred believing. But the difference between the knowing of the inner and of the outer world is not at issue at the moment. For that reason, a discussion of the term *believing* in the sense of a knowing that is concerned exclusively with the external world can be left aside for the moment. "Believing" in the present context means only "sacred believing"; for this reason, the adjective, being in a certain sense redundant, has been put in parentheses.

The question remains as to the meaning of the term *sacred belief,* the last word taken in the active sense, in other words, in the sense of "believing." This is to be understood as the acceptance of God's Word revelation or of whatever one looks upon as a word revelation. Such sacred belief is, therefore, not always Christian; in fact, in the case of most people, it is its opposite. This opposition is, of course, of the greatest importance, and philosophy can only gain by doing full justice to it. In the present study, we have, therefore, paid it the attention it deserves. For the moment, however, it is sufficient to observe that, as long as this belief has not been undermined by certain influences, every human being believes something, for example, that a favorable or unfavorable judgment of God on this life can be known.

Now this sacred believing comprises—as contemporary investigators are again generally inclined to acknowledge—an element of knowing (or erring). This knowing is, therefore, just as extensive as this believing. On the other hand, only an extremely small percentage of people are engaged in scientific activity. In fact, the number of those who do have some belief or other but lack every scientific capacity is quite large. Let this suffice as support for the thesis that knowing (or erring) believing belongs to the nonscientific life.

Nevertheless, it is a matter of knowing. Here, too, it holds that philosophy, however much it differs from this action and its correlate, must not only reflect on the place and task of each but be mindful that it is in accordance with both as well.

If philosophy neglects this, then it will leave its adherents behind as people whose life is rent by a struggle between science and belief. The history of philosophy accordingly shows us that such harmony has been sought with the greatest seriousness—not only by many Christians, but also in the circles of Jews and pagans.

12. *Philosophic knowing and believing the Word revelation of God*

Although we also find the need for such harmony and the attempt to satisfy this need elsewhere, it may certainly not be missing in the case of Christians.

Christians ground their *belief* regarding an unfavorable or favorable judgment of God, but also in a good deal more, in the acknowledgment of the true Word revelation, which, having been put into writing in Holy Scripture, rejects all other revelation as having arisen out of the human heart and which brands every belief in such an alleged revelation as *unbelief.*

Nevertheless, this completely justified sharp opposition within sacred belief does not abolish the similarity that exists between Christian and non-Christian belief. A consequence of this is that the sacred belief of non-Christians continues to be sacred belief (see A. Kuyper, *E Voto Dordraceno* I, 128; II, 296; and III, 534†). But it also follows that Christian belief and the knowing that is included in it are of a nonscientific character. Millions of people have died in Christ over the ages, and most of them have never been engaged in any science; in fact, many of them lacked every capacity for science. Equivocating Christian belief with science, even with its earliest stages, also does violence to the life of today and yesterday, misconstrues the glorious

---

† *Editor's note*: Vollenhoven repeatedly referenced page 536, but 534 is more likely.

reality and, when it comes to discerning the norm for faith-life, leads to an intellectualistic rigor that does nothing but foster a quasi-scientific attitude.

In the meantime, this rejection of scholasticism may not for a moment cause us to forget that the Christian revelation belief always inherently includes knowing, albeit a nonscientific knowing. A Christian philosophic conception must, therefore, not only contain thoughts concerning the nature and the task of Scripture belief but must also completely agree with this believing and with the knowledge that is correlated to it, that is, be scriptural or, if you prefer, in line with Scripture. And the deepest motive for our making this demand is not the desire to avoid the sorrow that any division of life brings with it, but respect for God, who forbids fragmenting life in any way.

13. Three questions to be posed and answered by scriptural belief

Scriptural belief adheres to Holy Scripture. The latter speaks in words that people are able to understand. Now, words have a meaning, by which they denote something and direct the attention of the hearer or reader to that which is denoted.

Holy Scripture is peculiar in that its words point toward created things as well as toward the Creator. As such, it also answers the following three questions: "Who is the Creator?" "What is that which is created in relation to him?" and "Where does the line between them lie?"

a. To the question "Who is the Creator?" Holy Scripture unambiguously answers, "God." Conversely, it never sees in him a regulative idea or a speculative concept, but always the living God with his all-predestining Counsel, his creating activity, his all-dominating will; in short, the Sovereign in the absolute sense of the word.

b. The answer to the second question, "What is the created in relation to him?", is determined by what was just found: That which is created is completely dependent on the Creator, that is to say, wholly subjected to his sovereign law, Word revelation, and guidance.

c. The third question that we as Christian revelation believers ask Scripture is: "What is the limit that marks off that which is created from the Creator?" One should understand "limit" as something such that one can say that everything that stands on that side of this line is God and everything that lies on this side is created.

(1) In this way, we highlight the relationship of God and cosmos, not their similarity and difference.

Comment 1: This means that we reject the following:

    a. The attempt to understand the basic relationship between God and cosmos purely in terms of their similarity. This happens when God and cosmos are seen as manifestations or phases of a "being" or "process": In this way, God as well as cosmos are subordinated, for example, as *coincidentia oppositorum* ([the coincidence of opposites] Nicholas of Cusa and Hegel), to something that stands above both and hence are coordinated with one another.

    b. The attempt to understand the basic relationship between God and cosmos purely in terms of their difference. This happens when people set God and cosmos over against each other as the divine and the nondivine and consequently call God *das ganz Andere* ([the "wholly Other"] K. Barth); in this way, the relationship becomes a contradictory one.

Comment 2: Carefully note the circumscription of this limit in the question asked. This limit marks off that which is created from God, but not God from that which is created. To accept the latter position would be incompatible with the acknowledgment of the infinity of God, who is always and everywhere acting in and upon—and certainly not only from within—the cosmos.

Comment 3: The word *line (grens)* should not be conceived of in spatial terms, for spatiality itself belongs to that which created. Hence, a spatial demarcation, or boundary, is always a limit, or extent, within the created and never between Creator and creation.

(2) Now, this demarcation is the law of God, which is permanently posited by God for that which is created. For the only being who sovereignly gives laws to the cosmos and maintains them is God; on the other hand, all that which is created is subjected to his laws. And it continues to be subjected because God's activity in the cosmos since the creation is never coupled with a violation of the law. Accordingly, it is impossible to mention anything divine that stands under the law or anything that is created that stands above the law.

Comment 4: This means that we reject the following:

    a. Realism (in the classical sense) with its doctrine that the law also holds for God. God is not subjected to the law, although he is held by virtue of his faithfulness to maintain his law once put to the creation. We find the combination of these thoughts already in Calvin: "*Deus legibus solutus est*" (God is not subject to the law) and "*Deus non exlex est*" (God is not without the law).

    b. The attempt to understand the basic relation between God and cosmos as that between whole and part. This viewpoint allows for a number of different elaborations.

        i. When consistently applied, there are two conceptions possible:

• God is the whole, the cosmos a part—for example, that part of him that is manifest: pantheism.

- The cosmos is the whole, God a part of the cosmos—for example, the resultant of the operation of many cosmic forces or else the result of pistic representation: pancosmism.
    ii. When inconsistently applied, we also find two views:
    - A part of the world is divine: partial theism.
    - A part of God is cosmic: partial cosmism.

  Comment 5: To speak of the law as the line between God and cosmos does not purport to indicate completely the difference between God and cosmos; "difference," as denoted by word pairs like Creator and creature, infinite and finite, is something other than "line" or "limit."

  Comment 6: The law's mode of being is that of "holding for." The law, therefore, always stands above and outside that for which it holds—a comment directed against objectivism and subjectivism. The law is, therefore, not "regularity," etc.: Processes subjected to the law are regular or irregular.

  Comment 7: The law of God holds for everything and, therefore, brooks no exceptions at all. This also holds for the normative laws: that these can be transgressed does not mean at all that they are thereby also abolished.

To acknowledge the law as the line between God and cosmos is a requirement of the fear of the Lord, which is of significance for much more than exclusively science, but which also may not be lacking in it either if science is not to lead to putative or pseudoknowledge, that is to say, to error rather than to genuine knowledge.

14. The significance of these answers for determining the place of philosophy

The answers to these questions are of great importance, including for philosophy. As we have seen, it is human striving and a result thereby obtained. Both belong to the created. They are not elevated above the law of God but subjected to it, to the Word revelation and to the guidance of the sovereign God.

In summary, the archè, in other words, the dominating beginning, of philosophy as well, is God. And the limit that it will never transcend is the law of God (more specifically, the law of God for philosophic knowing).

  Comment: This holds even where it is not acknowledged. The philosophy that declares itself autonomous, rejects the Word revelation, and does not mention the guidance of God in no way attains what it wants. As apparent from its present state, what it did attain is nothing but anarchy in its thinking as well as in its terms.

15. The significance of these answers for conceiving the task of philosophy

The answers to the questions, however, also imply a distinctive conception of the task of philosophy.

a. In the first place, the answers limit this task. Philosophy may never deny or seek to push aside that which exists, not even to the smallest degree: To do so would be to deny either God or all or part of his work or to fail to do justice to its nature.

(1) That is why, in the first place, philosophy cannot take the place of belief in the Word revelation of God. All of our knowledge about God rests directly or indirectly on that belief, and what a philosopher who rejects the Word of God claims to know about him turns out upon closer investigation to be pure speculation.

(2) Moreover, philosophy can not annex other parts of the nonscientific life either. Philosophers may at times have governed a state wisely, but they did not do that exclusively by virtue of their philosophic competence. For philosophy remains science. And although the person of science also received other gifts, the extension of his or her work is so demanding that at least a part usually does not have the opportunity of developing itself. That may be the case with another part—but even then, when there is a harmony between the various branches of his or her work, the difference remains.

(3) Finally, philosophy may also not push the special sciences to the side. If it does this anyway, then an ignominious defeat, as it suffered after Hegel, for example, is well deserved.

b. Even though its task is limited, the philosophy that keeps the line between God and cosmos in mind truly need not be in want of work. For a philosopher who believes that God created the cosmos proceeds every time again from the presupposition that the wealth in that which is created will be much greater than has been ascertained up to that time. For that reason, such a philosopher can never say, "I am ready, look here, a closed system." On the contrary, her result, though acquired systematically, is always a provisional one, for she remains filled with expectation, attuned to new surprises that will no doubt complement the main conception that agrees with belief, yet will time and again supplement and usually alter earlier findings.

16. The field of investigation for philosophy

The question remains as to what philosophy can investigate. This question can be completely answered only after a definition of "science," which is inappropriate here. Yet the preceding does offer sufficient basis to initially survey the field of investigation—the entire domain of the cosmos.

17. The point of orientation and the route of philosophy

a. Because the whole cosmos is subjected to God's law and, therefore, to God, this being-subject is our *point of orientation*. That is to say, all further determinants and differences are oriented to this being-subject.

b. This is also decisive for the route that we follow. Beginning with subjectivity in *this* sense of the word, we look for the further determinants of this being-subject and discern in them a great variety.

18. Division

Following the route mentioned above, we find first a twofold specification, for that which is subject to God is either heavenly (Part I) or earthly (Part II). Both contain what is initially a completely unsurveyable concrete wealth, of which that of the earth is best known to us. After analyzing the diversity in these two, we discuss the connection between the two (Part III).

An Appendix presents the result of applying what is found to several questions that are more complicated.

As was said, completeness is not to be had. The intention of the following is accordingly only to indicate with words, as clearly as I can, the most important determinants and diversity that I discern in the cosmos, so that others may also see them.

PART I

THE DIVERSITY AND CONNECTION OF THE DETERMINANTS OF THE HEAVENLY SUBJECT

19. The first determination of being-subject

Heaven and earth belong to that which is created. They are both similar in that they are subject to God. Nevertheless, the words *heaven* and *earth* say more than *being-created*. They both denote determinants of being-subject.

Upon comparison, we observe that the two are similar in that they are both created. There is, however, also difference.

20. The diversity in the heavenly subject

a. *Heaven*, provided that this word is taken as denoting the world of angels, is to be clearly distinguished from heaven in the sense of starry heaven and firmament, which belong to the earth (Genesis 1).

However, we know nothing concerning that heaven except by way of Word revelation, which is, therefore, based on belief.

It is true that the communications of Word revelation on this point are fairly scarce; nevertheless, they cast a light on this part of the cosmos that is completely different from what philosophers, at least to the extent they were (or are) interested in these matters, have thought.

In brief, the givens of Holy Scripture can be summarized as follows:

(1) Heaven and its dwellers belong to that which is created (Genesis 1:1).

> Comment: This is in contrast to the worship of heaven in many pagan religions.

(2) By virtue of creation, heaven is correlated with earth.

(3) In heaven, there exist spirits, angels, and messengers who differ by virtue of creation in individuality, task, and rank. The communications of Holy Scripture concerning these matters are, however, exceedingly sparing and even negative in part. That heaven and earth are very different can be deduced, for example, from the fact that Scripture not only fails to speak of female angels but also explicitly denies the existence of wedlock between angels (Matthew 22:30).

Nevertheless, the givens that Holy Scripture offers us about them are of great importance because we thus possess information about creatures that, however they may differ from earthly creatures, have that mere-being-creature in common with us.

b. This conception consequently forbids us to equate earthly being with created-being; it is only a part of that which is created.

21. *The antithesis and the world of the angels*

The difference in the world of angels between good and evil angels is a difference different from those mentioned above.

Holy Scripture informs us that this difference arose because one of the most important angels did not remain standing in the truth, that is to say, in the constancy, safety, and faithfulness of God. In this irreparable fall, many other angels followed him and he with them came to stand against the good angels.

In correlation with this difference, there arose the difference between heaven and hell. Also, this difference, therefore, does not exist by virtue of creation but by virtue of the judgment of God on account of the sin of the angels. It is important to make a clear distinction between those two lest we end up in an antithetic dualism (Parsiism or Zoroastrianism) or in a conception that views the lowest as demonic, the highest as heavenly, and the earth as the result of their combination (Babylonian world picture or astrology).

PART II

THE DIVERSITY AND CONNECTION OF THE DETERMINANTS OF THE EARTHLY SUBJECT

Introduction

22. The many determinants of earthly being

The word *earth* only implicitly refers to the wealth created in it by God. Holy Scripture denotes the relationship of "earth" to this variegated multiplicity as a relationship of that which was initially encompassing to that which was initially encompassed (Genesis 1:2) and the evolving of the latter out of the former as the work of the Spirit of God, who guides all of this, reciprocally connected, to development.

> Comment 1: This evolving has reference exclusively to earth, not to heaven and (certainly) not to God himself.
>
> Comment 2: This evolving is not to be identified with evolution. The latter presupposes the derivability of that which is higher out of that which is lower, whereas evolving presupposes the derivability of that which is later from that which is earlier.

Now the diversity that manifests itself thus is much too great to be able to survey without further analysis.

In the first place, there is that unique relation between the created earthly subject and God, which we call "the covenant," a relation in which humankind, as is evident from its *religion*, occupies the most important place when viewed from the side of what is created.

With this, the difference between humankind and that which is subject to it is indicated; apart from this, however, there exists a great diversity of *kingdoms* and *kinds*.

Within the kinds, we finally come upon *things* and *human beings*. These are not present separate and alongside each other but are connected with one another in all kinds of ways and accordingly demonstrate a clear similarity in the structure and diversity of their analytically irreducible determinants.

23. The need for a double investigation

The sequence in which we just mentioned the many determinants of earthly being was arrived at through resolution. Analyzing reality in its completeness, further and further, we finally arrive at diversities that cannot be further analyzed.

Having arrived at these, it is also possible to follow the reverse route. In this case, we begin where analysis ended, that is to say, with the analytically irreducible diversities and then proceed in the direction of ever-greater complexity.

> Comment: The analytically irreducible diversities are, therefore, not elemental in nature: To analyze is not the same as finding component parts.

As it stands, we could simply confine ourselves to the inquiry mentioned first, for it indeed has a greater advantage over the second. This advantage cannot lie in its being "creative," for that it is not. All human knowing is a part of that which is created and this investigation is no exception to this rule. The advantage I have in mind has to do simply with the fact that the "whole" comes to the foreground.

But precisely because this glimpse of the whole may not be lacking, we cannot confine ourselves to the second inquiry apart from the first. For a clear view of the determinants, which are discerned later, can only be had if their connection with that of which they are determinants is kept in mind: The earth, after all, is not a collection of kingdoms, a kingdom is not a collection of kinds, a kind is not a collection of things, and a thing is not a collection of analytically irreducible determinants.

There are, however, great advantages to be had when the second investigation follows the first. In the first place, we eliminate the danger of never getting beyond vague generalities and speaking of wholes without ever seeing the wealth that they contain. Secondly, in this manner, we clearly see that the whole we saw first cannot be built out of the "parts" obtained through resolution: What is lacking is precisely the connection that was kept in mind when following the first route.

24. *Nevertheless, a preference is necessary*

Meanwhile, the scope of this *Isagoge* does not permit us to devote an equal amount of time to both routes of this twofold investigation.

So as not to let the advantages of the second route elude us, after the brief treatment of the first route above, we now turn our full attention to the second.

25. Initially not discussing something does not imply its elimination

Hence, we continue the investigation in a moment by beginning with the analytically irreducible determinants of a thing, so as then to proceed ever further in the direction of that which is concrete.

In doing so, it is unavoidable that much that is of primary importance is not discussed initially. At the same time, we should keep in mind that we do not for a moment exclude any of this in our knowing activity. For example, that along this route religion is discussed last does *not* mean that we eliminate it from our investigat*ing*. On the contrary, religion also distinguishes our knowing from that of non-Christian thinkers. Our conception concerning the archè and limit, our expectation in which we do our investigation, always attuned to new surprises, and the determination both of the field that we can explore and of the point of orientation that dominates the entire route, all rely on the Word revelation of God, accepted through faith. But that is not all. We also owe to the Word of God the insight that what we, as a result of this postponement, examine first is not the full concrete life of everyday, whose wealth we will, precisely because of this detour, be better able to appreciate.

> Comment: The elimination of this knowledge and of the religion that obtained this knowledge is, therefore, not possible, and, hence, the question as to the desirability of the same cannot even come up for discussion.

The same also holds, however, with respect to everything else that is not discussed right away: It is tabled because it is simply not possible to deal with everything at once.

26. Subdivision

The subdivision of this second part follows from the above. We will discuss the following:

Division I   The structure and direction of things and humans
Division II   The structure and direction of the kingdoms and of humankind

Division I
Structure and Direction of Things and Humans

27. Subdivision

In the treatment of the structure and direction of thing and humans, we discuss the following:

Chapter 1 The two most simple determinants and their basic connections (the structure)

Chapter 2 The third determinant and its combination with the others (the direction)

Chapter 1
The Two Simplest Determinants and Their Basic Relations (the Structure)

28. Subdivision

In this chapter, we will discuss the following:

Section 1 The two simplest determinants, the diversity within both, and their combined occurrence

Section 2 The two basic connections within these determinants, the diversity in both, and their combined occurrence

Section 1
The Two Simplest Determinants, The Diversity in Them, and Their Combined Occurrence

29. Subdivision

Two of the simplest determinants are found in things. It is immaterial in what order we deal with them because they never occur separately. They must both be discussed, however, before treating their combined occurrence.

From this follows the subdivision:

A. The first most simple determinant and its diversity
B. The second most simple determinant and its diversity
C. The combined occurrence of both most simple determinants

A. The First Most Simple Determinant and Its Diversity

30. An example of the first determinant of earthly being-subject

When a person says "psychical," he is not denoting something that is not created earthly. Psychic being does not exclude being created earthly but presupposes it. It is a matter of *being created earthly* in a determinate way. Put differently, the word *psychic* denotes something that is created earthly with a further determination.

31. The diversity in the further determination of being earthly subject

Now, if all that which is created earthly were psychic, it would be impossible to speak of diversity in the determination of being earthly subject.

All that which is created earthly, however, is not psychic. Other determinants occur besides this one. In this regard, we distinguish the following: *arithmetic, spatial, physical, organic, psychic, analytic, historic, lingual, social, economic, aesthetic, juridic, ethical,* and *pistic*.

> Comment 1: By the arithmetic, we must understand the domain of (unnamed) magnitude. In other words, that of more and less.
>
> Comment 2: With reference to the spatial, the following observations are in order:
>
> a. The spatial is not a mode of intuition (Kant) but a property of all things.
>
> b. The spatial is not identical to "environment." This is because there are other things in the environment of a thing that share its spatiality but also possess other properties. And the thing alluded to is in turn in the environment of those other things; it, too, is spatial, but not exclusively.
>
> c. Spatial is not the same as extended. Figures, planes, and lines are extended. But also points, which have no extension, are spatial. A point is neither a number nor a movement.
>
> d. The spatial does not, as we might suppose based on tradition, have a Euclidian structure: Euclidian space is not truly spatial, as we shall discover later (see §65).
>
> Comment 3: The following considerations are to be kept in mind with reference to the physical:
>
> a. The term *the physical* is synonymous with terms such as "movement," "the energetic," "the kinetic," and "the mechanical."
>
> b. As far as the first and last terms are concerned, we must beware of misunderstanding.
>
> i. The movement in question here is not secondary or arbitrary, due for example to being thrown, but the primary movement that by vir-

tue of its being created by God is proper to the creature insofar as it is physical.

ii. The term *the mechanical* is not to be confused with "machinelike." The latter is found only where there are machines, that is to say "(material) culture"; it is not original but presupposes human activity. We must, therefore, reject every machine theory in the philosophy of nature; not only the "machine theory" concerning the organic but also that concerning the inorganic.

Comment 4: By the organic, we are not to understand exclusively or even in the first place the static features studied by morphology but primarily those dynamic features investigated by physiology.

Comment 5: By the psychic, we are to understand exclusively that which is studied by a scientific psychology that is mindful of its limits. That is to say, only the mode of behavior (in animals and humans) that is of a primary sensitive kind and that which (as object) is correlate with it (see §§65 and 66).

Comment 6: The analytic does not coincide with the logical, at least to the extent that the latter is understood as a collective term that, on the one hand, does not embrace all that which is analytic but only the result of analytic activity and, on the other hand, includes a good deal that is not analytic.

Comment 7: The historic is not the same as the genetic: It is true that the former never occurs without the latter, but genesis is also found in contexts where we cannot speak of history, as, for example, in the case of the splitting of stars and of the reproduction of plants and animals. The historic is to be understood as the province of power, including tradition and know-how (see §207).

Comment 8: By the lingual, we are to understand everything that is language, that is, not only the spoken but also the unspoken part of it.

Comment 9: The social has reference to intercourse and human interaction.

Comment 10: The economic is the domain of value-weighing thrift.

Comment 11: The aesthetic is the field of harmony.

Comment 12: The juridic is the domain of retribution.

Comment 13: By the ethical, we must understand that which has reference to troth in friendship and marriage.

Comment 14: With reference to the pistic or pisteutical, the following should be kept in mind:

a. Positively. These terms designate "sacred belief (or faith)."

b. Negatively. First, "belief (faith)" is not the same as "religion," which can only be dealt with later (see §115ff.). Second, as we have already observed, "belief (faith)" is not identical with faith in Christ; all people believe, but not everyone believes in the Christ of God (see §11).

It is plain that there is a rich diversity in this first determinant, and this rich abundance is perhaps even greater than we have seen so far.

32. Terminology
For the sake of brevity, we call the diversity discussed above the "thus–so difference."

33. The mutual irreducibility of the thus–so determination
Within one and the same *so*, further determination of *so* can occur, as we shall see below (§§37 and 60–63).

However, none of the thus–so determinations can be reduced to another. If we attempt to do so, we become involved in antinomies, which, however, by virtue of everything being-subject to a law that is correlate to it, cannot occur in the cosmos in a primary sense, that is to say, apart from human error. They are the result of a confusion we will discuss later (§§201 and 202).

34. Law determination
It makes no sense to speak of being-subject without accepting a law that holds for that which is subject to it. Hence, there is a determinant of law that corresponds to a determinant of being-subject. So, too, if it makes sense to speak of "psychic being-subject," then it makes just as much sense to speak of a "psychic law" that holds for the psychic, because this is subject to that law.

35. The diversity in law determination
It follows from this, however, that diversity in law determination runs parallel to the diversity in the determination of earthly being-subject. Consequently, an arithmetic law holds for that which is arithmetic, a spatial law for that which is spatial, a psychic law for that which is psychic.

In brief, the difference in being-subject is correlate with the difference in law.

B. THE SECOND (THIS–THAT) DETERMINANT
AND ITS DIVERSITY

36. The determinant denoted by "this"
To say "this number" is to say something other than simply "number"; and in this case, too, the difference in words corresponds

to a difference in that which is denoted by them. Let us take a closer look at this difference.

That which is denoted by the words *this number* can be, for example, the number three. The number three is a number. That is to say, it is subject to the arithmetic law. But we do not find this property only in the case of the number three, but in the case of everything that is number. The determinant denoted by the word *this* is not in conflict with the similarity between the number three and all other numbers. Nor does it do away with this similarity: It presupposes it. It is simply another determinant.

37. *The nature of this determinant*

This determinant, too, belongs to the analytically irreducible determinants. That is why it is difficult to circumscribe it.

To avoid confusion, however, it is good to show briefly that it does not coincide with what we already discerned in the earthly subject (§33), namely, the thus–so determinant (a) and its further specifications (b).

a. To this end, I first ask myself: Is this further determinant something other than a diversity in thus–so determination? Let us try to clarify the import of this question by a specific case. Thus, I can put it, for example, in the following way: Is the relationship between *number* and *this* the same as that between arithmetic and spatial?

To ask the question is to answer it negatively, for it is plain that what causes the number to be "the number three" is something other than spatiality, which is entirely lacking here.

b. Is it then perhaps the case, one might ask, that the determinant "this" is a further specification of "thus"?

This question also must be answered in the negative. To support this negation, it is sufficient to juxtapose the term *this number* and the term *rational number*. In the latter case, we have the designation of a further specification *of* number *as* number; however, there are many rational numbers, but there is only one number three. Consequently, this determinant does not further specify the numerality of three but is a determination that retains its significance even when all further specifications *of* its numerality have been added up.

38. *The diversity in this determination*

If no other number existed besides three, then it would be impossible to speak of diversity in the this determination of numbers. But since there are, in fact, more numbers than this one alone, we must also deal with this diversity.

As *this number,* three is different from all *other* numbers. The word *other* here denotes that all numbers that are subsumed under it lack the determination being-three. Nevertheless, they most certainly have a qualitative determination of their own that is entirely parallel to that of *this number.* This can be indicated by means of the terms *this, that,* and so on.

39. Terminology

In connection with what is noted above, we can typify this determinant briefly as the *this–that difference.*

40. The law-sphere

Therefore, the this–that difference is not incompatible with the possibility that *this* and *that* are alike in that the same law holds for both.

All thises and thats for which the same law holds together constitute the domain or the sphere of this law; they are *its law-sphere.* Because there are many laws, there also exist many such law-spheres.

Consequently, we may not deduce from the fact that we illustrated the existence of the this–that difference only in the case of the arithmetic law-sphere that this difference occurs only here. It occurs in all law-spheres. For it is also true that the one spatial figure is not the other and that a distinction can be made between this and that *energetic activity,* this and that *analytic activity,* this and that *ethical act,* and so on.

C. The Combined Occurrence of Diversities in Both Determinants

41. The line of thought

If it is to be possible that the diversities in both of the determinants that we have discussed so far can occur in combination, then they cannot be reduced to one another. We must, therefore, first discuss this mutual irreducibility.

42. The mutual irreducibility between the thus–so and the this–that difference

a. The this–that difference in a law-sphere presupposes the peculiar nature of the law-sphere (see §36). Therefore, the difference in nature between the law-spheres is certainly not to be reduced to that of this–that.

b. However, the nature of the this–that difference has been shown to be distinct from both every thus–so determination (see §37A) and all further specification *of* a thus or a so—it is an *additional* determination (see §37B).

c. For that reason, we can say that the thus–so difference and the this–that difference are mutually irreducible.

> Comment 1: To clarify the text, we will occasionally add a diagram. If we picture the difference between a *this* and a *that* as vertical lines, then the thus–so difference, given the fact that it is irreducible to the former difference, can be pictured most adequately by means of horizontal lines. We get, then:
> 1. Diagram for the difference of *this* and *that:* | |
> 2. Diagram for the difference of *thus* and *so:*   ———
>
> Comment 2: The reason the vertical lines are chosen for the former difference rather than for the latter can best be indicated later (§55).

43. *Clarification in terminology: The terms individual and modal*

Up to this point, we have made do with the expressions *this and that* and *thus and so*. However, these do not meet the requirement that holds for scientific language, namely that it must be unambiguous—every word may have only one meaning. Both words are easily used interchangeably and can refer to differences and properties that are of no importance for the structure of that which is created. But it is precisely with this structure that we are concerned here. Therefore, the continuance of our investigation will gain by the introduction of a clearer terminology.

What we need, based on the irreducibility that we have established, is two words, each of which has a meaning of their own. That which is designated by the one term must be the diversity between thus and so in the sense of those properties that are relevant for the structure of creation, whereas that which is designated by the second word must be the diversity between the thises and thats that are also relevant in the same sense for the structure of that which is created.

> Comment: The terms *quantitative* and *qualitative* may readily come to mind. On further reflection, however, this pair will not serve in this context.
> a. Of the two diversities in question, that between a thus and a so can certainly not be denoted by the word *quantitative*. But also for the designation of the difference between a this and a that, this term can only be used within the arithmetic. In this way, the whole difference between thises and thats in the nonarithmetic remains unnamed. Al-

though we can speak of "two stones," etc., the difference between the one stone and the other is no more quantitative than that between two plants, animals, or persons.

b. The term *quantitative,* therefore, can be applied in neither of the two cases, whereas the term *qualitative* can be used in both cases and is, therefore, inappropriate.

We could certainly explore several other terminological attempts at this point, but the scope of this study does not allow this and, in this division, it requires only a positive exposition. That is why I begin here by establishing the terminology and give only passing attention to the question of whether it meets insuperable objections.

I call the difference between thus and so *modal* and the difference between a this and a that *individual.*

Now, one might say, "Both terms are well known in philosophy and often mean something other than what is intended here." But that is not a problem. If one were to require of an unconventional conception that it only employ terms that have never occurred in other systems, then it would be obligated to introduce new words everywhere. This would certainly not enhance the readability of such a study (Richard Avenarius's attempt is an example of such an approach). If this rule were to be consistently applied, it would have the effect that no one would be able to understand anyone else. To be sure, it is not legitimate to deal arbitrarily with terminology, but it is questionable whether the line (*grens*) between nonarbitrary and arbitrary coincides with that between traditional and novel. Very often, because of all kinds of misconceptions, a term has acquired a traditional meaning, which can no longer be maintained once the mistake has been unmasked.

Of the two terms suggested here, the first is not likely to meet with resistance from the side of tradition. The modal diversity may be richer in my view than elsewhere, but this does not immediately affect the meaning of the term. There will be more resistance from the side of the philosophic tradition against the use of the second term: Is individuality not the exclusive privilege of humans? To counter this objection, however, we may point to the results of recent discoveries in arithmetic, geometry, physics, and so on in which the emphasis falls increasingly on the individual character of each number, each spatial figure, and each atom. Consequently, the objection we have in mind is not based on arbitrariness on our part but on the exaggerated importance attributed to humans by the advocates of the traditional usage. This can be documented in its historic development (for example, the Greeks) but is completely out of tune with all of those special sciences that have broken with this exaggerated view.

Because I cannot in the present context discuss the development of this misconception of the basic structures in the cosmos, let the counterargument I have just mentioned suffice.

44. The terms subject modality and law modality

After what we have said in §43, the terms *subject modality* and *law modality* will no doubt be clear. In connection with what was said at the end of §34 we must point out that the modality of being-subject is always the same as that of the law correlate with it.

45. The combined occurrence of both determinants

Being-individual and being-modal are different from one another and, therefore, have to be dealt with and named separately. But this difference does not involve being separate. In fact, neither of these determinants ever occurs alone. For example, a specific number is both arithmetic (that is, modally different from space, for example) and *this* number (that is, something that is individually other than every other number).

> Comment: The diagram for this occurrence in combination therefore becomes (per our comment in §42) the following:

46. The occurrence of diversity in modality in this combination

a. Every circle is subject to both arithmetic and spatial laws. Every stone is subject to these two as well as physical laws. In the case of a plant, besides the three subject modalities mentioned so far, we also distinguish an organic one. In the case of an animal, besides the four we came across in the plant, we also distinguish the psychical. A human being possesses, besides the five we have mentioned, all the others that were enumerated in §31.

b. Actually, what we have said so far is not even complete. For in all of these cases, the modalities that are not mentioned with them are nevertheless present, even though they are not present in the same sense as is the case in the examples we just mentioned. I hope to return to this point later (§65). Nevertheless, the examples mentioned in the first paragraph are in any case sufficient evidence that different subject modalities always exist together in any individual *this;* that was the point of this subsection.

Comment: The diagram for this more complicated combination therefore becomes:

47. *The term subject unit*

Taking into account what has just been said, an individual *this* can properly be called an "individual subject unit." Therefore, circles, atoms, organisms, animals, humans, the state, the church, and so on are all subject units; numbers, however, are not included.

Keep in mind that this term serves exclusively to indicate the fact that the individual determinant always occurs in combination with a *manifold* of modalities. Yet much more is involved in "things" than we have discerned up to this point.

48. *Modality and time*

Included in that "much more" is time, at least insofar as it is modal and can therefore be discussed at this point. My not discussing time was done advisedly. Only now is it possible to make clear the proposition that time is neither an individual nor a modal difference. Nevertheless we do find it in all the modalities of the subject units: in the arithmetic as succession, in the spatial as simultaneity, in the physical as the time of movement, in the organic as development, in the psychic as tension, in the analytic as *prius* and *posterius* (earlier/later), in the historic as period, in the lingual still as adverbs of time and the tense of a verb, in the social in the giving of priority [for example, "ladies first"], in the economic in the giving and receiving of interest, in the aesthetic as aesthetic (not pure) duration, in the juridic as length of validity (think of the retroactive force of a positive law), in the ethical in the choice of the "right" time, in the pistic in the alternation of liturgically festive and ordinary periods.

> Comment 1: Time is, therefore, not a mode of intuition—it exists independently of our mental activity.
> Comment 2: Time is not a modality; therefore, the juxtaposition of space and time is incorrect.

49. *The different modalities of the subject unit in time—the term subject function*

Because we are now also taking time into account, it becomes evident in retrospect that we have so far conceived of the different modalities of an individual subject unit as though they were timeless. We can now dispense with this abstraction—the modalities of an individual subject unit never exist outside of time.

Once this insight has been gained, it is also possible to introduce a shorter term for this being-subject of the individual subject unit to laws of differing modality, namely, "the functioning of the subject unit." Consequently, we can say concisely that a subject unit has more than one subject function.‡

The (subject) functions of a subject unit differ from each other, of course, modally.

SECTION 2
THE TWO FUNDAMENTAL CONNECTIONS IN BOTH DISTINCTIONS AND THEIR OCCURRENCE IN COMBINATION

50. Introduction and subdivision

We met with connection both between that which differs individually and between the subject modalities. These connections, too, almost always occur in combination. Consequently, we make the following subdivision:

    A. The connection between that which differs individually
    B. The connection between the subject functions
    C. The combined occurrence of both connections

A. THE CONNECTION BETWEEN ENTITIES THAT DIFFER INDIVIDUALLY

51. The being connected of a this and a that

We take our point of departure from the simplest case, namely, where two individually differing entities are similar in modality of subject functions and are, therefore, subjected to the same law. However, similarity is not the same as connection. Nevertheless, such connections do exist.

For example, in the arithmetic law-sphere, the numbers three and four stand in a certain relationship to one another. Two circles can intersect; in the energetic law-sphere, the one energy can be changed into another. Two organisms can live in symbiosis. I can be subject to psychic suggestion by my fellow human; in the analytic domain, two propositions can stand in the relationship of premise to conclusion.

---

‡ Editor's note: Read both uses of "subject" here in the sense of "subjected-to" (see §70 as well). After paragraph 59, there is also talk of subject functions in contrast to object functions.

52. The term interrelation

So far, we have talked only of connection. We are now in need of a term that denotes specifically the connection between that which differs individually. Let us choose the term *interrelation* for this.

> Comment: The diagram for an interrelation can best be drawn, following our earlier diagrams, as follows:

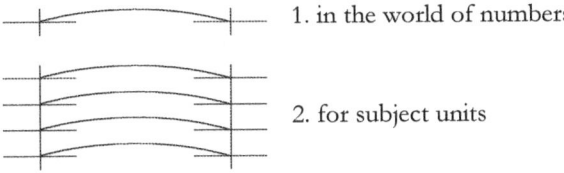

1. in the world of numbers
2. for subject units

53. The modality of the interrelation

It is possible to say that different numbers stand in a certain relationship to one another. But we cannot say of numbers that they do or do not intersect, that they are or are not of equal force, or that they live in symbiosis with each other. For numbers are something other than lines, forms of energy, and organisms. The interrelation between two or more numbers, therefore, turns out to be different from the connection between that which differs individually in the nonarithmetic law-spheres. In other words, the modality of an interrelation is the same as that of the law-sphere in which the interrelation occurs; and terms such as *intersecting, being of equal force,* and so on are, therefore, more concrete than the vague denotation *interrelation*.

B. THE CONNECTION BETWEEN SUBJECT FUNCTIONS

54. Introduction

That two entities that differ individually belong to a single law-sphere was not enough to establish the existence of a connection between them (see §51). Nor is sufficient reason given for the use of the term *connection* between subject functions if we simply refer to the fact that they often occur together (see §46). For surely it is one thing to observe that a circle is subject to both the arithmetic law and to the spatial law, but another thing if I am able to answer the questions: Is the spatial-being of the circle connected with its (modal) property or function of being-arithmetic? And, if so, what evidence is there of a connection between the arithmetic and the spatial subject function?

However, if we attempt to answer these questions, then it appears in both cases that there is something presupposed, namely a natural order of subject functions. Consequently, we must look at this first.

55. *The order of the subject functions*

Let us examine whether there exists any order between the arithmetic and the spatial, and, if so, what it is. A polyhedron, for example, is subject both to spatial and to arithmetic laws. It has a stereometric form, and its planes can be counted. But at the same time, there is more here than a "both-and." The fact is that spatial properties presuppose arithmetic ones and not vice versa. For it is possible to express the length of a line with the help of numbers, but it is not possible to clarify the relationship of numbers simply with the help of the relationship between radius and circumference. Therefore, when I calculate the length of a line, I do have interrelations between numbers at hand, but I have no use for the interrelations between lines when I am busy with numbers.

This indicates a certain order between the two. There are numbers everywhere where there are lines. But it is quite possible for spatiality to be absent when I speak exclusively about numbers. Numbers are, therefore, presupposed in the case of lines, but lines are not presupposed in the case of numbers. In the order of the subject functions, therefore, the arithmetic precedes the spatial.

Similarly, every movement presupposes spatiality. Every organic activity presupposes the conversion of energy. A psychic state presupposes organic life—a certain constitution of the blood. Analytic discernment presupposes a sensitive attention (sometimes only a very weak one) with reference to something. Historic life presupposes the presence of some analytic judgment. Speech, whether or not it comes to expression, presupposes historic activity. Social intercourse presupposes language, and so on. Conversely, it is not true that a line's being tangential to another presupposes conversion of energy: I can no more explain a tangential line in terms of the latter than I can explain the relationship of numbers in terms of lines.

> Comment 1: In the foregoing, I have only indicated for the sake of brevity that every function presupposes that which is next lower to it. However, this implies, of course, that it also rests upon all of the other lower functions. This becomes evident, for example, from the fact that when there is something wrong in those lower functions, the higher functions do not function well either. For example, an inflammation in the organic is accompanied by pain in the psychic. And certain kinds of brain damage disturb the function of thinking.

Thus, there appears to exist a natural order of subject functions in which that which is more complicated always presupposes the less complicated, but in which the lower does not presuppose the occurrence of the higher functions.

More specifically, it turns out that the subject functions occur in the order in which they were enumerated in §31. Moreover, it will be plain, based on this "being-presupposed," why I earlier (§42) chose horizontal lines for the denotation of thus–so differences.

Comment 2: In the first place, we can now incorporate this order of sequence in the diagram given in §46. To that end, one should begin with the listing of the functions from the bottom, that is, with the arithmetic. It also turns out that the differences between subject units, listed in §46A, can be represented by the differences in length in the vertical lines of the diagram above.

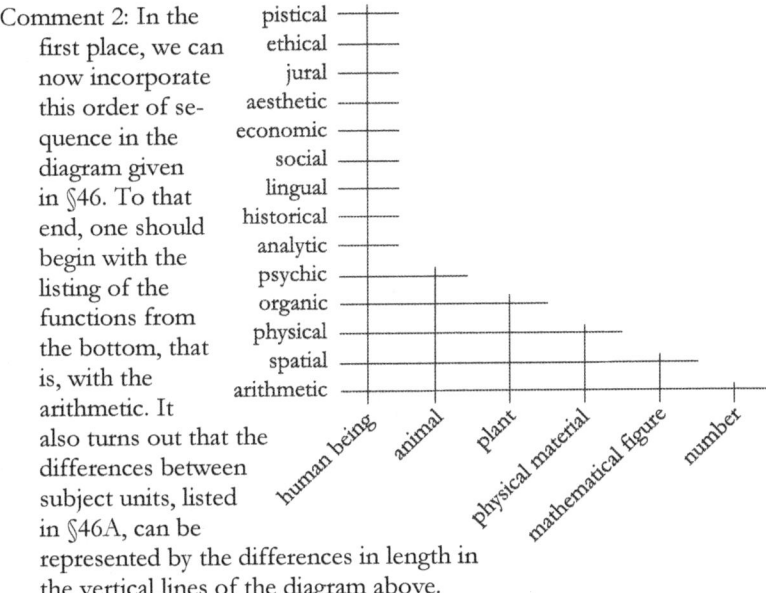

56. *The terms substrate and superstrate*

We may call those functions that are presupposed in a given function its *substrate* and those functions that are not presupposed its *superstrate*.

In this way, the substrate of the psychic function includes the arithmetic, spatial, physical, and organic functions. Whereas its superstrate includes all functions, except the four we have mentioned and the psychic function itself.

The more substrate functions a given function possesses, the less superstrate functions and vice versa.

For that reason, there are two limiting cases: The lowest function, the arithmetic, is without any substrate, whereas the highest is without any superstrate. All other functions possess substrate and superstrate.

57. Dichotomies and trichotomies of the total number of subject functions

If I now take any one function as a point of departure, then I can summarize all of the others as "not-thus." This negative expression indicates in the case of the arithmetic function only its superstrate and in the case of the pistic only its substrate. However, in the case of all other twofold divisions of the order of the subject functions, the negative term covers both substrate and superstrate without distinguishing them terminologically.

For that reason, it is clearer to avoid the negative circumscription.

a. If I then first take the lowest and the highest function, then all of the remaining functions can be designated positively, as its superstrate and substrate respectively.

In this way, without negation, I come to two dichotomies. There is no preference for either above the other.

b. However, if I take any one of the other functions—just as long as it is not the highest or the lowest—and avoid the negation, then I come to trichotomies. Examples of such trichotomies are: spatial, subspatial, and supraspatial; psychic, subpsychic, and suprapsychic; and so on.

If the number of subject functions is n, then there are, therefore, $n - 2$ trichotomies possible. There is no preference for any of these threefold divisions above another. And there is nothing given here beyond a terminological summary of substrate functions and superstrate functions.

> Comment 1: If one forgets this and considers two or three groups of functions of a thing as things, then one must infer the existence of things, for example, like the *res cogitans* (thinking thing) of Descartes, that are taken to possess higher functions but not lower functions. However, this is in conflict with the mutual connection between the functions the existence of which is evident in all kinds of ways.
>
> Comment 2: The two dichotomies and the $n - 2$ trichotomies of the total number of subject functions are not in conflict with one another but are compatible.

58. The evidence for the mutual connection between subject functions

The mutual connection between subject functions is evident on two sides, namely, on the subject side and on the object side.

59. The evidence of the mutual connection between subject functions on the subject side

This consists of the analogy of one function with other functions. This analogy is a double one, for a subject function is analogical on the one hand with its substrate (if any) and on the other hand with its superstrate (if any).

60. The analogy of the subject function with its substrate: Retrocipation

The more complicated subject function presupposes one or more less complicated subject function(s). This means not only that the latter precede(s) the function involved, being, in the order of the subject functions, (a part of) its substrate.§ But also that the more complicated subject function in its turn refers back to its substrate. Thus, a "dimension," for example, is definitely spatial in character. Nevertheless, space refers back, in the multiplicity of dimensions (which can always be multiplied), to number.

> Comment 1: The number of spatial dimensions can always be multiplied. Our preference in everyday life for three-dimensional space cannot be explained until later (see §65).

This reference back of a higher to a lower function can be given the perspicuous name *retrocipation*.

The examples of this connection—which does not occur in the arithmetic because it lacks a substrate—can be found everywhere in the cosmos. Thus, all of the supra-arithmetic functions retrocipate on the arithmetic: All of these functions possess a multiplicity that is inherent to them—a multiplicity of dimensions but also of forces, of organs, and so on. We discover something similar in the supraspatial spheres: They retrocipate on the spatial; their occurrence transverses a course on the basis of which it is possible to describe this occurrence, as far as this analogy is concerned, with a curve. Furthermore, all of the supraphysical retrocipates on the physical substrate: all of these functions bear a dynamic character—think of growth in the organic, emotion in the psychic, mobility in thinking, and so on. Further examples of retrocipation are: development in the supraorganic; the "feel" of things in the suprapsychic; the (nonscientific) cognitive element (of both thinking and knowing) in everything above the analytic; the role played by the scheme means–ends in the suprahistoric; the language of social intercourse, of commerce, of poetry, and such in the supralingual; commerce in the suprasocial; the thrift principle in the supraeconomic; the harmonization of interests [in the

---

§ *Editor's note*: All of the relevant versions of the text have "superstrate" here.

supraesthetic; doing one's duty]** in the suprajuridic; and the assurance of belief [in the supraethical, i.e.,] in the pistic.

It follows from the above that the higher a function is situated in the order of functions, the more retrocipations it possesses: Whereas the spatial has only one retrocipation, we find no fewer than thirteen retrocipations in the pistic.

> Comment 2: Of the retrocipations in the pistic, two have been prominent in history: the retrocipation of the analytic (knowing) and that of the ethical (trusting). However, these two are not the only retrocipations: another example is sacrifice, in which the pistic retrocipates the economic. It is, of course, completely incorrect to conceive of the first two retrocipations as the component factors of faith: They are only traits present in all faith alongside other features.

The number of retrocipations is, therefore, one (in the second function) plus two (in the third function) + . . . thirteen (in the fourteenth function), to make a total of ninety-one.

> Comment 3: A retrocipation can be represented schematically with the help of an arrow pointing downward in the following manner.††
>
> Comment 4: Since the retrocipations of a higher function onto substrate functions are

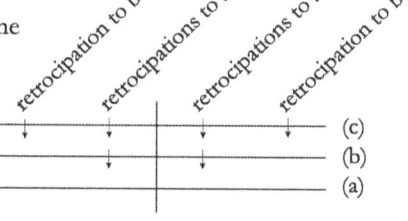

inherent to that function, it is possible to briefly denote which functions are present in this way in an individual subject unit in terms of its highest function. Thus, a circle is a spatial subject unit. A river is a physical one, and a plant an organic one, while the total of human functions can, for the time being, be called a pistic subject unit.

** *Editor's note*: These examples of retrocipations were added in 1941a. However, reference to the aesthetic as well as an indication of the retrocipations to the juridical were not included. Vollenhoven did not amend this in the copy he used for his lectures. "Doing one's duty" is the editor's suggestion.

†† The arrows represent the analogical structure among the functions and are repeated on the function line, to the right and to the left of the vertical line, which represents the subject unit. This repetition has to do with a distinction that will be made later—between the left and right direction of functions (see §91). Drawing them on each side of the vertical line makes clear that the analogical structure of the functions remains the same even when the direction changes.

61. *The analogy of a subject function with its superstrate: Anticipation*

The connection between subject functions is manifest, however, not only in the fact that a function refers back to its substrate, but also in that the substrate refers forward to its superstrate.

Someone going through the series of positive whole numbers in an orderly fashion for the first time will mention only natural numbers and hence count: one, two, three, four, and so on. But in doing so, she only mentions "natural" numbers and does not take into account the connection of these numbers to their superstrate. However, if she takes the retrocipation of space to number seriously, then she will discover by way of this detour that this enumeration is far from complete. For the length of every line can be divided in all kinds of ways into a number of parts, including the length of the hypotenuse of an isosceles right-angled triangle. Also in the case of this division, the rule holds that the smaller the divisor of a number, the greater the quotient. If we now postulate the length of the equal sides of the triangle to be one, then the length of the hypotenuse is $\sqrt{2}$. This $\sqrt{2}$ is a number as well, albeit an "irrational" number: It fits into the series of positive numbers without any difficulty. The same holds for $\sqrt{3}$, and so on. Evidently, the arithmetic, as number series, therefore refers forward in the irrational numbers to space. If we take this into consideration, then we no longer count one, two, three, four, [...] but $1(=\sqrt{1})$, $\sqrt{2}$, $\sqrt{3}$, $2(=\sqrt{4})$, $\sqrt{5}$, $\sqrt{6}$, $\sqrt{7}$, $\sqrt{8}$, $3(=\sqrt{9})$, and so on.

This forward reference of a function to its superstrate may be designated with a term formed analogous to "retrocipation," namely, "anticipation."

Anticipation, of course, occurs only where there is a superstrate present. For that reason, it is lacking in the pistic. But also elsewhere, the presence of a specific function does not guarantee that it here, too, anticipates; different from retrocipations, it only does this in subject units in which still higher functions are present.

Nevertheless, within this framework, we discover also a rich diversity of anticipations. The arithmetic of nonspatial subject units, for example, not only anticipates the spatial in the irrational numbers, but also the physical in differential and integral numbers. Similarly, the spatial anticipates the physical: Already Archimedes spoke of a gravitational "line" and a "center of gravity" in mathematical figures. In the case of organisms, the physical "anticipates" the higher. An example of this would be the fluids that occur in plants as well as in animals and humans. In the case of the plant, these fluids exclusively anticipate the organic, but as blood in animals and humans, they also anticipate the supraorganic. There is a further difference here between animals and humans: In the case of an animal, the blood exclusively anticipates the psychic, for example, in the acceleration of circulation when excited. But in the case of a human being, it also anticipates the suprapsychic, for example, in blushing. We find the same to be the case mutatis mutandis in the organic. Animals—at least the more highly developed ones—and humans possess a brain, which is organic in character. It is a part of the body and also displays organic defects, but it does not occur in plants. At the same time, there is once again a difference to be observed between animals and humans. In animals, the brain anticipates the psychic only; in humans, on the other hand, it also anticipates the suprapsychic—we need only think of the significance of this organ for thinking and speaking.

In the supraorganic subject, there are anticipations to be observed as well, albeit only in the functional existence of human beings. Some examples of this are the following: The psychic anticipates the suprapsychic as logical feeling (in the case of success or lack of it in analytic work), historic feeling, lingual feeling, aesthetic feeling, juridic feeling, and so on. The analytic anticipates in logical mastery, the historic; in the economy of thought, the economic; and in the compatibility of both actions and results of thought, the aesthetic. The historic anticipates the lingual in the recognition or denial of historic significance and anticipates the social in that culture is bound to society; the lingual anticipates the economic in economy of language and the aesthetic in harmony of language; the social anticipates the economic as effusiveness and reserve in the social graces. The economic anticipates the juridic in industrial regulations without juridic sanctions. The juridic anticipates the ethical in the consideration of extenuating circumstances in the making of a verdict.

Comment 1: Anticipations can be pictured schematically with the help of a vertical arrow pointing upward in the following manner:

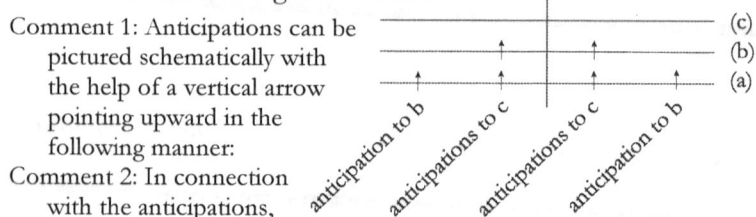

Comment 2: In connection with the anticipations, the *highest* function of a subject unit also fills the role of *leading* function.

Comment 3: The doctrine of anticipations has to date not been worked out with the same degree of clarity as that of retrocipations. This has to do in part with the state of affairs in the special sciences; arithmetic, for example, has not advanced beyond the discovery of the anticipation of the arithmetic to the physical.

62. *The combined occurrence of retrocipation and anticipation*

Whereas the highest subject function of a subject unit possesses only retrocipations and the lowest possesses nothing but anticipations, both occur in all of the other subject functions. They retrocipate their substrate and at the same time anticipate a superstrate (if present).

These remarks would seem to be nothing but a repetitive summary of our earlier findings, yet this is only an appearance. The fact is that here again, it is possible to obtain a deeper insight into the unity of subject units, more specifically with reference to retrocipations. After all, these everywhere refer back to the substrate. But in the doctrine of anticipations, it became evident that the substrate in the case of subject units with different leading functions is not the same. A corollary of this is that retrocipations to different substrates are also mutually different.

Once again, an illustration may illuminate our point. Both in the case of humans and animals, the psychic retrocipates the organic, whereas the latter in turn anticipates in both cases the supraorganic. However, because the anticipation in question—brains and senses—is anything but the same, the psychic in each case does not retrocipate a similar substrate, and, hence, this retrocipation is also not the same in humans and animals. Humans also suffer psychically in a different way than animals. Not only, for example, because humans' feeling for justice (which is lacking in animals) has been offended but partially also because the primary pain of a case of encephalitis (inflammation of the brain) differs because that inflammation, too, though it evidences points of agreement, is not the same in humans and animals.

The same is, of course, true for the retrocipations of the other sub-analytic functions and also for the retrocipations of these to their substrate.

> Comment 1: We must now introduce the indication of retrocipations and anticipations in our diagram of subject units. If we combine our earlier diagrams, we come up with the following:
> a. when no more than two functions are present:
>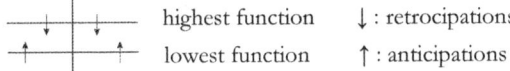
> highest function   ↓ : retrocipations
> lowest function   ↑ : anticipations

b. when three functions are present:

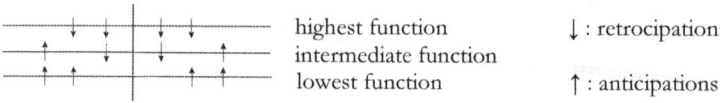
highest function
intermediate function
lowest function

↓ : retrocipations

↑ : anticipations

c. when more than three functions are present:

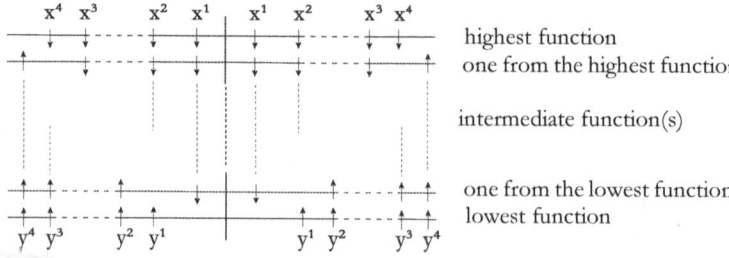

highest function
one from the highest function

intermediate function(s)

one from the lowest function
lowest function

x^1 : retrocipations to the lowest function
x^2 : retrocipations to the one from the lowest function
x^3 : retrocipations to the second from highest function
x^4 : retrocipation to the one from highest function
y^1 : anticipation to the one from the lowest function
y^2 : anticipations to the second from the lowest function
y^3 : anticipations to the one from the highest function
y^4 : anticipations to the highest function

63. *The modality of the subject function—in connection with retrocipations and anticipations*

The character of the subject function remains the same also in retrocipation and anticipation. Length remains spatial, that is, it is only subjected to the law for that which is spatial; a gesture remains organic, that is to say, it is only subjected to the law for that which is organic. The joy of faith is not pistic but psychic. And an association that has the advancement of its members' economic well-being as its goal (for example, labor organizations and management associations) is not itself a business enterprise: its president is not related to the other members as employer to employees.

> Comment: The analogies, then, are inherent to the subject function. If this basic thought is neglected, we fall into a dangerous dilemma, for then one of the following proves to be the case: either the retrocipations and anticipations become intermediate functions between the function in question and the two adjacent ones or the function in question becomes a collection of three subfunctions.
>
> In the first case, we end up with a *regressus ad infinitum*: the analogies that have been promoted to pseudofunctions in their turn require retrocipations and anticipations that again become intermediate functions between the original analogies and the original function, and so on.

In the second case, we end up with a strata-theory that opens the way to an arbitrary grouping of different functions. This happens, for example, when feeling, thinking, and willing are brought together under the heading "psychic."

64. *A more complete sense of the term subject unit*

Not every individual "this" is a subject unit. The latter name is only used to denote an individual this that possesses two or more subject functions. On the other hand, nothing further has been included in this term up to this point.

In the previous sections, however, there was talk of a connection between the different subject functions of a subject unit. Now that we have again seen something more of the fully concrete, it is evident that what seemed to be a terminal point before was no more than a resting spot. Having come further since leaving this point and looking back, seeing more, we can summarize the old with the new. Since no subject unit exists without such a connection between its functions, there is no reason to introduce a new term at this point. As long as I still need this term, I understand by it: an individual this with two or more functions that stand in vertical, mutual connection.

65. *Evidence of the mutual connection of subject functions on the object side:*
The repetition of the substrate in the superstrate

Nowadays, the common opinion is that the difference between subject and object is nothing more than a distinction, that is, the product of human thinking. Or else, if this is not considered to be correct, then in any case, this difference occurs for the first time in that which is analytic. However, this opinion is not consonant with the structure of the cosmos.

If the existence of objects is recognized, however, then it must be seen in its connection with the cosmos as a whole so as to prevent an exaggeration of its importance.

If we do this, it turns out that the object is not a relation of subjects, but the repetition of the substrate in the superstrate.

The simplest example of this can be found in the spatial law-sphere. A straight line, as long as it is not intersected by another straight line, is extended endlessly in a single direction or dimension. In the multiplicity of its dimensions, space retrocipates the arithmetic law-sphere. However, this multiplicity of dimensions has the implication that as soon as a straight line is intersected by another one drawn in another direction a point arises that they have in common.

We are here met with something that up until now we have only touched on in passing. For points do have spatial character, but unlike lines, they are discontinuous.

Let us take a closer look at these matters.

The discontinuity of points reminds us of that of numbers. We might, therefore, be inclined to speak here of a retrocipation. But this is precisely what is forbidden us by the discontinuity of points, since the character of the subject functions remains the same also in retrocipation, and the spatial subject, also in its retrocipation, always shows continuity. We therefore come upon something here that has to do with a connection with the arithmetic and yet does not coincide with the retrocipation.

Nevertheless, it is not isolated from retrocipation either: Without the multiplicity of dimensions, there are no points.

If we are to give account of what we have found, then we can say that the discontinuity of number is here repeated within space and that this repetition is rooted in the fact that space retrocipates the arithmetic.

The case that we have just dealt with is only one of many. This is already apparent in the case of the arithmetic function. For this function is repeated not only in the spatial but also in all of its remaining superstrate functions. As an example, we might adduce here the moment as the repetition of the arithmetic in the physical.

But the arithmetic function is not the only one with such object functions in their superstrate spheres. For example, space is repeated in the physical as physical space or distance. Other examples of a repetition of space are life space, perceptual space, analytic and representation space—in other words, space in an organic, psychic, analytic, and technical sense.

> Comment 1: Technical space is Euclidean space. In this way, it will be clear why space in itself is not Euclidean. Similarly, it becomes clear why every attempt to approach the existence of non-Euclidean space with the aid of representations is doomed to failure.

The supraspatial is also repeated in its superstrate. For example, physical movement is repeated in the organic as stimulus, in the psychic as sensibly perceptible (roughness, color, sound, taste, smell), in the analytic as the knowable, in the technical as formable, in the lingual as nameable, and so on.

The same holds for the leading function in plants and animals. In this way, an organism that possesses subject functions in none of the supraorganic spheres does possess an object function in all these spheres. A flower, for example, has no feeling, yet it is psychically perceptible. It does not think, but it is analyzable. It is not technically busy, but in a nursery does prove to be formable. Moreover, it can be given a name lingually. It has social usefulness, such as highlighting a canal or dike, and although it is not itself economically busy (lilies of the field do not toil, neither do they spin [Matthew 6:28]), it does have an economic value. It is also aesthetically beautiful or ugly; it can be legal property or *corpus delicti* (evidence presented in a court of law). It is an ethical symbol of troth in friendship and marriage ("Say it with flowers!"), and it is a pistic object of belief and unbelief.

> Comment 2: This also casts some light on the sacraments: As far as their leading function is concerned, they are nothing but water or wine and bread. In other words, they are physical and organic subject units (and not the body of the Lord as Luther believed, influenced as he was by the incorrect theory according to which every statement is a statement of identity). But they lend themselves as pistic object to be the sign and seal of something.

In summary, every subject function possesses an object function in every superstrate sphere.

> Comment 3: Objects can be modally classified, just as retrocipations can be within the subject—that is, they can be grouped as spatial objects, physical objects, and so on. Within every modal group, it again makes a difference as to which substrate function is repeated in a given case. The number of classes within the different groups is, therefore, not equal: The spatial law-sphere has only one class of objects, namely points. The physical already possesses two, the organic three, and so forth. The pistic law-sphere has the greatest number of classes of object functions, namely thirteen. The total number of these classes, therefore, amounts to ninety-one and is, therefore, as great as that of the retrocipations.
>
> Comment 4: Objects do not only play an important role in the cosmos and in our practical lives but also in the history of philosophy and the special sciences—we need only think of the debate about "secondary" qualities between subjectivism and objectivism.

If we do proceed not from the subject functions but from the subject units, then it is correct to say that all subject units, including those that do not possess all the subject functions that occur in the cosmos, have functions in all spheres.

Conversely, in any given law-sphere, every subject unit occurs, if not as subject, then as object. This is sometimes also called the universality of the law-sphere.

> Comment 5: It is under objects that we must classify a good number of the so-called "secondary qualities."

66. *The relationship of subject functions to object functions*

We have, therefore, learned to distinguish, apart from modal differences, two kinds of being-subject, namely, subject functions and object functions. Let us now look at the relationship of these two.

a. Concerning this relationship, it was already possible for us to say positively that what is lower owes its presence as object in the higher law-sphere to the fact that the higher function retrocipates its substrate.

b. Concerning the relationship of subject and object, we can say negatively that it is not possible to derive subject functions from object functions or vice versa, to derive object functions from subject functions: acknowledging also in this regard the wealth of the cosmos, we are bound to acknowledge each of them as existing next to each other.

(1) It is not possible to derive subject functions from object functions. Thus, a (continuous) line cannot be built up out of its (discontinuous) points. Attempts to do this anyway always rest on a failure to recognize the difference between subject functions and object functions. This is evident in that the latter are first viewed as a subject function, whereby their derivation is then an easy matter.

> Comment 1: This is the mistake made, for example, by someone who wants to construct a line out of its points and to this end begins by conceiving of points as spatial subjects, that is, looks upon them as very small lines. This mistake is often masked by saying that points are lines, smaller than any measure that can be laid next to them, and that it is, therefore, possible to build up the larger line only if one has an infinitely increasing number of such infinitely diminishing lines at his or her disposal. But one must choose between one of two alternatives: Either these "little lines" really are lines, in which case they are first of all continuous and secondly finite (that is, intersected by two lines of another direction), so that no more than a finite number of these finite little lines are necessary for the construction of a large finite line. Or else these "little lines" are not lines at all but points, and, in that case, even the infinite increase of them will not provide us with the continuity we are looking for.

(2) On the other hand, the derivation of object functions from subject functions is excluded as well. The theory of self-objectification forgets this, believing that the secondary qualities can be explained from the self-disintegration of a world subject.

Comment 2: One who avoids speculations about the origin of objects but classifies the object under the subject makes the same mistake indirectly. That is done, for example, by someone who considers the secondary qualities of physical things as an interrelation of different subjects or else takes these qualities, being nonphysical, to be intramental.

Comment 3: The expression *next to each other* in our text does not imply that subject and object always belong to different subject units. Besides subject–object relations where this is indeed the case (for example, in the case of the human cultivation of plants and animals), there are also subject–object relations in which subject and object belong to the same subject unit, as is the case, for example, with lines and points of the same figure or with someone's cultivating "a slim figure," and so on.

Comment 4: Let us attempt to also picture the object functions in a schematic diagram. Proceeding from the diagram of subject units found in §55, we can use dotted lines to indicate what has reference to objects in it. The horizontal dotted lines group the object functions♯ modally. The vertical ones do this in accordance with the substrate to which they belong. In this way, the intersecting points of the horizontal and vertical dotted lines indicate the classes of objects schematically.

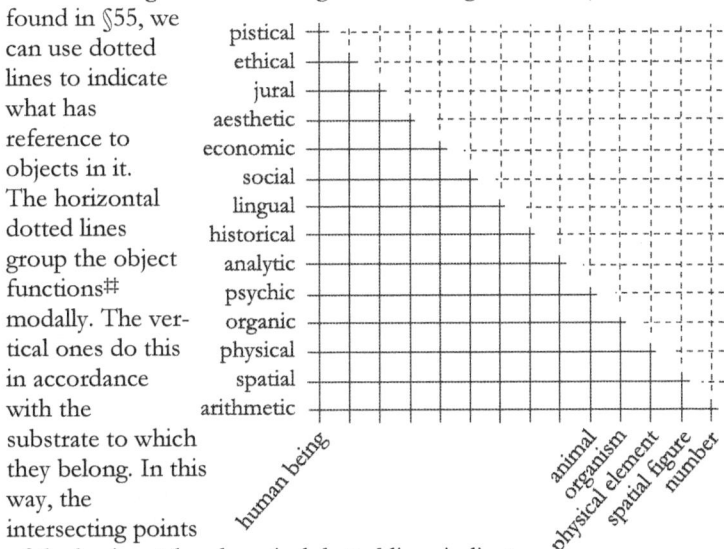

♯ *Editor's note*: The syllabus read "subject functions." In the diagram, the solid vertical lines represent the various subject functions and their substrata. These functions are subject functions only in combination with subject units (human being, animal, organism, etc.).

C. THE COMBINED OCCURRENCE OF BOTH CONNECTIONS

67. *The line of thought*

What turned out to be true of the combined occurrence of both determinants (see §41) also holds with respect to the two connections discussed in both preceding sections. For that reason, here, too, their mutual irreducibility is discussed first; thereafter, we discuss the combined occurrence of vertical and horizontal connections.

68. *The mutual irreducibility of both connections*

a. Just as the modal diversity cannot be reduced to individual diversity, so the connection between modally different functions cannot be reduced to the connection between individually differing thises. In other words, retrocipations, anticipations, and the repetition of the substrate in the superstrate cannot be reduced to interrelation.

b. The converse is also true. A connection between individual thises, that is, an interrelation, is a connection between two subjects in the same law-sphere; vertical connections, on the other hand, are connections between functions in different law-spheres. In other words, interrelation is not to be reduced to vertical connection.

c. The vertical connections (retrocipation, anticipation, and repetition of the substrate) on the one hand and the horizontal connection (interrelation) on the other are, therefore, irreducible one to the other.

> Comment: For this reason, it is illegitimate to use the same term to denote both horizontal and vertical connections. This happens very often in current philosophy. For example, the term *cause* is often used to denote at the same time a particular interrelation in the supraspatial spheres and the connections between the different functions in a single subject unit. Whatever the case may be, a choice will have to be made—keeping in mind, of course, that in scrapping an incorrect term for one of the two mutually irreducible connections, this connection most definitely continues to exist. How we determine our choice in such cases is a question that, from the point of view of the clarity of philosophic terminology, is of secondary importance. "Secondary," however, does not mean "arbitrary." Hence, I would recommend that, for example, the term *cause* (in view of its usage in the special sciences) be reserved for certain supraspatial interrelations that we will discuss below (see §78A comment).

69. The occurrence together of both connections

Here, as elsewhere, irreducibility does not mean being unconnected. On the contrary, vertical connections occur only in combination with horizontal ones.

70. Terminology: The terms figure and thing

To denote the combined occurrence of a "this" with more than one subject function, we earlier coined the name subject unit (§47). Subsequently, however, it turned out that this term was in many respects an abstraction: When we introduced it, we could not yet take into account the different connections that have now been discussed or, consequently, the combined occurrence of these connections. However, now that we can consider these things, the question presents itself whether there is not a fitting, more current term to be found that also denotes these additional implications. Such a term does, in fact, exist: In ordinary language, in referring to what is mathematical, we speak of "figure" and, in referring to what is more than mathematical, of "thing." Consequently, there is now nothing to prevent us from using these terms also in our philosophic work. "Figure" and "thing," therefore, include everything we understood by "subject unit," increased by that which we discovered in the theory about connections.

> Comment: The relationship of mathematical figures and things is this, that the former are always inherent in the latter and are gleaned from things by separate treatment in mathematical analysis.
>
> This analysis is not to be confused with "abstraction": The mathematical figure has the same concreteness as things, even though it does not occur outside of things.

71. Thing and interrelation

With the above, we have just gained the insight that although a thing is not taken up in its interrelations, a thing without interrelations (a *Ding an sich* in this sense) does not exist.

Because the emphasis falls in this way on the interrelations in which a thing stands, it is desirable to further investigate "interrelation." For in this term, we have hitherto taken together a good deal that is mutually different.

72. The direction in the interrelation

Until now, we only spoke of "the" interrelation between A and B. However, that is an abstraction. For two interrelations exist between

A and B, namely, the interrelation of A to B and that of B to A, for example, the relationship of the circumference of a circle to its radius = 2π, that of the radius to the circumference = $1/(2\pi)$. Likewise, the route from Haarlem to Amsterdam is different from that from Amsterdam to Haarlem.

It is already evident from these few examples that both interrelations are not equal but differ according to the direction of the relation. Now this direction is determined by the answer to the question as to which of both relata is the starting point for the relation. The same holds for the interrelation between a previous and a following moment and for the interrelation between two figures or two things.

Hence, the direction in the interrelation may not be neglected.

Two points follow from this:

i. When the relata remain the same, the one direction cannot be replaced by the other.

ii. When the direction remains the same, the relata are not interchangeable.

73. Interrelation between and in figures and things

Direction is present in every interrelation. Let us now examine the peculiarities that do not occur in all interrelations but that enable us to distinguish groups of interrelations.

a. Take, for example, the interrelation between two circles that are tangent to each other; or the interrelation that presents itself when the cheerfulness of a friend who wrote me a witty letter has a contagious effect upon me. In these cases, there is an interrelation between the subject functions, subjected to the same law, of *two or more* figures and things (or human beings).

b. However, when I take note of the relationship between the radius and circumference of a circle or of the case that at a given moment I remember an earlier analytic activity of mine, these prove to be cases in which I have to do with interrelations between relata. both of which lie in the *same* figure and in the *same* thing (or human being).

*74. Terminology: The terms interindividual relation and
    intraindividual relation*

The interrelations between two subject units and the interrelations in one subject unit can be distinguished as interindividual and intraindividual (inter)relations.

Comment: The diagram for the distinction of both sorts is:

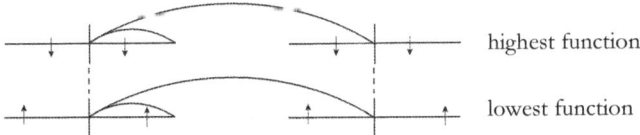

The large curves denote interindividual relations; the small curves denote intraindividual relations.

75. *Interrelations inside and outside a thing*

An interrelation can be inside a thing, for example, that between tongue and palate and that between tongue and food present in the mouth.

Besides these, there are also interrelations outside a thing, like that between hands and the head that rests on them or that between my eyes and the book I am reading.

76. *Terminology: The terms inner interrelation and outer interrelation*

It is appropriate to call interrelations inside a thing "inner," those outside a thing "outer."

> Comment: Do not confuse "inner" with "intraindividual" or "outer" with "interindividual." In both cases, the terms are not congruent, as is evident from the fact that they occur in all kinds of combinations. A few examples that show the untenability of such identification may suffice.
>
> 1. The interrelation, for example, between a needle that penetrated the body and the body itself is interindividual and inner; needle and body remain individual differences and yet their interrelation is an inner one.
>
> 2. The interrelation, for example, between two leaves from the same tree that touch each other, between the tongue of a cat that is licking itself and that part of its fur that is being washed, between someone's head that is resting on his or her hands and those hands, all of these are intraindividual and outer.

Distinguishing these four terms is especially important for the theory of knowledge (see §§160-162). In the meantime, the examples stated show that this diversity is significant as well as apart from all knowledge.

77. *Interrelation between simultaneous and nonsimultaneous relata*

Let us take a closer look at the examples used in §73.

a. The interrelation of a circle that touches another and the interrelation between the radius and circumference of the same circle differ mutually as interindividual and intraindividual. But they are nevertheless similar in that the relata are *simultaneous*.

b. The other two cases are completely different. The interrelation between the cheerfulness of my friend and of me on the one hand and the interrelation between my remembering and my remembered activity on the other differ mutually as interindividual and intraindividual. That does not, however, exclude a certain similarity in another point: The relata of both interrelations are *not simultaneous*.

78. Terminology: The terms contemporary interrelation and successive interrelation, constituent and moment

a. The difference between the two examples in §77 can be nailed down by the use of the terms *contemporary* and *successive*.

> Comment: The irreversibility of the direction of successive interrelations, for example, that of cause and effect and that of basis and consequence, rests on the successive interrelation being combined with the inconvertibility of its relata.

b. The difference between the relata in both interrelations can, correlate with the above, be denoted with the words *constituent* and *moment*. Constituents, therefore, are always contemporary with respect to each other; moments are always successive.

79. The combined occurrence of the differences that have been found

The differences found above occur together.

Cooperation when carrying a burden, for example, is *contemporary interindividual*; the causal connection *successive interindividual*; the connection between the center and circumference of a circle *contemporary intraindividual*; and the connection between two moments of the same existence *successive intraindividual*.

All these combinations are themselves combinable with the interrelations between subject functions as well as with those between a subject function and an object function.

Every interrelation has one direction, regardless of the group to which it belongs.

80. A fuller signification of the term thing

In order to deal with the cases denoted in §79, a number of distinctions must yet be made. But it is now already possible to give a sharper description of "thing." If we bear in mind what was found in §§72–79, it now appears that a thing is a subject unit, with a leading subject function, that possesses contemporary and successive intraindividual relations and stands in contemporary and successive interindividual relations with other things.

81. Active and passive: Introduction

In current philosophy, the active and passive correlation also plays a large role. For that reason, an introductory study should devote some attention to it as well.

All the same, one should be on the alert not to overestimate the significance due this correlation in the cosmos.

a. The active–passive correlation should not be equated with the difference between two groups of functions of the same subject unit nor with the difference between the active (supraspatial) and the nonactive (subphysical) functions. Its sole place is in the interrelations—and then only in those that are supraspatial.

b. But here, too, it has a much more discrete place than is often assumed.

(1) Active–passive does not always coincide with the difference in individuality. This correlation, therefore, is not inherent to the interindividual relation. When, for example, two things cooperate, both stand in interindividual relation, but both subject functions are active.

(2) Active–passive also does not coincide with the relationship between subject and object functions: The emotively perceptible object function color, for example, is not necessarily also a perceived color. On the other hand, subject functions can also be passive, such as in the case of remembered activity.

c. That is why the active–passive correlation ought to be explicitly mentioned as always something extra.

In the following paragraphs, I discuss a few combinations in which this schema occurs.

82. The active–passive correlation in the interrelation between subject functions

a. With interindividual relations. When one human suggests something to another, the one is suggesting or active, the other is receiving or passive.

b. With intraindividual relations. When someone remembers his or her own analytic action of an earlier moment as a later moment, the earlier moment is passive, the latter active.

> Comment: Both interrelations can occur simultaneously: A recollection can be contemporary with a suggestion.

83. The active–passive correlation in the interrelation between a subject function and an object function

a. With interindividual relations. When someone analytically perceives an animal, the latter is passive.

b. With intraindividual relations. When I got my hand dirty and now emotively perceive that, the intraindividual relationship between eye and hand is at the same time a relationship of active–passive.

84. Further distinction desirable both between ways of cooperation and between the differences in the active–passive correlation

The cooperation of two active subject functions as well as the correlation between an active function and a passive function evidence remarkable differences that first become clear when one takes into account the difference in the realms to which the things belong.

The discussion of this difference is availed, however, by first dealing with the third determinant found in the cosmos.

Chapter 2
THE THIRD DETERMINANT, ITS DIVERSITY, AND THE COMBINED OCCURRENCE OF THIS DETERMINANT WITH BOTH OF THE OTHERS (THE DIRECTION)

85. The third determinant

Besides the two simplest determinants discussed above, namely, that of individuality and modality, a third most simple determinant occurs in the earthly subject. It is that of "good" and "evil."

As in the case of the heavenly subject, here, too, the opposition in this determinant is not an original one. That is to say, its appearance is not by virtue of creation.

Meanwhile, since the Fall it does play an extremely important role in the earthly subject and especially in human existence.

86. The diversity in this determinant
   a. It is that of good and evil.
   b. The character borne by this diversity is not only a purely dual one; it is also antithetic. Evil stands *over against* good as disobedience over against obedience.

87. The relationship of this diversity in the case of humans to that discussed previously
As was the case regarding the relationship between the modal and the individual differences, here, too, we must first attend to the mutual irreducibility of the opposition good–evil and the diversities dealt with earlier, so as to then look for an answer to the question of how they are connected.

88. The irreducibility of this diversity to both of the others and to their connections
We will first discuss (A) the impossibility of reducing the antithetic duality to either of the other diversities as such and their combination; subsequently (B), the impossibility of such a reduction to the diversities that present themselves both in their connections and in their combination. In both parts of this discussion, we will investigate first whether there is any talk of duality; only when that is the case will we ask the question of whether this duality is also antithetical.

A. The impossibility of reducing the antithetic duality to either of the other diversities as such (1) and in combination (2).
   1. First of all, we take each of these separately. It is only by grouping these diversities that they can be placed in dual schemas.
   a. The modal diversity "thus–so" is genuinely dual in the dichotomies mentioned earlier: arithmetic/supra-arithmetic and pistic/subpistic. Of these two, the former does not pertain: the opposition good–evil minimally presupposes activity in both of the opposites. That leaves the dichotomy pistic/subpistic. This, too, does not coincide with the opposition good–evil: The pure good was and still is present in all law-spheres—think, for example, of the glorified and yet still-real human nature of Christ—and in the pistic sphere, evil is present just as elsewhere—think of the idolatry that is still present everywhere.

Comment 1: The verse that is quoted to support what is being rejected here, "everything that does not come from faith is sin" (Romans 14:23), of course does not say what people want to read there, namely, that Paul maintained a dualistic view of human functions according to which the pistic function was good and all of the lower functions, including also that of the state, would be sinful in contrast. Were this, in fact, the case, then according to Paul, either Christ would also be sinful according to the subpistic or the subpistic would be lacking in Christ! What Paul means, however, given the context, is something completely different. Paul, when dealing with Christians eating food offered to idols, eating what according to pagan conception is pistic food, distinguishes two groups: the strong and the weak. The strong, among whom he includes himself, know that an idol is nothing and thus deny all ties of any food to an idol and enjoy this food as a gift of God given them for Christ's sake. The weak, in contrast, are in a different position: They have not (yet) been able to free themselves completely from the pagan conceptions in their surroundings and, therefore, see this food as pistic, but, given the fact that they are Christians, also as pistically unclean. That is why they are offended by the attitude of the strong. If the weak, in spite of their own objections, would proceed to adopt the attitude of the strong and eat this food, then they would be eating what according to their own (limited) insight is pistically unclean. Such a use, therefore, would not take place as with the strong in the firm conviction (Greek: *pistis*) that they are not sinning, but in doubt. People eating meat and doing so without firm conviction is what Paul calls sin. Consequently, this text presupposes the antithesis in that which is pistic and is far from saying that the subpistic, in opposition to the pistic, should be called sinful!

b. The diversity in the schema "this–that" is also only dual when we form groups, for example, by the grouping in the schema "I/not-I," which changes every time one takes another I-sayer as starting point. This schema coincides, then, in only one instance with the opposition good–evil, namely, when Christ sets himself over against his surroundings: "Can any of you prove me guilty of sin?" (John 8:46). Consequently, the basis for this does not lie in this schema.

2. The irreducibility of the antithetic duality to either of the first diversities in combination.

In this structure, that of the subject unit, nothing is given that is dual, other than the difference between the two first diversities themselves. But this is in no way antithetic.

B. *The irreducibility of the antithetic duality to either of the basic connections as such (1) and their combined occurrence (2).*

1. Again, we first will discuss the irreducibility of the new diversity to each of the basic connections themselves.

a. In discussing interrelations, we talked more than once of dual differences, for example, of the dual difference between interindividual and intraindividual, between inner and outer, between contemporary and successive interrelations. However, none of the groups in these differences stand over against each other as good and evil. And this is no less the case when it comes to the duality of direction in the interrelation.

> Comment 2: The opinion, still often found among philosophers, that the marriage bond is something evil is to be rejected. This notion is rooted in the desire for autocracy (self-sufficiency), which, when consistently applied, must result in the destruction of every interrelation.

b. As for vertical connections, we distinguish subject (i) and object (ii) and the interrelation between these two (iii).

(i) The subject. Retrocipation and anticipation offer a point of connection to the extent that here again we are dealing with a dual difference that is, in addition, a difference of direction. It is, therefore, also not surprising that paganism repeatedly thought that it was here on the track of the opposition of good and evil. In this context, we should distinguish two conceptions. The one denies the schema of substratum and superstratum for one or more of the higher functions, hence maintaining a partial apriorism, and sees evil in the connection of what it takes to be a priori with that which is not a priori, while the higher, distancing itself from the lower (ascetically and in death), is seen as the good. The other conception, in contrast, thinks in an ascending manner: The higher is seen to be the later. Sometimes it sees the good in the connection of that which is lower with that which is higher—that which is highest here is not only that which is later but also the goal toward which that which is lower has to strive. Sometimes it takes the same connection to be evil: By directing itself to that which is higher, that which is lower denies its basis, to which it must return.

Both conceptions, the partial aprioristic as well as the ascending conception, are to be rejected: Retrocipation and anticipation have only to do with the mutual connection of the functions and not with the opposition between good and evil. Both theories, then, are also connected with uranic and tellurian themes of paganistic religion.

Comment 3: The retrocipation of that which is higher to that which is lower is, therefore, not "bodily," and the anticipation of that which is lower to that which is higher (or of that which is higher to that which is still higher) is not "spiritual"! In Holy Scriptures, these terms have a completely different meaning (see Colossians 2:23). So also, to "not be brought under the power of any" (1 Corinthians 6:12) is something completely different from partial aprioristic asceticism.

(ii) The object. This does not have anything dual about it and, therefore, does not lend itself to speculative connection with the good–evil schema.

(iii) The connection between subject and object. This has one dual difference, namely, the difference in the direction of both interrelations: Here and there it was also connected with the difference between good and evil. In this regard, there are even two conceptions that stand in opposition to each other. The one, objectivism, overestimates the object, making it the law for the subject; the other, in contrast, like, for example, the theory of self-objectification, subjectivistically conceives the relationship in the reverse way. Both conceptions are to be rejected: The law stands above the difference in subject and object, both of which are subject to the law, and hence does not lie in the object. On the other hand, the object proved above (§66) to be something completely other than the result of the breakdown of a world subject.

2. The irreducibility of the antithetic duality to both basic connections occurring together.

In this structure, namely, that of figure and thing, nothing is given that is dual other than the difference between the two basic connections themselves. But that is in no way antithetic.

In Summary: The antithetic diversity cannot be reduced to either of the other diversities or to their connections.

89. The irreducibility of both of the other diversities to the good–evil difference

The fact that it was possible to discuss these diversities, their connections and their combined occurrence in figure and thing, without taking into account the difference in the third schema, shows already that these cannot be reduced to the latter.

90. The mutual irreducibility of the diversities in the three schemas

This follows from the two previous paragraphs.

91. The combined occurrence of these diversities

Here, too, irreducibility does not exclude a combined occurrence. Obedience, just like disobedience, is neither a thing nor a function. In the case of humans, it is a direction of functions.

> Comment: The irreducibility requires that a "*third* dimension" be distinguished in the schemata. However, the combined occurrence requires that this be possible *in* the schemata. To that end, we now emphasize the difference between left and right, which was never rejected and was implicit in the schemata from the beginning. We limit ourselves to drawing this difference in the case of one function: denoting the two directions of the third determinant with horizontal arrows pointing in opposite directions, not in the curves of the interrelations, but in the function line. ←——|——→

92. Terminology: The terms heart, thing, and human

a. On earth, we meet the good–evil opposition *between* humans as well as *in* humans.

Because good and evil, in spite of the sharp opposition between them, are both included under the "direction of human life" and because the difference in direction does not originate in the functions, which are rather determined by this difference in antithetical direction, we must look for some indication of that which directs these functions for good and for evil and which must, hence, itself lie before—or, if you prefer, behind—all human functions.

Here, too, Holy Scripture points the way. Simply think of the passage "Out of the heart are the issues of life" (Proverbs 4:23; see also Matthew 12:34b–35; 15:18; Luke 6:45).

> Comment 1: The "issues of life" does not refer here to the functions as such—for then every thing would have a heart—but to the two religious directions in which the functions work in the case of humans.

b. Although the structure of a human being, if we overlook the heart, corresponds, as was seen, with that of things in that it, too, is functional, we now understand how it can be that a human being is more than a thing: What makes its structure differ from that of things is the heart in the sense of "that which is prefunctional."

> Comment 2: Instead of "heart" in this sense of the term—it does have another meaning—we can sometimes also say "soul" and "spirit." But if we use these words in the sense intended here, we must remember that they are identical with heart and not with higher functions, like the supraorganic, suprapsychic, or suprajuridic. If we who forget that,

we fall into functionalism, overlook what is peculiar about humans, and end up in a teleological or ascetic pseudoreligion.

93. *The relationship, in the case of humans, of heart (soul) and the rest (body)*

The above also throws scriptural light on the relationship between soul and body.

Both have in common with each other that they only occur with human beings (as members of the cosmos created with time).

The difference between these two, at least to the extent that it can be discussed here, lies in the fact that the soul is prefunctional, while the body, in contrast, is functional.

As far as the relationship of soul and body is concerned, it follows from the above that they are not related to each other as higher group functions and lower group functions, but as that which determines the direction and that which in the same person is so determined in its direction. Hence, the connection between them both is intraindividual. Yet it is not an intraindividual connection between functions or between constituents, moments, and so on. For while the connections discussed previously all lay in the area of the functions, this connection is one by which the *entire* cloak of the functions (2 Corinthians 5:1–8) is nothing more than one of the relata.

94. *The relationship of humans and things*

This can only be fruitfully discussed after the structure of the kingdoms and that of humankind in the cosmos is dealt with. That is why we now turn our attention to these manners.

DIVISION II
THE STRUCTURE [AND DIRECTION] OF THE KINGDOMS AND OF HUMANKIND

95. *Introduction*

In the previous division, we dealt with the structure [and direction] of things and humans. In so doing, the concrete existence of that which is subject in an earthly way was already approached in an important way. Yet in no way can it be said that we have arrived. Thing and human are, after all, individual creatures connected with each other, but both stand in genetic connection with other things and humans and they also take their own place in religion. Consequently, these two traits have to be discussed in any case if we want to see that which is subject in an earthly way in its concreteness.

Chapter 1
THE STRUCTURE OF THE KINGDOMS

96. Survey
That which is subject in an earthly way, thing and human, does not stand by itself but is included genetically under one or another kingdom.

Consequently, we have to discuss the variety of these kingdoms and then their mutual connection.

SECTION 1

THE VARIETY OF THE KINGDOMS

97. Introduction
That which is subject in an earthly way displays a variety of genetic connections or kingdoms: the kingdom of physical things, that of plants, that of animals, and that of human beings.

To the extent that these genetic connections are all "kingdoms," there is a similarity; to the extent a variety exists, there is also a diversity.

Let us first of all ask about what is clear concerning this similarity and this difference on the basis of what we have found up until now. Naturally, the answer obtained in this way will not be sufficient—the kingdom connection includes more. Yet that "more" stands out more clearly when we first see how far what we discussed above reaches.

98. Points of similarity and difference between the kingdoms to the extent that both can be clarified at this stage
a. We can state:

(1) Concerning similarity. The things that belong to one kingdom all have a leading function in the same modality.

(2) Concerning diversity. The things belonging to different kingdoms differ in the modality of the leading function.

b. Thinking through both statements further, we find:

(1) Similarity with the things of one kingdom in:

(a) The number of subject functions and object functions

(b) Evidence in everything of vertical connection between these functions

(c) The structure of each of these functions in connection with the number and the nature of the anticipations and retrocipations

(d) The modal determination of the intraindividual and interindividual interrelations

(2) Difference with the things belonging to diverse kingdoms in the same points

99. Another point of similarity and difference

Until now, we have not discussed the genetic connection in the case of things and human beings. However, this connection is present among both things and humans. If we consider that now as well, then we find two points.

a. All things, except for the first ones, arose and arise from previous things. In other words, the rule "nothing comes from nothing," which obviously does not hold for the creating of the first things—that being a work of God—does hold without limit for later things. There is only one exception, which we will get to below (see §102, Comment 4).

b. The genesis of these things takes place within the realm to which that thing belongs. That is to say, the things of one realm—and this holds for humans, too—agree in this that they are not genetically interrelated with the things of the other realms.

> Comment: This formulation is negative. That has to do with the fact that in the nonhuman realms we do find a variety of genetic series or true (genotypical, not phenotypical) species. While there is no compelling reason to assume that these series were previously genetically interrelated, that is the case for human blood groups.

100. What the genetic connection includes

What typifies the genetic connection is the evolving of the younger thing out of one or more previously existing things.

> Comment: This evolving is totally different from the process taught by supporters of the functionalistic theory of evolution and of a certain kind of metaphysics. Their claim is that the superstrate functions of the same thing proceed out of the substrate spheres (epiphenominalism) or, in the aforementioned metaphysics, that the lower set of the presumed a priori group of functions proceeds from the higher part of this group.

The genetic connection always includes the transition of one or more things out of an intraindividual interrelation into an interindividual interrelation.

When two or more are involved in the genesis of a younger thing, then an additional transition takes place. The constituents of the later thing, which originally were interrelated in an interindividual manner, together take on an intraindividual interrelation.

101. The transition from an intraindividual interrelation to an interindividual interrelation present in every case of genesis

This transition, which is not connected with the other one, is found among physical things as well as organisms and lower level animals.

An example of this transition in the realm of physical things is when atoms give off electrons. This process makes genetic sense also for the emitting stuff, the mother atom, because via this atomic "disintegration," as daughter atom, it becomes another element.

> Comment 1: "Individuality" does not mean "indivisibility."
> Comment 2: Due to a change in our concept of elements, the formerly popular view that physical matter was devoid of genesis proves to be unfounded. Matter is that which is physical in its technico-historic object function.

In the realms of organisms and lower animal species, we speak in analogous cases of asexual reproduction.

102. Genesis with transition from an interindividual to an intraindividual interrelation

a. We find this kind of transition with chemical compounds.

(1) In the simplest cases, this is a *total* connection between two or more differing things that each consist of only one element, each of which is different.

> Comment 1: The chemist is not at all interested in the individual occurrence of such a thing. He focuses on the how-to of the connection and on the practical uses of the resulting product. In contrast, the representatives of the relevant special sciences (physicists and mathematicians) are much more interested in questions having to do with the individuality of these physical things.

Both things first stood in an interindividual interrelation, but now take on an intraindividual interrelation so that they become one individual thing.

This change manifests itself in all the functions. Not only the physical function changes but also the spatial (a shift in configuration) and, likewise, the arithmetic (unit).

(2) In other cases, the connection is *not total*. Then only parts of the original things enter an intraindividual interrelation. Only these

parts make the transition from inter- to intraindividual interrelation; the remainder of the original things does not.

That is why, in these cases, these transitions are accompanied by transitions in the opposite direction. The parts that together took on an intraindividual interrelation now stand in interindividual interrelation to the rest of the things from which they came (chemical decomposition).

b. Analogies of these kinds of connections can be found in other realms as well.

(1) They are there in the realm of plants and animals to the extent that reproduction is sexual.

> Comment 2: Just as with a chemical connection, there is no increase for plants, animals, or human beings in the number of modally differing functions.
>
> Comment 3: The laws of Mendel deal with, among other things, changes in the supraphysical functions of organisms, animals, and human beings.

(2) With the respective differences being considered, the same happens with human reproduction. This, of course, has to do with human beings as living souls, in other words, with humans as whole, inclusive of the soul in the sense of heart.

> Comment 4: Reproduction for humans is not limited to the body. An (individualistic) clamor for the opposite opinion regarding the creation of Adam does not hold water. The origin of later human beings is different from that of Adam, for they all stem from Adam and Eve. There is only one exception to this rule, namely, the holy reception of the fatherly factor in the case of the Mediator according to his human nature. On the other hand, this occurrence does not contradict the rule. Rather it confirms it: Christ, in contrast to us, had to parallel Adam.

103. *The active–passive correlation in this transition*

Until now, we considered both constituents of the new thing as active; hence the expression *take on an intraindividual interrelation*. This terminology is also appropriate when the activity of one of the respective constituents develops earlier than the other.

The schema of active–passive, however, can have a part to play in these connections. That happens, for example, when the original things emit the future constituents of the new unit.

Section 2
The Connection between the Different Kingdoms

104. Introduction

Although there are no genetic connections between these kingdoms, they are, nevertheless, tied to each other. That is obvious from the many relations between things belonging to different realms.

These relations are primarily twofold. In the one case, there is an affinity among subjects from the various realms. In the other case, the subject–object relation predominates.

105. This connection with respect to the affinity of subjects from different kingdoms

There are many cases to distinguish here.

a. The connection is one of involuntary cooperation. The warmth generated by the sun, the ground loosened by the roots of lupines, and the collection of honey by bees are all examples. These fit in with certain expressions of human activity and, to that extent, work together with it.

> Comment: In these cases, avoid an anthropomorphic interpretation of the activity of the nonhuman things involved in this cooperation.

b. There is also a connection when the relation between subject functions of things from various realms is coupled with the active–passive correlation, as, for example, when growers and breeders intentionally promote the growth of plants and animals.

c. The affinity is even stronger when the interrelation between these kinds of subject functions moves from interindividual to intraindividual. These interrelations recently came to the forefront because of advances in nutrition theory. Many inorganic salts proved to be vital for the healthy functioning of organisms, animals, and human beings. So also, a number of vitamins are necessary for preserving the organic function—and therewith the existence—of humans and animals.

106. This connection in the subject–object relation

In by far the most cases, the connection between the different realms runs via the subject–object relation. Here, the activity of a member of a higher realm—human, animal, or plant—directs itself to one or more things of another realm in their object function. These kinds of interrelations exist between all realms. A plant will use a stone to support or protect itself and animals use plants for food and nests. But this connection plays an even more important part in the relationship of humans to things in the nonhuman realms.

107. The place of the subject–object relation in the relationship of human life to the things of the remaining kingdoms

In the organic law-sphere, humans, animals, and plants are subjects, while physical things are objects. In the psychic law-sphere, humans and animals function as subjects, while plants, in addition to physical things, function as objects. Qua subject (functions), there is a parallel between humans, plants, and animals in the organic, and likewise another parallel in the psychic between humans and animals.

There are no parallels in the suprapsychic spheres. Human beings alone are subject there. The things from all the other earthly realms are present only as objects. In addition, the number of object functions in these higher spheres is larger than in the lower ones. That explains the great significance of the subject–object relation in and for human life.

Complete insight into what this relation encompasses here obviously is not possible as long as the theory of objects is not yet elaborated. So I will limit myself here to outlining it briefly just for the analytic and historic law-spheres, both of which are of particular importance for human societal connections.

108. The subject–object relation specifically in the analytic and historic law-sphere

a. Human knowing, as will become clear when we deal with the theory of knowledge later, in no way depends entirely on the subject–object relation. Understanding one's neighbors and oneself are obvious counterexamples (see, e.g., §§160d, 161e, 164e, and 168e). Nevertheless, this relation plays an important part in human knowing. If physical things, plants, and animals did not function as objects in the analytic law-sphere, even non-scientific knowledge about these realms would be out of the question—not to mention that know-how would lack its immediate foundation.

b. The subject–object relation is likewise not the only relation in the historic law-sphere. Cooperation is primarily a relation of subject-to-cosubject. This is not to say that the subject–object relationship is any less important here. Of course, its character in the historic law-sphere is different from what it is in the analytic law-sphere: It is not directed to the subject knowing the object, but to the subject mastering the object; in so doing, it includes a mastery of analytic life. When attention turns to the past, the subject–object relation in the historic law-sphere is present as reconstruction; when human interest looks to the future, it is evident as know-how. This, too, given its significance for Western culture, requires broader discussion below (see §§207–215). But we note here already that know-how, too, stands or falls with the subject–object relation in the historic law-sphere. Without this relation, further mastery of physical things (in this case, matter), of plants, and of animals would be impossible.

Chapter 2
THE STRUCTURE [AND DIRECTION] OF HUMANKIND

109. Introduction

The human race is connected with other kingdoms. But God also gives humankind the task to construct, in part upon this basis, societal connections. The completion of this task is divided among many such connections.

Hence, even more important than these connections is the relation in which the human race religiously stands to God.

Consequently, we have now to deal with these connections and with religion.

SECTION 1
THE SOCIETAL CONNECTIONS

110. Survey

We will discuss respectively: the character of these connections, their diversity, their mutual relationship, and their relation to religion.

111. The character

The connections to be discussed occur only in human life. They are founded historically; contain, in addition to this function, also the lingual and social; and intend cooperation in a supralingual sense.

In like manner, all of these connections display the following traits. They are connections of power by virtue of their historic basis. Their lingual character comes out in the fact that consultation, conviction, and convincing are everywhere present as constitutive factors. These connections derive the common trait and presence of the authority–respect correlation from the social function. Furthermore, the leading function of such a connection determines its destination. Finally, those who bear authority—not without contact with those who pay respect, of course—have to positivize and to maintain the law that holds for that particular connection.

> Comment 1: To distinguish the (theory about the) connections from the (theory about the) things, we can better call the leading function of a connection the "prevailing function."
>
> Comment 2: Authority and those who bear authority should be clearly distinguished. The presence of the authority–respect correlation rests on the structure of the cosmos and, hence, goes back to a creation ordinance. Those who bear authority, however, are persons chosen to be in authority and acknowledged as such by others. The fact that the office exists and is filled "by the grace of God" in no way implies that office bearers have something divine within themselves, as the theory about "the kingship of God's grace," in the old German sense, posits.
>
> Comment 3: Part of the task of those who bear authority is to maintain the positivized laws. This includes two facets:
>
> a) If the positivized laws no longer fit in the changed constellation or if they display lacunas, then they ought to be replaced or amended. Maintaining laws that are out of date brings injustice.
>
> b) Office bearers have to maintain the connection against anyone belonging to that connection who tries to withdraw from requirements that the cooperation in this connection sets.
>
> For example, the state cannot limit itself to simply making a list of those who refuse to serve in the military. Whoever does this, whatever the motive, must also bear the consequences, for example, being declared stateless.

Given the fact that living together and ordered cooperation stand in the foreground in these connections, the interhuman relation, that of subject to subject, is dominant. Meanwhile, the subject–object relation is not absent here, either. The number of classes of object functions is, as we found earlier (see §§65 and 66), even greater in these spheres than in the subhistoric. This relation, too, is, in the societal connections, suprahistoric in nature, bearing a dominating character. An example may clarify this. Business is one such societal connection. Now physical things, plants, and animals possess an object function in the economic by virtue of their structure, hence, independent of all human activity. They are economic goods. Were this not the case, there could be no talk of price. Yet the price of these goods is something other than the goods themselves. The "price" is determined by the need of the human subjects, who can intentionally raise and lower it.

These connections then, clearly display their suprahistoric character in their primary interhuman relations as well as in their secondary relation to nonhuman things. Because of that, decision-making stands in the foreground of the first and activity in the foreground of the second. Given, however, that the social also relies on the analytic, both relations are in no way irrational in nature.

112. The diversity

Here, too, there is more than one of these connections. The foundation is the same for all. In addition, the same persons are often involved in different connections. Consequently, the basis for this diversity cannot lie here but must be sought elsewhere. Further investigation shows that this diversity must be attributed to the difference in prevailing function.

For clubs and associations, the prevailing function is the social; for businesses and factories, the economic; for the artist's guild, the aesthetic; for the state, the juridic; for the family, the ethical; and for the cultic connection, the pistic function.

Now, each of these connections includes all of the human functions between the historic and its destination function. Thus, most of these connections also agree with each other in that they have more than just the historic, lingual, and social function in common. Factory, artist's guild, state, family, and cultic connection all also possess an economic side; all of these connections except the factory [and artist guild], also a juridic aspect; and both family and cultic connection, an ethical function. Meanwhile, such communal areas, as well as the historic and the lingual, certainly do differ from each other, because all of these functions are also determined differently based on the difference in destination function. That is why, for example, justice for the cultic community is not the same as for the family and different again from that for the state.

Correlate with this double difference, namely, in destination function and in the functions in between, is also the fact that the task of the office bearers in each connection is unique. That is why a previous generation already, following Abraham Kuyper, rightly spoke of "sphere sovereignty."

In practical life, this adage soon got a strongly negative connotation. But sphere sovereignty, even today, is truly not devoid of meaning. Yet here, too, we ought to see the position as the basis for the negation. This principle means in the first place that those in authority in each institution have to positivize the laws holding for that connection in consultation with those who pay respect.

> Comment 1: Kuyper's adage has lost nothing of its power, even for our time. We can sooner say that its significance has increased. Think only of the response that this conception received elsewhere: the rise of "the subsidiarity principle" among Roman Catholics and the move for "functional decentralization" in socialistic circles. Its significance was also clarified in many ways now that the younger generation of Kuyper's followers took this thought seriously in the theory of functions.
>
> Comment 2: To avoid misunderstanding, we ought to distinguish sovereignty and autonomy more strongly than did Kuyper. The first has to do with modal differences, the second with individual differences. Family and factory are both sovereign in their own realm; the first is qualified ethically, the second is qualified economically. Within the circle of both connections, however, exists a great diversity: there are many families and many factories and businesses. Naturally, it makes no sense—in fact, it is confusing—to also call the freedom of the different families with respect to each other's internal rules "sovereignty." In any case, there is a difference here, and a distinction in terminology can only clarify things further. We find these differences elsewhere as well. States have the same sovereignty, namely, juridic sovereignty. However, with respect to each other, they are not sovereign but autonomous, as are the provinces within the territory of the same state.
>
> Comment 3: Autonomy should also be sharply distinguished from two other matters.
>
> a) From Autonomy in the sense of the self-sufficiency declaration of men with respect to God. This Autonomy stands over against Heteronomy, that is to say, the acknowledgment that the law is set by God and not by us, like autonomy in the sense of being qualified to formulate rules for one's own territory stands over against heteronomy, standing under the laws of another territory. In this way, we can understand that degenerate thought, basing itself on Autonomy, landed up repeatedly in heteronomy. In contrast, Calvinism, proceeding from Heteronomy, was able to maintain both sphere sovereignty and autonomy and, in so doing, in a land as ours, where it had great influence, became and remained the "origin and security of our constitutional freedoms."
>
> b) From autarky, that is to say, wanting to be self-sufficient. Included in autonomy is the acknowledgment of being juxtaposed with

other connections, but autarky, temporarily or not, denies this juxtaposition.

113. *The reciprocal relationship*

It is twofold, namely, genetic and static. Societal connections are given, albeit potentially, with the structure of the human body, by virtue of creation. But because they must become realized in their diversity by humanity itself, we will discuss the genetic relationship first.

a. The genetic relationship is determined by the genesis of full human life. It is rooted in sexual reproduction that, as we saw (§102), also has a prefunctional side to it. The family is the institution in which man and woman prove troth to each other. But that does not constitute the role of the family. For whenever husband and wife are also parents, they also nurture their children in the family connection. This nurturing aims to prepare their children for living not only in their own family but also in all of the other social institutions. That is why for the future unfolding of human life, immeasurably much depends on this nurturing, and likewise, in this nurturing, on answering the question whether this task is seen by both parents and whether in so doing they have an eye for the uniqueness of the different institutions.

> Comment 1: Nurturing is then the task of the family, primarily that of the parents, in the second place, that of eventual brothers, sisters, and family helpers. If the nurturing is endangered, by death, by sickness, or through neglect, then other families, first of all the relatives, have to lend a helping hand. Only when this kind of help is not present does the cultic connection have a task, and in its absence the state, because otherwise these connections, too, as well as the others, eventually will suffer. This task is, however, an extremely limited one. It does not imply that these connections take the nurturing upon themselves, but only that they entrust the child to another family.
>
> Comment 2: As children grow up, schools assist families with their children's education. This assistance, too, itself the result of the cooperation of many parents if things are right, is there not to take the place of the family but to lighten and support the nurturing of the children by the family.
>
> The principle of sphere sovereignty does have very special significance for the school. It affects its relative independence with respect to sister institutions, as is the case for the other life connections, but it also affects the goal of its work. Education aims primarily at sharpen-

ing the ability to distinguish and at conveying distinctions. But without distinguishing their destination, it is impossible to realize societal connections and, tied to that, the unfolding of human life in the following generation, which the school, of course, is there to help educate. Consequently, in the near future, the school plays only a supportive, but important, part in this realization.

b. The static relationship can be defined positively as well as negatively.

(1) Positively, this relationship ought to be one of genuine cooperation, for all of these connections aim at developing different components of human life.

This cooperation includes two things:

(a) Fulfilling one's own task. A state cannot flourish if economic life, organized by trade and industry, does not grow. Family life, too, languishes when the pistic connection falls short.

(b) Acknowledging the unique task of the other connections. After all, they owe neither their origin nor their continued existence to the goodwill of another connection. Consequently, none of these connections have to seek permission from any of the others to act or advance.

This double requirement does not only hold for the area of the prevailing function, but also for the activity of different societal connections in those law-spheres that they have in common. Hence, cooperation does not only imply that state, family, and cultic connection recognize each other's unique nature, but also that they respect each others' bylaws. That is why particularly those who recognize both stipulations in all of these connections have an important task. Loss is inevitable for those who do not acknowledge them.

(2) Negatively, two things are to be taken into account.

(a) In a preventive way, every connection has to keep from getting involved in the internal arrangements of areas where other connections have competence. This is especially true for those arenas characterized by the prevailing function of another societal connection. All the more so, any attempt to sideline another connection by going beyond one's own competence is forbidden.

(b) Once the correct relationship is disturbed, the threatened connection should oppose the high-handed moves of the other one with any fitting means available.

Comment 3: Repeatedly over the course of centuries, cultic connections, including pagan ones, were quick to guard against state interference in their domain—their ecclesiastical rights. On the other hand, more than a few times, a number of states waged a tough battle against the power politics of pistic office bearers in political affairs. Along the same lines, families in the nineteenth century protested against state-directed nurturing programs, while the state itself took action against the pretense of business and industry when the government had to prevent laborers from being so wrapped up in the demands of industry that they had no time left to participate in the life of the state.

This kind of resistance becomes more intense and varied when one connection in functional life strives to be totalitarian, which is to say, tries to crowd out all of the other connections; something that happens easiest with the state for it already includes all the citizens. This kind of struggle runs deepest, however, when, on top of this, one institution wants to be religious and also, in spite of its own functional character, attempts in totalitarian fashion to involve the heart.

114. The relation of these connections to religion

We have mentioned the human heart twice already: the first time when dealing with the structure of humans (§92) and the second when human genesis was being discussed (§102).

Societal connections, too, have something to do with the heart. Although they carry a functional character, the realization of these connections is rooted in the obedient execution of a task given by God—or disobedient lack thereof—and entrusted to the human race of all ages. It is here, in carrying out this task, that the direction of the human heart is decisive.

One case in point is how the struggle concerning the competence of connections has and continues to play a part in human life, particularly when the claim of totality from any connection also touches what is prefunctional in human life. But even irrespective of the confusion about competence, the question is always: In which direction is this or that (societal) connection headed?

Here, too, it is the law of God that decides what is good and evil. More specifically, the second table of the Ten Commandments, in contrast to the first, addresses humans not in their relationship with God directly, but in their relationship to other humans.

Hence, in the first place, we have to ask about the content of this law. It reads, in the summary given by Christ (Matthew 22:39) and in accordance with the Old Testament (Leviticus 19:18): "Love your neighbor as yourself." Three points respectively draw our attention here: the concept "neighbor," the "as," and the requirement "to love."

The neighbor, as well as those addressed in this commandment, is the whole person to the extent that we are placed in his or her proximity during the divinely directed course of our lives.

"As"—Greek *hoos*—is not talking about an amount, as if it were pointing in the direction of the "correct mean" between egoism and altruism. Scripture does not see things mathematical as law for the rest. This term means something else, namely, "in the same way as." This presupposes that we also ought to love ourselves—of course, in the same way as we love our neighbor. As a result, this *hoos* requires a criterion that lies beyond the one love, of self, as well as the other love, of neighbor. The intent is that we are to love our neighbor and ourselves as the image of God, that is, to the extent they, and we as children, are like unto the Father in Heaven.

Regarding love, take note of two things: love's antithetical structure and its prefunctional character.

The structure of this love is antithetical. That is, the command that requires me to love my neighbor and myself to the extent that we display traits of our Father also requires that I hate my neighbor and myself to the extent that we display the opposite.

The character of this love is prefunctional. It does not coincide with our functional existence, because love—or hate—defines that existence. Nor should we equate this love with a specific functional relationship, such as ethical relationships, and certainly not with a sexual-ethical relationship—although this love also permeates both of these. Scripture never refers to the second table of the law—and certainly not all of the Ten Commandments together—as the "moral law."

If we summarize the above, then it appears that the task of bringing life connections to realization ought to be carried out according to the second table of the Ten Commandments. That is what the law requires. Which is not to say that this law is always observed. For even in relationship to that part of the law that has to do with the relationship to one's neighbor, obedience as well as disobedience is present.

Ultimately, these two do not stand alone. The same is true for the correlate part of the law. For just as the law, to the extent that it demands loving our neighbor, is dominated by the command to love God above all, so also is one's relationship to one's neighbor dependent on religion.

Consequently, practicing the task of neighborly love is not identical with religion. But it is directly determined by religion.

With that, we come to our discussion of religion.

Section 2
Religion

A. Introduction

115. The line of thought

As Bible believers, we continually reckoned with the word of God in the foregoing. But the actions of God it presupposes and their correlation on the part of humans have not yet been discussed in detail.

The reason for this was primarily that not everything that can be observed in creation could be dealt with at the same time. But why postpone the discussion of religion to the very end? Certainly not because it is of little significance. Rather, because it dominates the whole of human existence, it was appropriate to first analyze that which is dominated.

We must now also examine religion more closely. For however great the diversity we have found so far in the basic structure of the earthly subject, we have certainly not grasped the earthly subject in its full concreteness as long as religion has not been discussed.

In addressing ourselves to this part of our task, we must emphasize beforehand that it is impossible, in a study like this one, to give anything approaching a complete discussion of religion. We will restrict ourselves to a summary of essentials. For the time being, we must limit ourselves to the most important questions in this regard, namely, (a) What is religion? (b) What does it presuppose? and (c) What is its structure? When these questions are answered, the division of the remaining material will also be clear.

116. What religion is

Religion is the relationship of humankind to the first and great commandment: "You shall love the Lord your God with all your heart, and with all your soul, and with all your mind, and with all your might."

From this summary of the first table of the law, which was given by Christ (Matthew 22:37)—following the Old Testament (Deuteronomy 6:5)—it is plain that God appears here as the God of the covenant. Therefore, religion is the relationship of humankind to the God of the covenant in obedience and disobedience to his fundamental law of love.

117. What is presupposed in such a covenant

In such a covenant, the following are presupposed:

a. The existence of God and his creative activity

The activity of Logos and Spirit play a special role in the latter (Psalm 33:6). This creating does not, of course, presuppose the existence of anything apart from God, such as matter that can be formed.

b. The result of this activity, in other words, the existence of heaven and earth and specifically (as far as the earth is concerned) the existence of human beings.

These humans, with all of their interrelated functions, who God formed out of the earth and who became living souls by God's breathing into their nostrils the breath of life, already with respect to this structure of theirs, differ from all other creatures. Moreover, they were created from the beginning in the image of God, so that their nature was good and they, being created, addressed, and directed to the good by God, could reflect in the covenant, as the concrete correlate of the Triune God, his glory on earth (cf. 2 Corinthians 3:18), and could satisfy the requirement of his law in original righteousness.

> Comment 1: The text cited refers not to beholding but to reflecting the glory of God (specifically in the Mediator).
>
> Comment 2: The formulation *being (created) in the image of God*, indicating a relational state, is to be preferred over *the image of God*, because the latter is an abstraction, a usage that has proved historically to have its dangers. This danger became particularly acute when some who laid the emphasis on "image" then also lost sight of its being related to God, subsequently began to ask what that image might be and sometimes ended up identifying it with a specific group of functions or even with a supposedly innate understanding.

c. The establishment of the covenant between God and humans on the part of God, including the appointment of an office bearer

> Comment 3: We should distinguish here God and his covenant relation to the human race—a possible absolutization of the covenant is thereby ruled out.

Comment 4: In the case of humans, we should likewise distinguish being-in-the-image (initially of God) and office. The former belongs to the nature of being human and is, therefore, to be found in every human, whereas only the first and the second Adam were invested with the prefunctional office here referred to. The mutual relationship of being God's image and office bearer is that the first makes possible the second and is, therefore, presupposed in it.

A failure to observe the difference in question can occur in two ways:
a. Being-in-the-image is subsumed under office; in that case, the former does not belong to the nature of being human, and can, like the office, be lost (Roman Catholicism).
b. Office is subsumed under being-in-the-image; in that case, the difference between Adam and us is removed.

118. The structure of such a covenant

In a religious covenant as in every covenant, there are, after its establishment, two parties: God and the human race in its religion, resulting in (dis)obedience.

Comment 1: After what was said above, there can be no room for misconstruing the term *party*: though humans, being both created by God and put in covenant with him, are the correlate of God in this covenant, they are, of course, in no way God's equals. The instituting of the covenant is consequently "unilateral," its structure is "bilateral."

a. Present in the covenant from God's side is Logos revelation. It always involves: on the one hand, the promise of blessing in the case of covenant faithfulness and, on the other hand, the threat of curse in the case of covenant breaking.

Comment 2: These two "sides" must be clearly distinguished from the two "parties."

b. From the side of the human race in its religion, there is always an appointed bearer of the prefunctional office who must act before God in the things that must be performed on behalf of those comprehended in the covenant.

Comment 3: This office, therefore, has to do with the relationship of the office bearer, and those represented, to God on the one hand, and, on the other, with the relation of the office bearer to those comprehended in the covenant.

Besides the features indicated, we can find others in the history of religion that are not constant. These features have to do, on the side of the law, with the content of the Logos revelation and, on the side of religion, with the person invested with the office, with his or her relationship to the Word of God, and with the relation of those comprehended in the covenant to the office bearer.

119. Division

Based on the differences indicated, we must distinguish two covenants in the history of religion: the covenant of creation and the covenant of re-creation.

B. THE COVENANT OF CREATION

120. Introduction

a. Character. This covenant has two characteristics: With respect to Logos revelation, there is no reference to grace (in the sense of forgiveness) or to re-creation, and, as far as religion is concerned, we may note that the person invested with office was the first man, that his relationship to the Word of God did not prove constant, and that all those who were represented by this office bearer in this office descended from him or were to descend from him.

b. Division: Because this covenant was not kept by the office bearer concerned, we must distinguish here two phases, namely, that before and that after the Fall.

121. The covenant of creation before the Fall

Two stages are to be distinguished in this period. The correlation of Logos revelation and religion occurs in both.

A. *The first stage: Before the creation of Eve*

1. The Logos revelation to Adam

When the Triune God called Adam into being, as the initial execution of his plan to create humans "in our image, after our likeness" (Genesis 1:26), God spoke as "LORD" (Yahweh), that is, as God of the covenant, and God mandated him to till and keep the Garden of Eden (Genesis 2:15).

The first part of this mandate, which among other things meant that Adam was to examine the life of other earthly creatures, referred primarily to the relationship of Adam to an (admittedly limited number of) his fellow creatures (in a field that was still very restricted).

As to the second part, matters were different. It evidently referred to a danger that was threatening from elsewhere and consisted of this, that a part of the world of angels had not remained standing in the truth, or constancy (John 8:44), and were threatening earthly life in the garden. For this part of the mandate is followed immediately by the probationary command (Genesis 2:16 and 17), in which the region is indicated where the attack of the enemy can be expected. The revelation of the death penalty in case of transgression was an additional incentive to stand firm in the face of a possible temptation and thus to gain the blessing—to live eternally in God's favor. This "keeping," therefore, directly touched Adam's relationship to God and his pre-functional office, as prophet, priest, and king, to be faithful to him.

This mandate was in both parts a demonstration of God's favor.

> Comment 1: Hence, the covenant of creation can also be called a "covenant of favor," although, in my opinion, the former term is to be preferred, both because it is more comprehensive and because "grace" is sometimes used in a broader sense than that of "favor forfeited by sin." Whichever term is chosen, however, the doing of works in this covenant was not an earning of God's favor but the execution of a double task that was assigned to Adam by virtue of that favor. (The term *covenant of works*, which did not arise until later, does not mean what, judging from experience, it tends to suggest.) Obeying the covenant of creation held the promise of blessing (victory over the enemy and the inability any longer to die); as punishment for disobedience, on the other hand, was fixed the curse (being worsted in the struggle and suffering God's wrath in the [first] death).

2. Religion

The acceptance, in faith, of task and office

> Comment 2: Then, just as now, faith meant holding for truth all that God has revealed in his Word and relying on his favor; on the other hand, of course, there is not yet any question of faith in "grace" (in the sense of forgiveness).

When Adam named the animals, he also paid attention to the genetic connection between the older and younger generation, and, on that basis, the cooperation of the sexes. He then noticed that he lacked the possibility of such cooperation (Genesis 2:20).

> Comment 3: Holy Scripture does not represent Adam as an asexual being who preceded the differentiation of the sexes or was elevated above it (monogenic in the speculative sense attached to it by Parmenides and others): Adam is a male, who feels keenly the need of a woman as helper.

Consequently, after Adam noticed this lack and God supplied him with what was missing, in accordance with his plan (Genesis 1:26), Adam immediately acknowledges this joyfully as the fulfillment of his desire (Genesis 2:23).

> Comment 4: The information that Eve was created out of Adam tells us that God did not call the second human being into being separately, from the first, but preserved the unity of humankind from the outset.

B. The second stage: *After the creation of Eve*

1. The first Logos revelation to Adam and Eve

This revelation comprised the command of fruitfulness and an extension of the task.

(a) The command the Logos issues is "Be fruitful and multiply!" This already is a clear indication that the depreciation of marriage that is endemic to many schools of current philosophy finds no support in Scripture. We can gain a sound perspective on marital life only if, preserving the Word of God, we look with wonder upon the genetic development of human life as the result of the Spirit's action, which causes human life to flourish (Psalm 127 and 128), both through the proliferation of human lives and through the flourishing of the life of plants and animals that keeps pace with the former (Deuteronomy 7:13 and many other places).

(b) Following immediately upon the command of fruitfulness is the mandate "subdue the earth and have dominion over the fish of the sea," and so on. If we compare this task with the task Adam had been entrusted with before the creation of Eve, then it appears that it has been considerably enlarged: The mandate is no longer confined to the garden but also has reference to the earth and the sea. This extension is no doubt related to the possibility of the development of the human race given with the creation of Eve.

2. Religion

(a) It is no longer the religion of a single person but of a married couple. This has two consequences. The first spiritual institution is rooted from the outset in the prefunctional: Wedlock is viewed here as a relationship of two humans, both of whom are created in the image of God.

> Comment 5: We must, of course, be careful not to identify "being-in-the-image-of-God" with this interhuman institution: There is no trace in Scripture (unlike the conceptions prevalent among many pagan peoples) of a sexual bond in God.

On the other hand, it is only here that Adam's prefunctional office finds its completion. For it was not until after the creation of Eve that Adam could act before God on behalf of another in the things that must be performed before him on behalf of that other (those others) and thus could become "a type of the one who was to come" (Romans 5:14).

(b) With respect to their knowledge of the antithesis of good and evil, the following should be kept in mind. Before the Fall, Adam and Eve had through experience that which was "good," namely, to live as children of God who showed the love of their heart through obedience and through observing the warnings of the Logos against the danger that threatened from the world of the spirits. One of the ways in which they did this was that both, in their relationship to their neighbor, did not live for themselves, as a little world in themselves (microcosmos) or as individuals that shut themselves off from their environment, but in mutual relationship with their neighbor. That neighbor was equipped in a different way but stood in the same relationship to God and was subjected to the same law(s).

Nevertheless, in this period, some knowledge of evil was not lacking. To be sure, the first human beings did not possess this knowledge through experience, unlike their knowledge of the good. Yet an easily pictured act had been forbidden them. They were aware of this prohibition and of the death that was threatened in case the act in question was performed.

Thus, even before the Fall, life was not without the threat of danger. Nor was it without the royal battle in fulfilling the task in service to God, the struggle that constitutes the meaning of history. For the future of humankind, therefore, everything depended on the question of whether Adam, the office bearer, would stand in obedience on God's side in this battle against the evil one or would be disobedient to his Creator.

122. The covenant of creation after the Fall
   a. Human life in and immediately after the Fall

Holy Scripture, the only source for our knowledge about these things, informs us that Satan tempted humans. More specifically, they were tempted with the help of cunning and delusion. For by the question "Did God say?" the covenant relationship was swept aside as well as the Word of God robbed of its character as law. With this, the road was paved for the proclamation of the ideal of autonomy: *eritis sicut Deus* ("You will be like God").

The actual catastrophe took place when, after Eve, Adam also succumbed. For with that the head of the covenant also proved to be unfaithful to God, willfully disobedient to his law, and the weaker one vis-à-vis the enemy.

As a result of the forbidden deed, Adam and Eve no longer stood in a relationship of trust to God: They now feared his wrath. But the reciprocal interrelation also suffered the consequences: Because they first imagined, in their delusion of sovereignty, that they would become God, they were now alienated from each other: One who denies that she is subject to the laws imposed by God will also fail to see the interrelationship, for this stands subject to the laws.

Good and evil now no longer stood in their life in the relationship of that which is present to that which is denoted but in that of past to present. Tainted by sin and no longer able to do the good that the commandment continued to require of them—and, therefore, also guilty in that inability—they were now subject to death. Based on Adam's position of office, this penalty also spread to Eve and all her descendants (Romans 5:12).

The Fall, of course, did not elevate men above the law: The transgression of the law occurs under the law. Nor did the change in the world's state affect the structure of humans and humankind: Adam and Eve would soon become the ancestors of their descendants.

The nature of being human, however, was something that, though it was not lost, did undergo a great change. As we have seen (§117), being-in-the-image-of-God and standing in original righteousness to his law were initially inherent to human nature. Now both of those relational states turned into their opposite at the Fall. As far as the former is concerned, the statement of Zacharias Ursinus applies: "Man is transformed by the Fall from a glorious image of God to an abominable image of Satan." And as to the second state, original righteousness was now replaced by unrighteousness.

> Comment 1: This twofold refusal can be represented diagrammatically as follows:

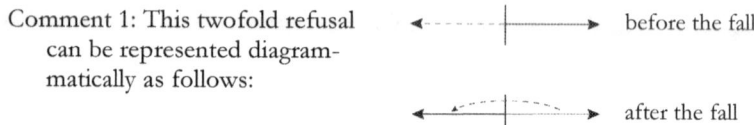

It goes without saying that a man with such a radically altered nature could no longer occupy the prefunctional office, in other words, that Adam had to be relieved of his office (Genesis 3:17ff.).

> Comment 2: On the strength of the distinction between being-image and office, the Reformation here asserted against Roman Catholicism that human nature, though transformed in the bad sense, was not lost; whereas its office was.

b. The first Logos revelation after the Fall

It is primarily, after investigation, the pronouncement of punishment.

Part of this, as far as human life is concerned, affected Adam and Eve together; another part, Adam alone.

The former consisted in this, that the human living souls suffered death. This does not mean that they are annihilated (this part of his work, too, God preserves against Satan) but that their entire existence, despite procreation (which is made more difficult), is a constant death, until by the sundering of body and soul as unity, they disappear temporarily out of the earthly coherence. This misery is made even more onerous during our lives by the curse that God pronounced not only over the serpent but also over the ground, so that the latter would henceforth seriously impede human cultivation.

> Comment 3: As far as this subdivision is concerned, therefore, the curse does not consist in our connection to the earth but in the connection of the lot of the earth to human beings.

The second punishment applied to Adam alone, specifically his holding of office. Since he had not fought on God's side against Satan, his office was taken away from him in the prediction of the conflict between the seed of the woman and the seed of the serpent. This office was destined for another, who would, via Eve, be joined to Adam in the state of innocence but would have nothing to do with him in his double capacity of unfaithful office bearer and fallen ancestor.

But this last point already belongs in part to what follows.

C. THE COVENANT OF RE-CREATION
1. INTRODUCTION

123. *Line of thought*

With respect to this covenant, we must first discuss its character, the way it is worked out in time, and the principle of division for that which requires further treatment.

124. *The character of this covenant*

Here, too, we must distinguish points of similarity (A) and of difference (B) with the earlier covenant.

A. This covenant has in common with the first both that which is presupposed in it and the covenant structure.

(1) As to the first point, re-creation is not the work of a God other than the God of creation (gnosticism); nor does the second covenant have reference to something other than that which was created before (Anabaptism); finally, the second covenant came into being because it was instituted and an office bearer was appointed exclusively on God's initiative.

> Comment 1: As we have seen above (§117b), the existence of the cosmos belongs to that which is presupposed of every covenant. Now this existence, in the case of the second covenant, is, of course, a continued existence. All the same, this continued existence remains something presupposed in the second covenant. Consequently, it is not the fruit of the latter, and thus not a result of re-creation or of grace: For the punishment for breaking the first covenant was not the annihilation of God's work but the death of the transgressor. And these two do not cover each other. The transgressor was only a component of creation, though a very important part, and to die is to continue to exist under the wrath of God and is in no way a not-existing.

(2) Concerning the structure of the covenant, here, too, Logos revelation and religion, evident in the obedience of the faith in the promises of God, are correlate with each other.

B. Obviously, it is very important to keep in mind the points in which the second covenant differs from the first.

(1) In the Logos revelation there is now, different from the covenant with Adam, talk of grace and re-creation.

> Comment 2: Distinguish grace and gift of grace. Grace is a disposition of God and the opposite of wrath. It does not stand over against sin. Grace is, with wrath, not the opposite of sin, but one of its correlates. Even less so does grace stand over against "nature," which, without further specification philosophically, can in this context be best taken in the sense of "that which has been created in a specific direction." "Gift of grace" is everything that the recipient of grace receives on the basis of grace.

(2) As far as religion is concerned, there is a difference in the first covenant in office bearer (a), in his relationship to the Word of God (b), and in the relation of those comprehended in the covenant to the one invested with the office (c).

(a) The office bearer. Because the covenant structure remained unchanged, once the initial office bearer had proved unfaithful, the first Adam was replaced by the second. His work was also the execution of the task of the office to acquire the promised blessing: to live eternally in God's favor. This task meant that the second Adam, unlike his predecessor, had to stand firm in temptation. But since re-creation is not a second creation, he also had to bear on behalf of his own the punishment that had been fixed for breaking the first covenant so as to satisfy God's justice and to propitiate his wrath.

If we compare this task with that of the first Adam, then we observe that it has become immensely more difficult. For the weight of God's wrath against the sin of the entire human race could not be borne by any human being: Consequently, the office bearer of the second covenant had also to be God. As man, as the seed of the woman, he had on the one hand to be joined with Adam in the state of innocence, and on the other hand to be parallel with him, that is, to be free from his sin. Therefore, we must distinguish in the Mediator the unification of the Logos with a concrete, hence individual human nature and the conception of the paternal factor of the latter from the Holy Spirit, although these two were not separate in time. Furthermore, a distinction must be made between these two, which made the execution of the task of office possible and the investiture with the office.

> Comment 3: The church here spoke of "nature," not of "person" (in distinction from Nestorius), to indicate that, supposing the concept of person was serviceable in anthropology, the human constituent in the Mediator never existed separately, that is as component, because its very origination was subservient to the incarnation of the Word.
>
> Consequently, the positive correlate of the rejection of the view advocated by Nestorius is that the Person of the Son has united himself with the human nature, and that the result of this unification (*henosis*) is a unity (*henotes*), not a unit.
>
> This formula is to be distinguished from a completely different one, according to which the human nature of the Mediator is said to be "impersonal" (*anhypostatos*). For this expression (which moreover has at least three senses and thus can hardly be called univocal) means in essence that either something of the nature in question is denied (either its individuality or its integrity) or this nature is seen as a duality that requires a *vinculum substantiale* ("substantial means of connection"), a role assumed in this case by the Son of God. None of these constructions, therefore, agrees with Holy Scripture or with dogma.
>
> Comment 4: The virgin birth, therefore, does not imply contempt for marriage (as P. A. Kohnstamm and his followers believe) but on the contrary, served the salvation of all of human life, including marriage.

(b) The relationship of the office bearer to the Word of God. In contrast to the case of the first Adam, this relation is constant: In life and death, the Mediator, according to his human nature, placed his reliance on the Word of God—and does this still. Thus, in the hour of temptation, he proved stronger than Satan, for which reason the angels came to serve him (Matthew 4:1–11).

(c) The relationship of the office bearer to those comprehended in him: This relation as well is different from formerly. Because while all those comprehended in the first covenant were to descend from Adam—and he did, in fact, become, through Eve, the ancestor of us all—one participates in the Christ only by imputation. This imputation is two-sided: "God made him who knew no sin to be sin for us, so that in him we might become the righteousness of God" (2 Corinthians 5:21; cf. Romans 8:3; Galatians 3:13; 1 Peter 2:22–24).

With respect to both sides (that is, also as far as the second part, being declared righteous, is concerned), this imputation is anchored in election, which is distinguished from predestination—the former is only a decision for good, the latter is a decision for both good and ill.

Scripture tells us that both predestination and election exist. However, it does not tell us by name who are included in election, except in a few cases, and then only of persons who have died long ago (compare Genesis 25:23 with Malachi 1:2–3 and with Romans 9:12–13). Yet we are not in the dark in this regard. Predestination and election are worked out in time, a process in which the God of the covenant adheres in all kinds of ways to the structure of his own work of creation.

125. The covenant worked out in time

In the process of working out the covenant, being declared righteous becomes a being-made-righteous (justification).

The latter takes place first in the Mediator, specifically in the acceptance of his suffering and death at his resurrection from the dead (Romans 4:25).

This fruit of his work is now conferred by the glorified Christ on all who belong to him in their justification, which is comprised in that calling by which he makes the spiritually dead alive. For this making alive or regeneration is the turning around of the heart, which has the effect that the renewed person, acquitted of guilt and punishment and having a right to eternal life, begins to walk according to all of God's commandments.

> Comment 1: This act of God takes place "immediately," that is, not by means of the persuasion of the will (Remonstrants) or of the conviction of practical reason (school of Saumur), but directly by the Word of God, in the sense of *vocatio efficax* (effectual call). It is God who gives life to the dead and calls things that are not as though they were (Romans 4:17).
> This turnabout can be diagrammed as follows:

This act of God is not to be identified with the preaching of his Word by the envoys of the Christ, for regeneration precedes the opening of the heart to the word of their preaching.

> Comment 2: The revival of this insight since the end of the previous century is especially due to the influence of Abraham Kuyper.
> However, this given of the Scriptures is combined in Kuyper with two other statements that can in any case be distinguished from it and, therefore, ought to be considered separately.
> The content of these statements was that regeneration was the embryonic seed and, furthermore, that it was accompanied by a testimony of the Spirit to the effect that Scripture is God's Word. With reference to the first statement, it may be remarked that Scripture (Luke 8:11ff.) compares the (open) heart with the (prepared) earth, but relates the image of the seed to the preached word: the word "produced" (Mark 4:8). With respect to the second notion, we observe the following: It was Kuyper's intention to keep the testimony in question purely "formal" in opposition to the doctrine of the "inner light," of which he was a vigorous opponent. His conception regarding the (special) testimony of the Holy Spirit (*testimonium Spiritus Sancti speciale*) must not be confused with the theory of a general testimony of the Holy Spirit (*testimonium Spiritus Sancti generale*). Nonetheless, the former was certainly not without content either, which is not surprising because a "testimony" simply cannot be formal. Moreover, such a testimony is superfluous: Scripture in itself is credible and must be acknowledged by the regenerate without such a testimony; what it tells us about the testimony of the Spirit does not come until after Christian faith and, therefore, is not dealt with in this study until later. For that reason, both additions are to be rejected.
> However, this criticism may not lead to a rejection of the basic statement: In the struggle against the overestimation of ecclesiastic office on the remote and recent past, the latter constitutes an important gain.

Regeneration also effects a turnabout in the pistic function (the *fides qua creditur,* in other words, faith by which a person believes). By virtue of this turnabout, faith is now directed to the Word of God that is preached, by the ecclesiastic office bearer, especially to its essence, namely the Gospel. In this way, faith, now in the sense of that which is believed (*fides quae creditur*), is awakened by the preached Word.

Strengthening follows this awakening. This takes place partially by that same preached Word, partially by the use (in faith) of the sacraments.

The preached Word, which is always unconditional, comprises partially prediction, partially promise.

The prediction concerns the first or second coming of Christ, which took place (will take place) despite unbelief among God's people (Genesis 18:12, Isaiah 7:12ff., Luke 1:18 and 18:8).

The promise, on the other hand, has a different character. As promise, it is directed not only to the believers but also to their children and to those who have been taken up together with them into the fellowship of the church; and now, as the promise of God, who is the faithful One, it demands that it will be believed. Thus, this promise comes as a command to the covenant community (cf. *Kort begrip der Christelijke religie,* question 20: "promised and commanded to believe").

Like every norm, this law has a double character: It promises blessing to the obedient and threatens the disobedient with the vengeance of the covenant.

The blessing consists in growth in grace, accompanied by the witness of the Spirit with our spirit that we are children of God (Romans 8:16, (cf.) 2 Corinthians 1:22 and 5:5, Ephesians 1:13–14 and 4:30). This blessing awaits the obedient, that is, the elect insofar as they did not die young.

The curse, on the other hand, consists in this, that the breakers of the covenant will suffer a more severe judgment (Leviticus 26:15ff, cf. 24; Deuteronomy 31:20; Romans 11:28–30; Hebrews 10:28–31 and 12:25).

> Comment 3: For the strengthening of his faith, the Bible believer has recourse not only to the guidance that the preaching of the norm of faith provides but also the use of the sacraments, which have been instituted in connection with the structure of the pistic object.
>
> Comment 4: The sacraments have been given to the church; they therefore presuppose, besides the preaching of the Word of God, the existence of the church and, thus, the operation of the regenerating power of the

Spirit on earth. To prevent misunderstanding, however, we must distinguish between receiving the sacraments and using them. Not only in the circumcision and baptism of adults, but also at the Passover and Eucharist, using and receiving went together if the life of faith was healthy. In the case of the circumcision and baptism of children, on the other hand, matters were and are somewhat different: Whereas the children of believers receive this sacrament, the faith-strengthening use takes place especially on the part of the parents and the congregation. And insofar as the recipients are not born again until after receiving the said sacrament, there cannot be any question of a faith-strengthening use (claiming the promise that was given) while baptism is being received.

The proclamation within the church, both in the service of the Word and in catechism, must keep in mind the nature of the church as Christian pistic institution. Consequently, it is not evangelism (proclamation of the prediction to those outside) but administration of the power of the keys, both to open and to close. Conceived in this way, it is a great influence on the religion of the heart with its prayer and makes the congregation a courageous people—and at the same time one that is careful in its walk with God.

The significance of the church, then, which has existed ever since the Fall, is great. It is, therefore, of great importance to conceive correctly of its relationship both to religion and to the other institutions of human life.

The church is the Christian pistic institution of human life. On the one hand, this means that it does not coincide with Christendom, for the latter manifests its Christianity in other human institutions as well, for example, in Christian family life.

Comment 5: This difference is sometimes indicated with the help of the terms *church as organism* and *church as institution*. This way of distinguishing is not particularly felicitous: "organism" has an established sense for the life of plants and "institution" for the result of juridic action. It is, therefore, preferable to speak of Church and church or else (perhaps this even clearer) of Christendom and church. We must keep in mind, however, that criticism of terms that lack clarity does not do away with the difference that they intend to formulate. This is especially important in the present context, because the alternative would be for all Christian action to be reduced to ecclesiastic projects that would not only hinder such action but would also involve the church in all kinds of questions that are not its concern, because its task consists exclusively in the awakening and strengthening of Christian faith through the administration of the Word of God and the sacraments, as well as through its discerned work. Especially as far as Christian science and scholarship is concerned, the church should take care not to venture into the latter's area; whereas the latter must investigate, besides Scripture, the entire cosmos, ecclesiastic dogma is bound exclusively to Scripture and, moreover, is nonscientific in character.

On the other hand, the church is different from any other human institution. This is rooted partially in its destination function, partially in its direction.

It is already by virtue of possessing a destination function of her own that the church does not derive its right to exist from any other human institution: A pistic institution is peculiar, *sui generis,* and differs on that basis from family and school, state, business, and so on.

Moreover, the church in its entirety is directed to the right, for it is the Christian pistic institution. This makes it different from the synagogue and other non-Christian pistic institutions. But, furthermore, on this basis, there is no room for Christian action in the church parallel to that in the state. The state includes all citizens, while the church can recognize as members only Christ-believers and their children. It is for this reason that a "national church" must always lead a contradictory existence.

The church ought to be one and, therefore, may differ only according to lingual boundaries (*grenzen*) in connection with its preaching. We must not, therefore, find excuses for what does not live up to this requirement. Once again, however, we must not confuse law and subject: In many lands, there exists a variety of Christian pistic institutions alongside each other, all of whom claim the name "church." This situation arose through all kinds of conflicts in the past, partially the remote past. Moreover, many of these schisms have roots that go quite deep. Consequently, they cannot be ignored; much less can they be removed in short order. However, if that which is subject in this case is ever to conform to the law again, then this will only come about as the fruit of a penetrating study of the history of the schisms involved and of continuing reformation in one's own circle. Nor will a reunion based on a compromise that levels the difference in question improve matters—this would only increase the multiplicity by one. Here, too, there is no other yardstick than the law.

Particular care must be taken, meanwhile, that nothing not found in Scripture be introduced into dogma, because this especially often fosters division and delays reunion.

> Comment 6: The study we here have in mind cannot neglect the influence of the many differences in the philosophy current at the time: Conse-

quently, a genuinely Calvinian philosophy will in many ways be able to promote the efforts toward a reunion correctly understood.

In all of these efforts, however, the antithesis must be maintained: It is certainly to the advantage of Christian and non-Christian pistic institutions to gain a clearer insight into what is common to the structure of both and to take this into consideration in their actions; but such reflection, if it takes place in the light of Scripture, will only throw into sharper relief the irreconcilable opposition between the church, on the one hand, and the synagogue and other non-Christian pistic institutions on the other.

126. *Division*

In connection with the fact that the second Adam did not appear immediately, a distinction must be made in the covenant of re-creation between two main periods, namely the one before the incarnation of the Logos and the one thereafter.

2. BEFORE THE INCARNATION OF THE WORD

127. *Introduction*

Character: Prominent in the Logos revelation is the announcement of the second Adam.

Division: In this connection, we must distinguish two periods within this main period, namely the one before the differentiation of the revelation in question and the one thereafter.

a. The period of the nondifferentiated Logos revelation

128. *Introduction*

Character. During these centuries, the revelation of the Logos is still the same for all humans.

Division. Within this period, we must again distinguish two phases, namely the one before and the one after the Flood.

129. *Before the Flood*

a. The Logos revelation

Because Satan seduced man, the first rapprochement (if there was to be any question of living with God again) had to come from God's side, something that was only possible through the love of God.

God did, in fact, come. Taking the new situation into account, his love has the character of grace: Already in Paradise, he announces the

Mediator of the New Covenant. This Mediator, as the seed of the woman, will live in enmity with the seed of the serpent but will be victorious in that struggle.

b. Religion

(1) Correlate with this change in revelation is a change in religion: Though saved from debasement, it is not restored to the old situation but becomes religion appropriate to the new situation, religion of grace. The renewed faith, likewise, holds for truth not only the Word of God spoken before but also the promise of God concerning the deliverance of all who believe this promise (as the Heidelberg Catechism puts it [Q & A 21]: "not only to others, but to me also").

(2) Not all, however, participate in this faith—not a few arrogantly reject the promises of God.

That difference can already be observed empirically in the life of the first family: Eve accepts the promise and relies on the God of the Covenant (Genesis 4:1). Cain, on the other hand, is arrogant: When God does not accept his sacrifice, Cain burns with anger, does not listen to the warning against a new sin, and does not concern himself, even after his evil deed, with anything but the preservation of his own life, now struck by a special curse (Genesis 4:3–14).

> Comment: The council of God also includes this difference. Predestination, which has reference to all development, is, of course, double (*gemina*) with reference to the taking of these two ways; when it concerns a decision for good, it is called election. Accordingly, election is not *gemina*, provided it is distinguished from predestination.

(3) In connection with this difference in the human race, the antithesis now reveals itself therein. This is, of course, also discernible in the working out of the task that was assigned to humankind and in the cultural results of its efforts.

130. *After the Flood*

a. The Logos revelation supplemented at the time of Noah

(1) Although faith in the promises of God remained (Genesis 5:24), sin gained ground rapidly, and the earth was even filled with violence. Therefore, God repented that he had made the creatures. Yet he did not destroy his work but decided to mitigate the outbreak of sin.

(2) Simultaneously with this announcement of his instruction to Noah, God also makes known to him the term *covenant* (Genesis

6:18) to give an indication of life after the Flood in reliance on this grace. In administering the covenant with a severely chastised humankind, which was preserved in that very chastisement, God not only refrains from punishing men with a second Flood but also communicates this intention of his, proclaiming the appearance of the rainbow as a reminder of his promise. He also allows the consumption of animal meat for food, promises a regular alternation of seasons, and bridles sin by including in governmental law the blood revenge that had already been exercised before (Genesis 4:23).

b. Religion

(1) By faith (which is not only found among the Semites!) in this enriched promise, the periodic cultivation of the land and of the animals that are required for it, becomes possible. Presupposed in this faith is trust in the basic promise of deliverance.

(2) At the same time, unbelief (which is also found among the descendants of Shem!) has the effect that some regard as divine certain interrelations (such as between sky and earth or between the two sexes), offices (office bearers), things (sun and moon), or functions (thinking, imagination). Unbelief also attaches itself to the periodicity of seasonal change by dishonoring God in the worship of plant gods. As a result of all of this, the assurance of faith is replaced by a sense of insecurity. Thus, we understand how animism could forget that the nonhuman earthly creatures stand in religious relation to God, only by way of humankind, and, proceeding from the correct assumption that there is psychic life also in animals, explained this fact to be a result of the transmigration of the soul. In this way, animism led to the prohibition of slaughtering, by which the benefits of the Noachian covenant were largely nullified.

> Comment 1: The confusion of soul and psychic life is an ancient error.
> Comment 2: The covenant with Noah is, therefore, a phase in the covenant of grace—the second in the period of nondifferentiated Logos revelation.
>
> The denial of this character is related to two misconceptions. According to the first of these, life between Fall and Flood had brought the late flowering of the covenant of creation; according to the second, the covenant of grace did not begin until Abraham. Neither of these views is correct: The main incision of history is found not at the Flood but at the Fall, and the covenant of grace already begins in Paradise, when God, in the absence of a worthy office bearer, promises provision in the mother promise.

This also disposes of the possibility of fitting the relationship between the covenant with Noah and that with Abraham into the scheme nature–grace.

b. The period of the differentiated Logos revelation

131. Introduction

a. Character. Whereas the supplementation in Logos revelation had still been made known to all of humankind in the time of Noah, a remarkable change occurs in the time of Abraham: The new supplementation in Logos revelation is furnished to only a small circle.

b. Once again, two phases are to be distinguished, namely the patriarchal and the national phase.

132. The patriarchal phase

a. The Logos revelation

It has immediate reference to the birth of the promised Messiah, who is announced as the seed first of Abraham, then of Isaac, thereafter of Jacob, and finally of Judah.

This revelation presupposes the revelation given to Noah but also incorporates the assurance given to Abraham, or to one of his descendants, that in him all of the families of the earth will be blessed (cf. Genesis 12:3), over against which Abraham, next to the requirement "walk before me, and be blameless" (cf. Genesis 17:1), which always holds, is confronted with the requirement of faith, particularly faith in this promise also. Circumcision serves as sacrament that signifies and seals the eradication of sin.

b. Religion

(1) Unbelief and faith with particular reference also to this promise are in conflict in the hearts of Abraham and Sarah and in the hearts of their offspring.

(2) Meanwhile, the exclusively Noachian religion also continues (Melchizedek, etc.). In large measure, however, it has only a lingering existence. Yet, though the nations are increasingly estranged from the true religion through immorality, animism, and idealism, God does not withhold his goodness from them: Tangible judgment falls only on certain regions in cases of outrageous excrescences of sin (Sodom).

133. The national phase

a. The Logos revelation

(1) The Logos addresses himself first to Moses and Aaron and calls them to lead Abraham's seed out of Egypt. The Passover serves

as sacrament, the meal of the sacrificial lamb, which reminded Israel of how the angel of perdition passed by their blood-marked houses.

(2) The inculcation of the law of the Ten Commandments presupposes, apart from the foregoing, the deliverance out of Egypt.

Distinct from this law are the commandments for public life, which now restrain blood revenge in family law, and the prescriptions concerning ceremonial practices that certified promises or that served to recall the mighty acts of the God of the Covenant and to avert mingling with the pagans living in the area (for example, the command not to eat certain animals that played a prominent part in many heathen religions precisely on the basis of their connection with the grave and death).

> Comment: In sharp contrast to a fascination with death found among some nations in the vicinity that considered death to open the possibility for extraordinary development, the Word of God continued to see death as punishment. That Israel, in time, also came to know some things about the difference in the situation after death, between those who embraced and those who rejected God's promises, and especially with regard to the difference after the resurrection (Psalm 49), is obviously something completely different.

(3) The prefunctional office of the Messiah is foreshadowed in the three offices of prophet, priest, and king, which stand next to each other. The Messiah, however, will fill all three together. He will be a prophet like Moses and a king like David. The priesthood proved to be more difficult, for that was tied to a tribe other than Judah. Hence, the prediction about the Messiah as priest and king talks of a future in which the differentiation of the revelation to Abraham will be removed: The Messiah will be a priest in the order of Melchizedek (Psalm 110). These prophecies are secure, even if they are not believed, not even by those who, as members of the holy line, will be most affected when they are fulfilled (Isaiah 7:1–17).

b. Religion

(1) The special promises to Israel also require a special faith. Unbelief and the breach of faith on the part of members of the national community are soundly rebuked. If they do not take the warning to heart, then the curse will come for breaking covenant. Differences remain. The sin is more serious as the promises are repeated (Deuteronomy 29:20–21), the covenant is renewed (Joshua 5:1–9), the command becomes more specific (Joshua 6:18 and 7:1), the promise narrows to one family (2 Samuel 7 and Isaiah 7:17), prophecy be-

comes less scarce (Isaiah 24:6), or the reformation among the people was more robust (Zechariah 5:3)—and with that the break more resolute. The punishment, too, is correlated with the difference in guilt. Sometimes, the curse even affects the culture of those being punished (Joshua 7:24, Zechariah 5:4)!

(2) At the same time, God remains a God of the nations who do not know these rights (Psalm 147:20), live without the law, that is, this law (Romans 2:12), but are then, without being judged by this law, also lost simply by not believing the promises that were revealed to them. That does not take away from the fact that God is good to individual aliens, who are outside of Israel's community and excluded from their paschal feast (Exodus 12:43 and Deuteronomy 10:18), as well as to whole groups. For example, the heavy punishment that strikes Egypt and Babylon stands over against God's goodness toward Nineveh when only the threat of judgment brings them to repentance.

3. AFTER THE INCARNATION OF THE LOGOS

134. The abrogation of the differentiation in the Logos revelation with the preaching of the Christ

a. The Logos revelation

(1) The promised Messiah was conceived by the Holy Spirit (Matthew 1:18) and born of the virgin Mary. He is, then, the head of the new humanity, yet, different from the first Adam, without sin. Just as he possessed all of the functions, so also he satisfied in everything the requirement of obedience, including all of the special laws holding for the Jewish people, for he was, of course, born under and bound by the Jewish law. By being united in a unique way with the Logos, who took on the very form of a servant (Philippians 2:7), he also bore the wrath of God against sin. In this way, he saved his own from the curse of the law, that is, from the curse that comes to the transgressor of the laws God gave. After that, raised from the dead, he will die no more, and he sent the Spirit's gifts he acquired out upon his people. Giving to them in this way from his Spirit, the spirit of obedience, he himself is called the head of this body (Colossians 1:18) and the Spirit (2 Corinthians 3:17) that preserves his people in communion with himself.

(2) Correlated with the fulfillment of the promise, there is also a change in the law for the covenant people. First of all, with the promise fulfilled, carrying out the ceremonial activities that pointed

toward this fulfillment becomes meaningless. Christians are free from the commands in question. The political difference between Israel and the peoples, to the extent it still existed, is maintained; Christians from among the Gentiles were not subjected to Jewish political law. And yet, the religious difference is abolished; the preaching of the covenant of grace again links up with the form for those not bound to Abraham and Israel.

b. Religion

(1) Christians from the Jews and from the Gentiles now live next to each other in the communion of Christ. To the extent that both believed the old promises, they had only to discover the fulfillment of these assurances in the Christ—hence, on the one hand, the penetrating question of Nathanael (John 1:48) and, on the other hand, the conversion of three thousand souls on one day (Acts 2:41). In contrast, a radical change was required when they previously had not understood the promises (Paul) or had rejected them (the Gentiles). But now all live as justified and purified through the Christ.

(2) As believers, they now know all things (1 John 2:20), that is to say, with respect to the previously and for the most part hidden will of God concerning salvation, and yield fruits of the Spirit in thanksgiving.

(3) Moreover, they live and die in the expectation of Christ's return. For, now that they can distinguish the two comings of God's Son, a clearer light also falls on their dying. Dying, still now, involves a being disengaged from one's context. People dread that (2 Corinthians 5:1–4). They prefer that the Christ would return, so that the way to the grave would be replaced with a sudden and, they will admit, necessary change. But two prospects will comfort Christians who die young. The first is this, that the punishment that will also befall them, as children of Adam, comes along with a blessing. For them too, life's unity will be broken. But at the same time, the struggle between "spirit" and "flesh," which consumed their life, is over. While on earth evil desires sprang from their hearts too, now their soul, purified of these things, lives with the Lord (2 Corinthians 5:8). And their body will soon follow suit. Though buried in corruption, dishonor, and weakness, their body, like their soul, will not fall prey to death. This seed, connected as it is to the Holy Spirit, will be raised as a spiritual body (1 Corinthians 15:42–44). The believers who do

experience the return of the Christ will, up until that moment, likewise be mortal and have to "put on" immortality.

Both groups of Christians, those raised and those changed, are then freed from the power of the second death to which the remainder will be subjected (Revelation 20:14 and 21:8, compared to 2:11 and 20:6).

> Comment: "To be subjected to the second death" is not "to be annihilated," just as "continue to exist" is not the same as "be immortal." Both confusions can be found among advocates of what they call "conditional immortality." To refute them soundly, one must not only avoid the first mistake but the second as well. Scripture teaches that all human beings continue to exist in soul and body after death. But, departing from humanistic usage, which attributes immortality *only* to the higher part, but then also to the higher part of *all* human beings already on this side of the grave(!), Scripture also teaches that only believers in Christ will put on immortality, just after the resurrection and as whole persons.

135. *The struggle in the life of a Christian*

The center of our life, then, lies beyond us; so also beyond the first Adam, with whom we are, meanwhile, connected as living souls. Restored by God into a right relationship to him, we learn to be obedient to the love command through the spirit of Christ, who pours out the love in our heart that God requires from everyone.

All the same, this rest, too, is not without a struggle that is parallel with the preaching of blessing and curse in the full Logos revelation. Under God's restorative activity, our pistic function takes to be true and certain what this revelation says to us, namely, that we have an eternal covenant with God, and that what it says about the blessing and curse of that covenant, therefore, also holds for us. As long as we keep this covenant and put to death our flesh, all things will work together for our good and, in spite of our sins and as apparent from the chastisement, we will belong in life and death to the Lord, irrespective of whether we know that or not (when sleeping or unconscious). But if we turn away from the Christ, God will hide his face from us as well and, if we do not return, we can expect a stiffer judgment than those who have disregarded a narrower revelation. Accordingly, the struggle rages precisely in the life of the Christian between flesh and spirit (Romans 7), that is, between the old and the new person.

Comment: This struggle does not exclude that of one function against the hypertrophy of another. That kind of difficulty, although an effect of the Fall, is also evident among those who are entirely oblivious to the struggle of the Christian. They consider the solution to this difficulty to be the most important one and try with their own power to become its master. However, this is what Paul refers to as "carnal."

136. The struggle between church and world

Since opposition from the outside, that is to say, from the side of the world and especially from Satan, comes on top of the inner struggle, Christians are dependent first of all upon prayer. In addition, they have to help each other in this struggle. The presence of the body (= trunk) of the Christ (= head) manifests itself in the co-operation among believers, not the least in the familial nurturing of the next generation.

Associations as well as organizations are eligible means for lending this help to each other in circles broader than the family.

Christian corporate life intends that association members help each other sharpen their sensitivity for the opposition between church and world and for the structure of the cosmos, so that the members of the church will themselves clearly distinguish the different arenas and, as a result, also the different life connections, with the prevailing functions that typify them.

In addition, organization is also necessary. Its goal is to resist open attacks and the gradual debilitation of these structures through lies and deceit by mobilizing all of the forces that cooperating Christians have at their disposal.

When organizational life has need of more permanent channels, it moves from organizing to instituting, and the product of its action is an institution. These institutions are not tranquil shrines but "bodies" in which humans work under a certain mandate and, at the same time, through their work, influence those who have given them their mandate.

Here, too, in all of these different forms of cooperation, God's Word remains the norm. That is why the Logos requires that this Word be preached everywhere with the administration of the sacraments, which point toward the fulfillment of the promise in the past, while the sacraments themselves indicate and promise his support of the faith in the present. It is, then, also very important that, where this is still or again necessary, believers in Christ unite to establish and maintain an institute that has the regular proclamation of the Word and sacraments in view. In so doing, they are bound to have this institutional function according to the offices that Christ established for it.

> Comment: That some, already early on, disregarded this requirement and often persisted in this failure up until today reflects very poorly on Christian cooperation in associations and organizations.

This institution is the Christian church (as institution). It presupposes not only election and the covenant but also the continued acceptance of that covenant. That is why, though colored locally and nationally, it can only seldom—and then only very briefly—include all of the members of one nation or people. And even then, it is not simply a pistic institution but really a Christian pistic institution.

This Christian institution would have never sprung up without the action of an organized Christian endeavor. With its pistic objective, this institution stands, as does its power to organize, on a historic basis. It is active in the arena of language, has its own forms of social conduct (house visitation), goods under its care, a unique beauty (with a calling to its own church art), and its own kind of justice (church law) and morals. Its aim, however, is pistic. That is why the offices of this institution lie exclusively in the pistic sphere and may not be confused either with the prefunctional office of Adam and the Christ or with the post of office bearers in (general or Christian) institutions whose prevailing function is supralingual but not pistic. That confusion only leads to tyranny and the obstruction of reformation, which is always needed. On the other hand, that's also why all of this institution's activity in nonpistic arenas is to be subservient to the undisturbed activity of the (Christian) pistic function. This means, for example, that the church's training of its future office bearers ought to be limited to preparing them for their future practical work (through ministerial internships).

This cooperation of Christians takes places on earth and is perceptible in time. However, in its internal struggle, invisible powers aid the fight. But these, too, stand in service of its invisible King. That brings us to the connection between heaven and earth.

PART III

THE CONNECTION BETWEEN HEAVEN AND EARTH

137. Introduction

We have now dealt with the most prominent structures known to us of that which is created. In Part I, we discussed the few givens about heaven, and in Part II, those concerning the earth.

It remains for us to turn our attention for a moment to the connection between these two.

138. The givens concerning this connection

Little is known concerning this connection. We gain knowledge about it exclusively from the Word of God, which on this point, however, is extremely restrained.

Basically, the givens provided amount to this, that angels make a difference in earthly life, for better and for worse, but that this influence, ever since resisting the temptation (Matthew 4:11), stands at the disposal of the Christ, who after his ascension sometimes opens heaven in order to encourage those who suffer for his sake (Acts 7:55 and Revelation 3:8).

> Comment: As far as angelic influence "for worse," being "possessed" is its most abnormal form.

139. The negative significance of these givens

However sparse these givens may be, they do have great value; not only for practical life but for philosophy as well.

For while it is true that philosophy has little more to say about this connection than that it differs from all of the other connections discussed up until now, this tidbit is enough to cut off negation as well as a number of speculations.

a. Negation appears when one forgets, with some currents in contemporary philosophy, that there is a world of angels. They negate the correlate of the earthly creation and hence do not see the earthly part of the cosmos as it is (compare the third petition; see Heidelberg Catechism, Sunday 49).

b. Speculation comes in more varieties. The most prominent types are mentioned here.

(1) The dualistic-trichotomistic type.

This view sees the cosmos as threefold: heaven, earth, and hell. Earth—humans in particular—is also taken to be threefold: The lowest is demonic, the highest is supposed to be heavenly, and what lies in between, if it is not a mixture of these two, then is subjected to both of their influence.

(2) The functionalistic-dichotomistic type.

The connection between heaven and earth is often equated with the connection between the higher and lower functions of humans. The claim is, then, that human beings are made up of a spiritual and a material substance, with the spiritual substance displaying varying degrees of affinity with the heavenly spirits.

Against that, the following can be noted.

(a) In our investigation of the cosmos, we have come across many things but no substances.

> Comment: "Hypostasis" in Holy Scripture is, in its religious sense, "firm foundation."
>
> In its use outside of Scripture, distinguish this word's nonscientific and scientific usage, and within the latter, between special scientific and philosophic usage.
>
> Here, of course, we are dealing exclusively with its philosophic usage, where the word always implies possessing a self-sufficient ground (self-sufficiency not in the sense of disposition). Its use in this sense is, then, obviously out of the question.

(b) This standpoint does not distinguish the spirit of men from the higher functions. In other words, it honors a functionalistic conception of the human heart.

(c) This approach does not bring out that the individual human being, also functionally, is an unbroken subject unit.

(d) Religion, in this view, is linked either to a presumed goal built into things or to asceticism.

(e) The genetic connection in which the individual human being stands to Adam is denied for the higher functions.

(3) Trying to avoid functionalism, some equate the difference between heaven and earth with the intraindividual connection between the human heart (soul, spirit) and the cloak of human functions (body). What they do keep, however, is the idea of a composition.

One should be warned about this position on the following grounds.

(a) "Spirit" in Holy Scripture means directional principle. This is why it can be used in the sense of the religious center of earthly and heavenly creatures that are directed, obediently or not, to serve God. There are simply no grounds (also not in Holy Scripture) for concluding on the basis of this common designation of creatures, which in this usage are named after one side only, while actually belonging to different worlds, that there exists a much more comprehensive connection. When spiritualism, true to its individualistic roots, negates the [reality of] office, it ought to realize that the realists (in the medieval sense of the word) had as much (or as little) right, based on the name of the office *angel* (= messenger), to postulate the connection between heavenly and earthly hierarchy.

(b) The connection between heart and function is at bottom intra-individual, not interindividual. The heart is likewise not an addendum. Only after dying does it come to be a separately existing individual soul. Those who forget this deny the connection between Adam and humanity as a whole.

(c) Also, after death, the soul awaits the revival of the body, differing in this again from the angels. The ideal for the Christian is not "the return of souls to their home" but inhabiting the new earth, upon which justice lives.

(d) Likewise, when it comes to eschatology, the paganistic conception of salvation is diametrically opposed to the Christian view, which only finds rest once it grasps that heaven and earth will be liberated from injustice.

(4) Some equate the connection between heaven and earth with the connection between God and the Christian. In response, think of the following: (a) that heaven, too, is a creature, and a longing for heaven is not the same thing as true religion; and (b) that the longing of the Christian for heaven has primarily to do, not with heaven, but with the glorified Christ.

140. The positive significance of these givens

a. Concerning the structure of this connection (between heaven and earth).

The Christ as creature is given all power in heaven and on earth. He is then not only the second Adam but also the head of the angels. The connection between heaven and earth should, therefore, not be sought in each person, as does individualism, but exclusively in the office of the Christ.

b. Concerning the nature of this connection.

This connection is the most inclusive within the cosmos. At the same time, it is still entirely intracosmic.

c. Concerning the limit of this connection.

The Christian religion, although it cannot do without this connection, therefore also has a deeper foundation. It rests in the connection, which reaches still further, between the Son and the human nature that he assumed, in the sense of *homo assumptus, integer, perfectus, singularis*. This connection is no longer intracosmic: It forms the tie between the Sovereign and the love-filled, surrendering, completely spiritual subject. Precisely for that reason, it guarantees us the bond of God to all that which is re-created, which is included in this man, the man Jesus Christ, and with that, to the church, the victory of her (for now still) unseen King.

APPENDIX

A NUMBER OF THE MORE COMPLICATED QUESTIONS OF PHILOSOPHY

141. Introduction

The preceding was devoted to the first, necessary distinctions. Now we come to a number of more complicated philosophic questions. A complete systematic elaboration of these thoughts would undoubtedly make this Appendix longer than what precedes it. But that is not possible in an introduction and also not desirable. So I will confine myself to questions that need to be clarified to understand the Second Main Part, which is devoted to the provisional negative result.

142. Subdivision and sequence

a. Subdivision

I will deal here only with the results following from the application of the main schemata in the theory about knowledge and in the theory about know-how (*technè*) and art. I devote one part to each of these three.

b. Sequence

(1) There are two reasons for the priority of theory of knowledge: Neither expertise nor art is possible without knowledge. Hence, it is good to start by studying the latter. Moreover, to do so is urgently needed in light of the confusing, but nevertheless recurrent, equation of philosophy and theory of knowledge.

(2) It also speaks for itself that in discussing skill and art, the former should be dealt with first: No art is possible without some skill.

PART I

HUMAN KNOWING

Introduction

143. Here, too, the limit is maintained
The theory about knowledge is the answer to the question: What is knowledge?

This question, however, should reckon with what was found earlier. "Knowledge," after all, is a word with many significations. For example, we can speak of knowledge that God has and knowledge that creatures have.

144. Terminology: The terms knowledge of and knowledge about
If the theory about knowledge is not to get entangled immediately in a limit-transcending conception, we have to make a strict distinction between knowledge *of* (one who possesses this knowledge) and knowledge *about* (that which is known).

145. The knowledge of God and that of the creatures
The knowledge of God about himself and his creatures can be sharply distinguished from that of the creatures about him and that which is created. We know only through Word revelation that God knows. But Scripture also tells us that this knowledge is not the same as ours. Only what God has wanted to communicate to us in human language about these things is knowable for us.

146. The knowledge of creatures
Here, too, we can distinguish the following:

a. We know through Word revelation that the angels know as well, for example, that they understand what God says to them, and also that they make distinctions when speaking to him. But even though this knowledge, which is creaturely, can be distinguished from divine knowledge, we know extremely little about it.

b. Lastly, we also find knowledge on the part of earthly creatures, specifically in the case of humans and animals.

(1) Everyone familiar with animals knows that they know as well: They know their master, their feeding trough, the path they have

taken once or more often, and so on (cf. also Job 28:7 and Isaiah 1:3). This knowing, which especially of late is being investigated by psychologists, bears a purely emotional character and implies perception, reaction, the perseverance of previous moments in the following moments, and a memory that can react afresh to that which lingers.

(2) Human knowing is different; if for no other reason than that here everything in the psychic is connected with the analytic. Moreover, the nature of human knowing is not only emotive; in fact, the emotions play a subservient role in human knowing. Yet it is good to have briefly mentioned the knowledge of animals. Doing so prevents thoughts from slipping into the theory about human knowing that are rooted in a view as though humans were composed of a psychosomatic substance, with which they would approach the animal, and of a spiritual substance, through which they would liken unto the angels: The human being is a unity and belongs to the earthly creatures. And even though humans' knowing far surpasses that of the animals, not only in the suprapsychic but also in the psychic, no instance of human functional knowing in the suprapsychic functions can be found in which the psychic substrate is not present.

147. The theory about human knowing: Its place in philosophy

a. We confine ourselves now to the theory about human knowing and accordingly use the term *theory of knowledge* below exclusively in this narrow sense.

b. We now direct ourselves to the question as to the place of the theory of knowledge, in its limited sense, in philosophy.

Many often equate philosophizing as an activity with reflecting on the question: What is human knowing? In correlation with this question, they then have to equate philosophy with theory of knowledge.

However, whoever sees that knowing is subsumed under being and takes stock of the results that were previously summarized, also understands then that answering the question "What is knowing?" can simply bring to light the fact that the distinctions obtained also continue in the case of knowing.

148. Subdivision

a. There are two kinds of knowing: a nonscientific and a scientific knowing (see §9).

b. Seeing as that scientific knowing relies on nonscientific knowing, the latter should be discussed first.

Division I

Nonscientific Knowing

149. Introduction
Regarding nonscientific knowing, we can distinguish its structure and its development. A chapter is devoted to the discussion of each of these two.

Chapter 1
THE STRUCTURE OF NONSCIENTIFIC KNOWING

150. What knowing is
Knowing is having knowledge, hence enjoying a state of rest.

151. Knowing and coming to know
This state of rest follows on a state of greater or smaller effort, during which one "comes to know."

152. What coming to know presupposes
A person only comes to know something when, in suprapsychic awareness, correct-distinguishing of what differs takes place in conjunction with the preserving, remembering, ordering, and so on of distinctions already made. This process therefore presupposes:
  (a) Being connected under the law of God with the entire cosmos
  (b) Being subjected to the analytic and supra-analytic laws
  (c) The activity of coming to know
  (d) That which is knowable
  (e) The resulting content of knowledge
  (f) The assimilation of a number of matters

153. Subdivision
Of the above-mentioned prerequisites, (a) and (b) were dealt with earlier, and (f) can be attended to only later. Hence, we now have to deal with:
  A. The activity of coming to know
  B. That which is knowable
  C. The result

A. THE ACTIVITY OF COMING TO KNOW

154. *The line of thought*
In the nature of the case, coming to know differs modally according to the law-spheres within which it takes place.

For the sake of clarity, I begin with the cognitive interrelation in the lowest suprapsychic, in other words, analytic, law-sphere: The advantage in doing so is that I can temporarily confine myself to a discussion of the cognitive interrelation in this particular sphere and, in this context, leave the more complicated supra-analytic spheres to the side.

155. *The constituents of analytically coming to know*
a. It is suprapsychic distinguishing. By denoting this distinguishing as "suprapsychic," we achieve two things:

(1) We remember that the psychic belongs to the substrate of all the higher functions.

(2) The mention of that which is analytic as well as that which is supra-analytic. We obstruct our own ability to discern the richness in nonscientific knowing when we do not acknowledge these supra-analytic functions or, as the apriorists, take them to be preanalytic and, in so doing, have no place for retrocipations to that which is analytic.

b. It is correct distinguishing. If analytic functioning is poor, for example, due to exhaustion, then mistakes are made and the result is not knowledge but error.

c. It is always a distinguishing of that which is different from the other with which it is connected horizontally and vertically.

156. *Division*
In connection with the last point, we must take note of the role of the analytic interrelation (1) as well as of the vertical connection in the activity of coming to know (2).

1. THE ROLE OF THE INTERRELATION IN ANALYTIC COMING TO KNOW

157. *Introduction*
The diversity within the analytic interrelation is just as great as the diversity in the horizontal connections of any other modality. We distinguish the contemporary synchronic (a) and the successive diachronic (b) interrelations.

a. The synchronic interrelations in the analytic law-sphere

158. Division
These interrelations are interindividual or intraindividual.

159. The synchronic interindividual relations in the analytic law-sphere
There are two cases to be distinguished here.

(1) Sometimes the correlates are both active. Then we have a case of analytic cooperation, for example, in a discussion that centers around nonscientific distinctions, such as between God and cosmos, animal and plant, one person and another, business and state, and so on.

(2) In other cases, the one correlate is active, the other passive. Interindividual perceiving and being perceived is a case in point. This instance has to be dealt with further.

160. Interindividual analytic perception
a. First, a few remarks in connection with the terminology, which, especially here, cannot be clear enough.

(1) It only makes sense to speak of in*ter*individual perception when an in*tra*individual perception exists as well. That is indeed the case, as is evident from the following paragraph.

(2) The distinction of interindividual and intraindividual here, too, does not coincide with that of outer and inner (cf. §76). Limiting myself to the interindividual, I perceive the food I eat as long as it is still in my mouth with a perception that is interindividual as well as inner.

(3) Many are of the opinion that the word *perception* denotes something that only occurs with that which is psychic. Of course, one can fix this term in this way, and the analyst will then have to look around for another word. But is this limited use of the word actually in agreement with the state of affairs? One says, after all, that Kepler by perceiving the Martian orbit and Galileo by gleaning from his experiments found answers to questions that were keeping them busy. What they were looking for, however, was not the emotional effects of the color of the stars or the noise of rolling balls on their senses! Even though both were present, they were there only as the substrate of something else. And that something else was the answer to the questions that Kepler was asking of stars and that Galileo was first asking of mechanical things here on earth. And so, what we find

here is almost the same as when I apprehend a result that someone else arrived at. In that case, too, the point is not—assuming it happens by means of symbols (spoken, written, or printed words)—whether the tone or typeset was pleasing to me. What I am interested in keenly is the thought that the words refer to, which can provide me with a link still missing in my demonstration, or an example that illustrates one of my expositions, or possibly a counterexample prompting me to be more careful when defending a particular thesis.

When, as in instances like these, language plays a part, we talk about "apprehending" (*vernemen:* to learn, hear, be told, understand). But when language does not perform the service of medium, we speak of "perceiving." This usage is sufficient to support the claim that this perceiving is not purely psychic but is surely also analytic in nature, hence justifying the use of the term *perception*.

> Comment 1: Perceiving and apprehending can go together, for example, when I hear and see a speaker and understand what he says.

b. What is active in this interrelation of perceiving is the perceiver, who directs her analytic subject function to that which is perceptible for her in something that differs from her in individuality.

c. As a result, what was simply perceptible becomes now-also-perceived, and, to that extent, becomes something that is passive.

> Comment 2: The passivity of that which is perceived is simply the being-perceived. The term *passive*, then, should certainly not be taken here in a broader sense. Hence, it is possible that what is being perceived is very active, maybe even more so than the one perceiving. Listeners perceive an orator on a platform if they take notice of him. The orator climbed the rostrum to be noticeable for many and articulates clearly for the same reason. His standing and speaking is together one activity. And yet the fact that he is perceived ultimately depends on the activity of the perceiver.

d. What the perceiver perceives interindividually can also be an object. But it certainly need not be. Two cases are possible.

(1) What is perceived is an analytic subject. For example, an instructor perceives that a student is alert. She does that directly when the student is in front of her and indirectly when she apprehends the same by means of an intermediate, for example, via well-posed written questions.

(2) What is perceived is an analytic object, for example, a pearl, an elm, a dog, or a psychic emotion of my neighbor's that I distinguish from his other emotions.

> Comment 3: Equating what is perceived with an "object" is often due to sloppy use of the language. It is worse when we come across this in philosophic works as well. Then it is either due to a lack of critical reflection on the validity of current theories of knowledge or, if we are talking about a primary source, a symptom of a one-sided orientation to sciences about the subanalytic (so-called epistemological "naturalism").

e. Direct interindividual perception of earlier moments is not possible. Perceiving is always synchronous with what is perceived. Perception of earlier moments is always perception of direct or indirect recollection (symbols).

In summary, interindividual perception is going on where an analytic subject function directs the attention to something that is analytically perceptible, in other words, to something that stands with this subject function in a contemporary analytic interrelation.

> Comment 4: Distinguish the perception from its interpretation. For example, during a storm, we perceive the lightning's flash before the thunder's rumble. But we would be mistaken if, based on the contemporaneous character of the interrelation of perception, we would also conclude that the beam of light originated before the sound waves. Both came about at the same time. That they did not reach us at the same time has to do with the difference in the speed of light and sound.

161. *Intraindividual perception*

a. The analytic subject function can also perceptually direct itself to something that is both perceptible and, at the same time, also intraindividually connected with the perceiver. We speak then of intraindividual perception.

b. Here, too, we find that the distinction of interindividual and intraindividual does not coincide with the distinction of outer and inner. With external perception, I can analytically perceive my hands, distinguishing, for example, right and left hand, even though they are intraindividually connected with the perceiver.

c. What is active in this interrelation of perceiving is the perceiver, who directs her analytic subject function to what for her by herself is perceptible.

d. As a result, what was simply perceptible becomes now-also-perceived, and, to that extent, becomes something that is passive.

e. Here, too, it is not necessary that what is perceived be an object.

(1) When my hands, for example, touch a piece of cloth and I perceive them doing so, then they are, though perceived, quite obviously busy in an analytic function. What I am interested in is not whether the cloth feels pleasant but whether it is what they say it is, for example, whether it feels like "real linen."

(2) What is perceived intraindividually can, however, also be an object. Then I am dealing with an intraindividual object function of myself, for example, when I perceive my own psychic emotion as analyzable.

> Comment 1: The inner object is a psychic one, but as object it is in the analytic sphere. In its quality of psychic subject function, then, it is not passive.
>
> Comment 2: As far as the disallowed equation of what is perceived with "object," what held for interindividual perception (see the comment in §160 D) holds here as well.

f. Intraindividual perception, too, is always contemporaneous with what is perceived.

162. *Interindividual and intraindividual perception*

When we compare both, we find points of similarity and of difference. These can easily be summarized. The points of similarity are listed above. A few words about the difference follow.

a. It is rooted in the this–that difference that we found everywhere in the cosmos. That is why it is impossible to reduce the one group of perceptions to the other.

b. The distribution of analytic perceptions into outer and inner does not coincide with that of interindividual and intraindividual, which crosses it. Hence, there are, when we take both distinctions into account, not two groups but four.

> Comment: We have to be very careful with the use of the terms *inner* and *outer* as adjectives of "perception."
>
> 1. They may never be used to refer to a difference in the function of what is perceived; as in, for example, inner perception being perception of the psychic and outer being of the physical.
>
> 2. To say exactly what is meant when using these terms, mention should also always be made of whether the interrelation of perception is intraindividual or interindividual; in other words, whether one is perceiving something of oneself or of someone or something else.

b. The successive interrelations in that which is analytic

163. Introduction and division

Both of the correlates in the cognitive interrelations we have dealt with fit the schema active–passive. Time-wise, they were contemporaneous.

However, there would be no talk of coming to know were there not still other analytic interrelations to which the schema active–passive does apply, but which are successive, not contemporaneous.

Because the knower stands in successive connection with the past as well as the future, we distinguish here two interrelations, namely, recollection and expectation.

164. The interrelation of recollection

a. The schema active–passive works here, too. Recollecting is analytically active, and what is recalled is analytically passive.

b. The successive connection here is such that what is recollectable is the earlier and the recollecting is the later.

c. What is active in the interrelation of recollection is the rememberer, who directs his or her analytic subject function to what is earlier and recollectable for him or her, with the result that what was simply recollectable becomes now-also-remembered, and, to that extent, becomes something that is passive.

> Comment: As with the interrelation of perception, what is passive here can be stronger, even much stronger than what is active. A peculiar instance of that is evident with eidetic phenomena, which, because they are so complicated, can only be discussed later (see §167).

d. Can we distinguish recollections, just as we did perceptions, into intraindividual and interindividual?

In all probability, the initial inclination is to answer this question in the affirmative. For example, if yesterday I looked at some prints, I can now remember both that I looked and what I saw. The first of these was an activity on my part, the looking that I now recollect. Hence, that looking stands in a successive intraindividual connection with my remembering this. The second was what I perceived analytically at the time, namely, the prints with which I then stood in an interindividual connection. The conclusion would seem to be valid that there exist both interindividual and intraindividual interrelations of recollection.

However, further reflection brings to light that the cases are not the same. It is possible that I recall that I saw something without knowing exactly what I saw, in other words, what precisely that something was. For example, when I have to prove my alibi for the hour during which I was busy with that looking or am looking for a pencil that I think I have lost in the meantime, then what I saw not only moves completely into the background, but recalling it is simply not included in the recollection of my action. But now the other case: It can certainly happen that I remember very well what I saw and barely that I saw it. That will happen often when what I am looking at during the interindividual perception of my looking had my complete attention. And yet it is not possible for me to recollect what I saw as seen without having the other recollection, namely, the recollection of the seeing, inherent to this recollection.

That is why an intraindividual action is primary when it comes to recollection.

e. What is recalled can be a subject as well as an object.

(1) In the example just introduced, I remember my seeing of yesterday. What is passive in this interrelation, then, is the functioning of a subject in the past.

(2) In contrast, when I remember my biotic reaction to a previous change in climate, what is being recalled is an intraindividual analytic object.

f. In discussing perceptions, we noted that there are perceptions of perceptions (see §160d1 and §161e1). Something similar is the case with recollection. I can remember that yesterday I was involved in a conversation filled with recollections of my youth. In these cases, what is remembered is always an action of the subject.

165. *The mutual irreducibility of recollection and perception*

Recollection establishes an interrelation between successive correlates; perception, including intraindividual perceiving, does the same between contemporary correlates. That is why neither can be reduced to the other. There is no transition from even the sharpest recollection to the weakest of perceptions.

This irreducibility does not exclude the possibility that both can be there at the same time (see §166) and occur together (see §167).

166. The simultaneity of some recollections with some perceptions

Someone can recall something and perceive something in the same moment. I can see a speaker and at the same time recall the argument that she has presented so far.

This coincidence of recollection and perception as elements in one moment does not negate the difference between the two interrelations, in each of which both of the elements of this moment make up one of the relata.

167. The combined occurrence of recollection and perception

Two things are to be distinguished here: There is recollection of analytic perception (a) and analytic perception of recollection (b).

a. Recalling analytic perceiving is direct or indirect.

(1) It is direct when someone remembers his own earlier perception.

> Comment: In this case as well, what is remembered can be so strong that the recalling itself stands entirely in the background. When, in addition, what is remembered was an interrelation of perception in which I just recently stood and in which what was perceived demanded my complete attention, then "eidetic seeing" can occur. I am no longer perceiving but, from the remembered interrelation of perception, am able to talk now about what was perceived then with a precision that shows that the recalled perception, the "eidetic image of recollection," still so entirely grips my attention that I am oblivious to the cessation of the perceiving and to my having set the interrelation of perception as passive correlate in an interrelation of recollection. Eidetic seeing, then, testifies to weak analytic activity.

(2) It is indirect when someone via her earlier perception remembers her perception at the time of someone else's perception.

b. Perception of recollection

(1) Perceiving someone else's recalling is possible only by means of his expressions. I note that someone remembers something because I hear him say, "Oh, yeah, now I remember," or see from his happiness or shock that he recognizes someone.

(2) Perceiving recollection on the part of the perceiver occurs when she remembers something and at the same time perceives this (intraindividual) act of recollection.

168. The expectation interrelation

a. Here, too, the schema active–passive can be used: The expecting is active, that which is expected is passive (analytically).

b. The diachronic connection, also present in expecting, is here, however, different from the case of recollection: The moment expected lies in the future and is, therefore, the later and the expecting is the earlier.

c. The active constituent in the expectation interrelation is the expectant who directs his analytic subject function to the future that he expects. In so doing, what is "to be expected" (expect-able) becomes "expected."

> Comment: Here, too, what is expected can be stronger than the expectation, for example, when what is expected is very desirable or very much feared.

d. That which is expected need not be intraindividual, but it is possible.

(1) I expect someone who wrote me that she would visit me for the first time: That which is expected stands in interindividual interrelation to me.

(2) That, in contrast, is not the case when I am busy perceiving something and, on the basis of my recollection of earlier perceptions of a previously perceived course of affairs, do or do not now expect to perceive the same thing. In such a case, where recollection via expectation codetermines the future perception, we speak of apperception. I see someone who visits me for the second time differently than I did the first time.

e. That which is expected is, as such, passive and can be either a subject (1) or an object (2).

(1) In the example above, I expect that the person in question will, in fact, come.

(2) When she comes again, I expect that the perception as well as the then-to-be-perceived object will or will not be the repetition of the earlier one.

f. The expectation of expectation also occurs. When someone gets ready to make a trip abroad, he expects to see many things. If he gets sick in the meantime, stifling the realization of his plans, then the expectation dies. But when his doctor wants to keep the severity of the situation a secret and appeases him with the promise of such a speedy recovery that the trip can proceed as planned, even though the patient, who would like that, does not himself think it probable, it can happen that he says to the doctor, "Please don't say that, otherwise I'll once again start to count on enjoying the trip." In other words, he expects that when the doctor repeats her optimistic words, his expectations will be reawakened.

In such cases of expecting expectations, what is expected is an action of a subject.

169. *Recollection and expectation connected but not mutually reducible*

Expectation is not possible without recollection, for example, recalling a promise. And when what is expected actually presents itself and is perceived by the one who was expecting it, the expectation later becomes recollectable. But however closely connected with each other, the act of recollection never becomes expectation, nor the latter a recollection: They continue to differ in time direction.

2. THE ROLE OF THE VERTICAL CONNECTION IN ANALYTIC COMING TO KNOW

170. *Introduction*

Until now, I discussed only the horizontal connections in knowing. Here, too, however, evidence of vertical connection is not absent. We find it in thinking as well as in the knowable; for that which is analytic is far from an isolated chamber of consciousness or categorial apparatus. I will discuss only thinking here.

If there is to be talk of connection, however, then there must also be difference. That is why I first take up the difference and then the evidence of connection.

171. *The difference between the analytic and the other functions*

It is not necessary to work out the difference between the analytic function and all of the others: An exposition of the difference between it and a few of the others, mainly immediately adjacent functions, is sufficient but also needed because of the prevailing confusion.

a. The difference between the analytic function and a few lower ones

(1) The analytic function is often identified with things mathematical. This identification is rooted in different causes. Some call both the analytic as well as things mathematical "abstract" (a); on the other hand, others view both as "a priori" (b).

(a) The first way of speaking appeals to the fact things mathematical are never present other than in nonmathematically qualified things and, thus, must be separated out from these. But this process is entirely different from that of abstracting, for example, from individuality when thinking about mathematic figures and nonmathematic things.

(b) One who calls things analytic and mathematical both a priori is first of all of the opinion that the analytic does not rest on the subanalytic but is joined to the latter as an added gift (*donum superadditum*) and then connects this outlook with the fact that that which is supramathematic presupposes things mathematical. But against the first claim, it can be remarked that nothing in the cosmos is a priori and, against the second, that "being presupposed" signifies here "being substrate" and, thus, implies the exact opposite of this supposed apriority.

(2) The still-frequent confusion of the analytic with the psychic is usually rooted in the lack of clarity concerning that which is psychic, so that when we summarize all of the suprabiotic under the term *psychic*, thinking will naturally fall under this psychic. That is why many of those busy with the psychology of thinking, in fact, also study the analytic (for example, the eidetic). It is sufficient to recall here that psychic life is that which is emotive and, be it differently, is also present in animals, and that the analytic is nothing other than basic thinking, which we find on earth only among human beings.

b. The difference between the analytic function and the next higher function

Because of the prevailing confusion, we have to mention here the difference between the analytic function and the two next higher ones.

(1) The difference between the analytic and historic function

Because many equate the historic and the genetic, the difference between the analytic and historic function is also often wrongly posed. It can be briefly expressed as follows: Thinking is not the same as cultivating, and, hence, nonscientific knowing, though presupposed in it, is also not the same as know-how (*technē*).

(2) The difference between the analytic and lingual function

If acknowledged, many look for this difference in that the thought is not spoken while the word is spoken. But this answer is not satisfactory. Every person formulates many statements in language without ever uttering them. The difference does not lie here, either, but in the meaning through words, both of things outside us as well as of thoughts. That we often think and know without putting the thought and the knowledge into words is evident from the recollection and expectation with which we view daily life. When we get up in the morning, we expect that everything will be in the same place as last night. But we hardly ever put that expectation into words except when it is not fulfilled, for example, because the wind blew something from its place or because thieves, disturbed in their work, have left a room in disorder.

172. The evidences of connection between the analytic and the other functions

Here again, we have to distinguish the analytic subject with its retrocipations and anticipations and the analytic object.

a. The analytic subject

(1) Retrocipations. That the analytic retrocipates to the arithmetic is evident from the multiplicity in thinking; to the spatial from comparison; to the physical from thought's strides, from basis to consequence (analogous to the causal correlation of cause and effect in the physical); to the organic from the brainpower; to the psychic from the mind's will.

(2) Anticipations. That the analytic anticipates the higher functions is evident, among other things, from concepts and statements. With concepts, the analytic anticipates technical use, with statements, formulation in language.

b. The analytic object

Because the meaning of the subanalytic repeats itself in all of the higher law-spheres, this is also the case in the analytic law-sphere.

This analytic object has great significance. It is true that the theory of knowledge has difficulty accounting for knowing the analytic object, but, to gain knowledge about the subanalytic, the analytic subject has to direct itself in the first place to the analytic perception of the analytic object.

B. THE KNOWABLE

173. What is knowable

Perceiving, recollecting, expecting: these all proved to be a directing of oneself to what is knowable in the present, the past, and the future. For us to give account of what knowledge is, we must also ask what is knowable in that toward which suprapsychic distinguishing is directed.

The following are knowable:

a. God, to the extent that he has revealed himself both through his Word as well as through his creatures, to the extent we can know these.

> Comment 1: God, therefore, can be known through two means. If one uses the terms *Scripture* and *nature* for these means, one ought to keep in mind:
> > a) that there was a time when the Word of God was not yet written;
> > b) that nature should be understood to be all the work of God and especially not only one group of earthly creatures. In this sense, nature also includes all institutions and the genetic course of affairs therein, for better and for worse.
>
> Comment 2: Not all of the works of God are knowable for us, as will be seen below.

b. His law governing the cosmos and knowable by the light of the word of God from the cosmos

c. The cosmos; more specifically:

(1) Heaven, in the sense of the world of spirits, to the extent we receive communication about it from the Word of God

(2) Earth, a) to the extent we receive communication about it from the Word of God, and b) to the extent we can investigate its past, present, and future

As for the latter, we ought to distinguish further: (a) the primary state of affairs, that is to say, what in that which is knowable is not itself knowledge or error, and (b) the secondary state of affairs, that is to say, what is knowable but is also itself subsumed under knowledge or error about a primary state of affairs.

> Comment 3: Earth, therefore, can also be known through two means. Those who do not accept this deny the possibility of Christian science.
>
> Comment 4: It is better not to call either of these means through which we can know God, his law, and (a part of) the cosmos a "source of knowledge." This term leaves the impression that human knowledge exists independent of us not only in the as-humanly-communicated Word of God and in the knowledge of our fellow humans but in all of nature, such that one runs the risk of losing sight of the difference between that which is humanly knowable and the knowledge obtained by humans.

174. The connection between the activity in coming to know and what is knowable

The thinking subject belongs to the cosmos.

That is why, negatively, it cannot transcend the limits of the cosmos.

On the other hand, positively, it stands connected with all that is knowable:

a. With God, who also calls coming to know into his service an expression of love-filled obedience;

b. With God's law—the relationship to God's law is not simply contemplative: This law is there neither exclusively nor even primarily to be pondered but to be obeyed;

c. With the cosmos, to the extent that it is knowable. That is why we turn against skepticism, which still has ideals for knowing but despairs of their realization, as well as against mysticism, which disqualifies coming to know what lies outside of us as being "external" and considers the knowing process to be introspective.

> Comment: This connection is a direct one. In other words, it is not the case that things or humans first create impressions in the thinking person and that he then arrives at results by abstracting from the impressions present within him. No, the person thinking focuses his attention on what is knowable, be it thing or human being, and analyzes it, abstractly or not, there where it is and, in so doing, arrives at results.
>
> For that reason, contrary to what the copy theory claims, the connection between what is knowable and the result is not direct. In between what is knowable and the related result, there is always the analysis of the person thinking, who analyzes what is knowable correctly or not and, in turn, comes to knowledge or error concerning what is knowable. On this score, Plato and not Aristotle is right.
>
> Meanwhile, keep in mind that this activity is analytic in character. Rejecting the copy theory, given the aforementioned grounds, in no way implies that this activity is creative or even productive. We do not bring forth knowledge or error from ourselves but come to these two as though they were results, to be gained only through the analysis of something knowable.

C. THE RESULT

175. *Two kinds of result*

We distinguish here *concept* and *statement*.

In the concept, we know a state of affairs; in a statement, a state of affairs in relation to something (namely, the subject of the statement).

176. *Concept and statement, being determined by the norm, by that which is known, and by the analytic activity*

a. Concept

(1) Being determined by the norm. Not only the activity but also

the result is normed. That is why we speak of contradictory and noncontradictory concepts.

(2) Being determined from the side of that which is known. In this connection, we distinguish:

(a) Primary concepts, that is to say, concepts about states of affairs that are themselves not knowledge or error and secondary concepts. The latter are concepts about states of affairs that are conceptual.

(b) Extensions of concepts. That the extension of the concept *human* is broader than that of the concept *woman* is rooted in the relationship of the number of women to the number of human beings.

(3) Being determined from the side of the knower. We distinguish here (a) perceptual and abstracted concepts and (b) simple and composite concepts.

b. The statement

(1) Being determined by the norm. Distinguish contradictory and noncontradictory statements. Being contradictory or not has to do neither with the statement's subject nor with its predicate but with their relation. A statement is contradictory only when a predicate is and is not attributed to a subject at the same time. Of the following three statements, only the last one conflicts with the norm of *principium contradictionis* (principle of contradiction): "Truth and falsehood are incompatible," "This argument is contradictory," and "This is true and not true in the same respect."

(2) Being determined by that which is known. This determines the quality of the statement as well as its extension. Quality here has to do with a statement's relation being positive or negative. The extension of a statement's field has to do with the range covered by the statement's subject.

(3) Being determined from the side of the thinking activity. Distinguish here between immediate and mediate, that is to say, between statements that are not gotten through proofs and those that are.

Chapter 2
THE DEVELOPMENT OF NONSCIENTIFIC KNOWING

177. Introduction

Until now, I have limited myself to discussing the structure of knowing at one moment. What was said already, then, also stood in connection with the past and the future. But so as to not confuse things, I proceeded as though the moment of now would not soon belong to the past and, so also, as though the past did not increase and the present did not shift. This, naturally, was an abstraction, only permissible for the sake of clarity and under the condition that I abandon it as soon as possible. Now that I have reached that goal, I will let go of that abstraction completely so as to concentrate now on what was disregarded in what was knowable and in knowing, namely, on what is genetic in both.

178. That which is genetic in the knowable

a. We saw previously (§§121–134) that the Word of God did not remain stationary but increased and changed. We also noted (§173) that the Word of God is written in human language and, hence, is knowable for us. Combining both of these givens, we find that in the *historia revelationis,* the Word of God, and hence what is knowable for humans, increased.

b. Likewise, that which is accessible in the cosmos to human investigation does not remain the same. Atoms disintegrate and stars collapse and melt together; plants, animals, and humans interbreed, evolve, and vary. A second important element is that we can know the past better than we can the future; hence, as the past grows, what can be known better does as well. Finally, do not forget the changes and expansion of that which is knowable that arises from human endeavor: We no longer speak of the *Zuiderzee* (South Sea) but of the *IJsselmeer* (Lake IJssel); on the polders of tomorrow there will be obviously much more to distinguish geographically than there is today. Here, too, then, there is an increase and change in what is knowable for nonscientific thinking.

> Comment: Tracing the evolving of humankind leads to a knowledge that, in the footsteps of Holy Scripture, was also often found in nonscientific circles (family trees recorded on the front page of the old Bible).

179. That which is genetic in the knower

In the theory of knowledge, humankind appears not only as part of that which is knowable but also as knower. Here, too, genesis can be detected.

180. The beginning of that which is genetic in our knowing

This beginning was not always tied to early youth. Holy Scripture sketches Adam (and Eve) as adults and lets us see how his (and her) knowledge increased. Insight into the difficulties that accompany the growth of our knowledge increases when we compare both processes with each other.

a. The development of knowledge for Adam

(1) In the foreground for Adam was knowing the God who created him. We also find that he observed the difference in sex among the animals and had some knowledge of good and evil.

(2) As far as his self-knowledge is concerned, he knew that he stood under God's law, differed from the animals, and later, after the creation of Eve, that he was her fellow human.

In both series, then, we find knowledge about being a creature; furthermore, a knowledge about belonging to a kingdom, or sort of animal and human being, based on perceiving sexual interrelations; and finally knowledge about the individual differences within such a realm.

b. For those whose increase in knowledge begins in early youth, the process is different. The sequence in which what they (and others) experience comes to their knowledge differs, because of, but not simply because of, the Fall. The most drastic difference, however, is the alienation, found in differing degrees, from the Word revelation.

(1) It is the intracosmic differences that stand in the foreground. This is true not only for perceiving, remembering, and expecting but also for the arranging that goes on with primary concept formation, which is not only interested in the number of the repetitions of a perception and in the strength with which what is perceived draws one's attention, but especially in the place that what one perceives occupies in the cosmos. In this way, the ordering of what we know happens in a completely different way than it did for the first human, in the areas of both self-knowledge and knowledge of all the rest.

In addition, there is the increase of what is knowable, particularly of what can be recollected, due to the communication of others. Especially when children grow up in an environment that is not uprooted from the past, their recollection of the things they have experienced is enriched by first- or secondhand stories of what happened to others.

(2) All of this does not mean that knowing becomes burdensome. How one arranges what one knows might well differ from the order in which one came to know it, but the experience of those who are older can also shorten the process of knowledge about oneself and others. What does encumber this process is the lack of knowledge too often evident about the Word revelation, either because parents themselves lack this knowledge or because they have forgotten it or deliberately keep it from their child. The deprivation or withdrawal of this light will cloud the mind.

181. *The assimilation of that which is remembered*

What is remembered also gets assimilated.

What is of primary consequence here are the historic will to order concepts and statements, the lingual formulation and sociodidactic ordering of these formulations, and the social use in discourse of what is gained in this way.

A theory of knowledge should likewise attend to each of these three actions.

182. *The ordering of concepts*

The ordering of concepts is not a compendium of characteristics (Hobbes) nor a deduction of the individual from the realm of possibilities (Leibniz) but an arranging of concepts according to the extension with regard to which they hold.

> Comment 1: "Hold with regard to" may not be confused (as do the Neokantians) with "hold for," and "holding according to" may not be confused with "holding by virtue or because of."

The principle according to which concepts are ordered, then, is no longer that of the genetic order in which they came to the knower at the time but another one entirely. The significance of the arenas involved depends on the extension they have according to the knower. As a result, it is crucial that when ordering these concepts one sees their extensions and their mutual relations correctly. For example, if you take the area of that which is created too narrowly, you will end up deifying that part of the cosmos that, as you see it, falls outside it and you will begin to ask all kinds of questions about the relationship between the parts of the one cosmos, which in this way have been thrown asunder, and so on. That makes it clear why whether one bows to the Word revelation helps to decide about the value of such an ordering. One who obeys God's Word can certainly still err when it comes to details, but one who does not arrives at concepts that are false in their basic structure.

> Comment 2: The basic distinctions do not always stand in the foreground. When defining a birch, the concept *tree that* . . . will usually be sufficient. But things are different when speculation grips nonscientific knowing. Then even knowledge about the subanalytic is not safe: A tree is set as "living" over against "dead" matter, and the like. These and similar distortions in concept formation are especially dangerous for suprahistoric life because the forming of concepts belongs to its substrate. Malformed concepts will lead to a fault in the foundation that will prove to be devastating for the edifice built upon it. Owing to this, government, family, school, and church are continually undermined by an anthropology that places a part of the human being above God's law.

183. Statements and formulating statements

To discern (*oordelen zelf*) is an analytic activity, specifically, to acknowledge that a state of affairs (the predicate) is joined (the stated relation) with something (the statement's subject).

Discerning presupposes conceiving as a less complicated phase in the process of knowing. That is not to say that discerning always has to do with concepts. Only seldom is it a matter of ascribing a predicate to a concept, for example, when I state, "This concept is a contradictory one." Even less often does it involve the connecting of concepts, as, for example, in the statement, "The concepts *a* and *b* coincide."

Discerning is, nonetheless, distinct from lingually formulating and didactically ordering simple statements as well as from connecting the constituents and presuppositions of simple statements.

184. The lingual formulation of statements

The simplest schema of a statement is: S (the subject of the statement) is (the stated relation) P (the predicate).

> Comment: The "is" of a statement's relation is not the same as the "is equal to" of mathematics. It has any number of meanings.

185. The sociodidactic ordering of statements (theory of categories)

Statements are organized by a conception's theory of categories in connection with the ontic order it accepts. That is also why this part of philosophy is certainly not neutral.

In conjunction with the *Isagoge*, we order these as follows:
I. Primary statements, that is to say, statements that, although they presuppose knowledge, do not themselves deal with knowledge
   A. About God
   B. About the law
   C. About that which is subject
      1. About that which is subject in a heavenly way
      2. About that which is subject in a earthly way
         a. About religion, for example, "You are of Christ, and Christ is of God."
         b. About value, for example, "It is good to speak truth."
         c. About the kingdoms:
            1) Statements about their structure, for example, "The leading function of animals is the psychic."
            2) Statements about their genesis, for example, "This kind proliferates quickly."
         d. About inherence, for example, "Bees collect honey."
         e. About relations, for example, "This child grows faster than that one."
II. Secondary statements
   A. About conceiving and concepts
   B. About discerning and statements

Comment: Realism's theory of categories reduces all or almost all statements to statements about (primary and secondary) classes. This, however, is a misconception of the diversity in the cosmos and overestimates the class concept. "Bees collect honey" is not the same as "Bees belong to the class of honey-collecting animals." The first of these is a simple statement, specifically one of inherence. The second statement is neither of these and presupposes the following:
   1. One or more statements about other animals: "They collect honey"
   2. Connecting these two (or more) statements into a new one: "Bees and other animals collect honey"
   3. Elevating the inherence of a particular characteristic occurring with a number of animal species into a class that, in contrast to all species, does not presuppose an actual reproductive interrelation but owes its being there to an abstract organizing principle
   4. Subsuming one of these actual species under this class

186. *Making composite statements*

Our discussion until now was limited to formulating and ordering simple statements. There are, however, also composite statements.

Composite statements rest on the analysis of one simple statement or on connecting more than one such statement.

187. Making composite statements on the basis of analyzing a simple statement

This analysis sometimes has to do with inferences, sometimes with the epistemological assumptions of the statement.

That is why we have to look at these two more closely.

188. Implications and epistemological presuppositions of the simple statement
a. The implications are:

(1) With respect to the predicate, the truth claim (to be noncontradictory)

(2) With respect to stated relation, the quality—a statement is positive or negative

(3) With respect to the statement's subject: (a) regarding its character, it is mathematic, dynamic, and either genetic or not, and (b) regarding its extension, it is universal or particular

b. The epistemological suppositions are:

(1) The statement is immediate or mediate; that is, had without or owing to demonstration.

(2) The statement is made with or without certainty.

189. The composition of statements resting on the analysis of a simple statement according to its implications

Distinguish here the following:

a. Someone analyzing focuses on the truth claim of the predicate (to be noncontradictory) and discerns, "This simple statement is true" (1), or "It is false" (2). The first composite statement is one of assent, the second of dissent.

> Comment 1: Distinguish assent and dissent from being positive and being negative. The first two occur only with composite statements and, in addition, are not always tied to the quality of the simple statement. So, every assent is, as such, positive and every dissent is, as such, negative, but not every positive statement is an assent and not every negative statement is a dissent.

Comment 2: If a dissenting statement A rightly claims that a dissenting statement B is simple, then B should be rejected as not true.

b. Someone analyzing focuses on the stated relation, making a simple statement into the subject of a composite statement and the quality of the simple statement into the predicate of the composite one, for example, "The statement 'S did not pass by recently' is negative." Such statements sometimes only have logical sense, as in this case. In an everyday context, they are usually an observational introduction to something else, for example, to a question like, "But who was it then that did pass by?"

Comment 3: Distinguish such statements of quality from more composite, observational statements, for example, "It is not true that the statement x is negative." This is a dissenting statement in which the truth of the predicate "negative" in x_1, [which is about x] and not the quality of the stated relation of x, is directly at issue. For example, let's say x was, "That man is being unsocial," and x_1, "That statement [namely, x] is negative." Then x_2 can claim, with an eye to the difference between being unsocial and nonsocial, "x_1, that predicated the quality of x as being negative, is contradictory." After all, being unsocial is being social in a wrong way, but is, nonetheless, social, so that whoever considers unsocial to be nonsocial is indeed claiming that something unsocial is both social and not social.

Here, too, it is helpful to distinguish assent and dissent (when discerning) from positive and negative (statements). Given that assent is, as such, positive and dissent, as such, negative, assent leaves the quality of what is proposed unchanged, but dissent turns this quality into its opposite.

c. When the analysis focuses on the statement's subject, distinguish the following:

(1) Analysis is looking at the character of the subject of the statement—among other things, whether it is genetic. If it is genetic, then possibility plays a part, if it is not genetic, then it is not a factor.

Comment 4: Possibility is neither "contingency" (Boethius) nor functionalistic-a priori conceivability with *epochè* ("suspension of judgment") concerning physical existence (logicism), rather it is the ability of what comes later to develop from what is earlier (not what is lower towards what is higher).

(2) Analysis is looking at the extension of the subject of the statement, for example, "The statement 'All men are mortal' is a universal statement," and "The statements 'Adam was created mortal' and 'Some people speak Dutch' are particular."

190. The composition of statements resting on the analysis of simple statements: According to epistemological presuppositions

Distinguish two cases:

a. Analysis focuses on the logical path by which the statement was discerned, namely, with or without the means of demonstration, for example, "It is proven that . . ." and "It is not proven that . . . ."

> Comment 1: The first of these statements are called "apodictic," the pertinent simple statement is called a "conclusion."

b. Analysis focuses on the (un)certainty of the person doing the discerning. When the condition is one of certainty, it does not draw attention to itself and one speaks and acts with assurance. "I believed; therefore I have spoken." It is when uncertainty arises that the attention slips from what is known toward the knowing subject, hence, (problematic and assertive) statements like, "It is still uncertain whether . . ." or "Once again, it is certain that . . . ."

> Comment 2: Note the difference in the conjunctions: "Whether" indicates uncertainty and "that" certainty.

191. The relationship of simple statements

a. Statements are compatible with each other or not.

b. Special relationships can be found [among simple statements].

(1) If predicates or the subjects of the statements are identical:

(a) When two statements have the same predicate, they can be conjugated. Schema: $S_1 + S_2 = P$. Example: "John and Fred are blond."

(b) When two statements have the same subject, they are copulable. Schema: $S = P_1 + P_2$. Example: "John is blond and large."

(2) When for two statements the subject of the one is the predicate of the other and the predicate of the first is the subject of the other, they are called each other's converse. Discussion of the conditions under which the converse of a true statement will also be true, and so on, would take me too far afield.

(3) Based on extension and quality, distinguish among statements between universal-negative, universal-positive, particular-positive, and particular-negative. The relationships of these four groups play an important part in the doctrine of proofs. This division is faulty in that it does not take into account the difference between genetic and nongenetic statements, which is very important when it comes to proofs. Here, too, I cannot now afford to elaborate.

192. The relationships of specific composite statements

When the extensions of the subjects of two particular statements with opposing predicates together include all of the relevant subjects, then the dilemmatic statement holds, "*S* is either *P* or not-*P*," and there is no third possibility. If these conditions are not met, then there is no dilemma and the *principium exclusi tertii* (principle of excluded middle) does not hold.

193. Proofs and verification

a. On the basis of relationships between two statements, it is possible to derive another one. The first two are called "premises" and the latter "conclusion."

Proofs are also found in nonscientific life. The simplest case is when a conclusion can be derived from two statements that are themselves conclusions from still other statements. In many cases, a proof does not mean so much; the proven statement can often be reached through invention. For example, from "2 times 2 = 4" and "3 times 2 = 6" I conclude that "5 times 2 = 10."

b. An exception to this rule is the conclusion that deals with something expected in the future. Such a proof has a hypothetical character but is often an aid to invention (discovery). Confirming the conclusion through perception is called "verification." When, for example, A says to B, "Watch out, you can't trust C. I've done *x;* now he's going to react by doing *y*," B is going to watch C's behavior and will be able to verify whether the conclusion A drew is correct.

194. Demonstration

Demonstrations are social in nature. They use proofs, among other things, but also all of the nonscientific knowledge available. By presenting an argument one tries to convince one's neighbor squarely, sometimes just to persuade in a less objective manner. It is possible to convince someone on sound grounds but also on those that are less so. The means one uses to achieve one's goal make up one of the factors that form a tradition. These ways and means are of paramount importance for gaining insight into one part of nonscientific knowledge.

> Comment: There is so much more to social life than demonstrative proofs! Leaders in this area, fortunately, also have other means at their

disposal. Maintaining invested authority does not stand or fall with the dexterity of the office bearer in arguing what she considers to be right!

195. *The supra-analytic interrelations in nonscientific knowledge*

Nonscientific knowledge includes so much more than current books on logic§§ deal with. And it is the person with a wealth of experience who always eclipses the beginner; "experience" taken here in its everyday sense includes a keen memory, a trained eye, and a cache of recollections and perceptions.

196. *Distinguishing functions within nonscientific thinking*

Nonscientific knowing also distinguishes a number of functions, primarily prevailing and leading functions.

That is especially true of the supra-analytic spheres, particularly in the supralingual fields, where the use of language, when clear, supports discernment. For example, without the help of science, people distinguish business, state, family, and pistic institution (church). Where Calvinism has made inroads, people earnestly resist mixing up these arenas and denounce, for example, political strikes, ecclesiastical science, and the like.

But also with respect to the subanalytic, nonscientific thinking does a good job of distinguishing. A farmer distinguishes stones, plants, animals, and humans more clearly than many who are stuck with an impoverished theory of knowledge that in quasi simplicity only knows a subject–object relationship and understands this to be the relationship of thinking and what sense perceives. (See §160d, Comment 3, and §171a2.)

197. *Nonscientific knowing and the theory of knowledge*

Obviously, those who are not keen in analyzing nonscientific knowledge will be unable to keep all of this straight: *primum vivere deinde philosophari* ("first live, then philosophize"). Nevertheless, what is analyzed here as nonscientific knowledge belongs without a doubt to the *vivere* and is present in an abundance more varied than indi-

---

§§ To understand the terminology current in scientific handbooks, one needs to know more about logic than can be dealt with here. For a more extensive elaboration I would refer to my *Hoodlijnen der logica* (Kampen: Kok, 1948). [A note revised in the 1967 edition.]

cated here. No one, even those who also work at a scientific level, can ever get too much nonscientific knowledge.

Division II

Scientific Knowing

198. Introduction

Scientific knowing everywhere relies on nonscientific knowing.

For now, I can only indicate very briefly what ought to be discussed in a theory about scientific knowing.

199. Division

We distinguish special-scientific and nonspecial-scientific (scientific) knowing. I devote a chapter to the discussion of each.

Chapter 1
Special Scientific Knowing

200. The connection between nonspecial-scientific and special-scientific knowing

Knowing in the special sciences distinguishes itself from nonspecial-scientific knowing by its ongoing isolation of increasingly refined interrelations in the several law-spheres. We speak of a *special* science when no more than one nonanalytic modality is investigated.

> Comment: "Mathematics," "astronomy," "zoology," and so on are terms, formed at a time prior to a sharp demarcation of fields of investigation, that indicate sciences in an earlier stage. Today, they are separating more and more into true special sciences, for example, mathematics into arithmetic and geometry or theology into pistology and ethics. Ethics in this context, then, is always theological ethics, but not all theology is Christian or sacred theology.

201. Method

Being busy in a special scientific way implies, then, that the analysis of the investigator is directed to a nonanalytic law-sphere.

a. Through analysis, and aided by the *principium exclusae antinomiae* (principle of excluded antinomy), such a law-sphere first needs to be analyzed out of the cosmic context in which it is found. In doing so, it becomes a "field of investigation."

> Comment 1: With respect to the connection seeking analytic activity, what is being investigated is not active; it is, if you will, noetically passive. This passivity in no way restricts the eventual nonnoetic activity of the functions being investigated. So, for example, energy is certainly active, even though it is noetically passive in the propositions of energet*ics* and phys*ics*.

The method of the special sciences is always binary, that is to say, *synthetic*. Only analytics (logic) lacks this synthetic character, at least in part, namely, to the extent that we do not approach it via the theory of knowledge.

b. Then analysis proceeds in a noetically active fashion within the field that was first analyzed out of its cosmic context.

> Comment 2: Within the entire field of investigation of a special science, it is possible to focus just on a part, for example, the physical aspect of only stars and the organic aspect of just one person, like myself or someone else. But we may not forget that such a part, in spite of this limitation, remains standing in limited and more open interrelations with all of the rest.
>
> So, after the field has been isolated, it is possible to introduce a second isolation, either in a vertical direction (as above) or in a horizontal direction. For example, scientific research can focus particularly on the anticipations or retrocipations within one sphere, as do differential calculus and integral calculus or social psychology and the psychosociology.
>
> Comment 3: The division of the sciences among faculties is rooted more in tradition than in a cogent theory of knowledge. Studies in some fields never developed, making it difficult in later years to incorporate them into existing curricula.

202. The diversity in method

The plurality of methods used to analyze these fields is as large as the diversity of nonanalytic functions. Because there are no dichotomous groups of functions in the cosmos, it is also impossible to split the sciences into two groups, like the "natural" sciences and the humanities. The distinction of a priori and a posteriori knowledge also lacks credibility. That 2 times 2 equals 4 might "speak for itself" to us, but this insight rests on nothing more than that the arithmetic function is the least complex. A child, however, does not simply discover this proposition without any effort. The division of the sciences into those of nature and of culture must likewise be rejected. Culture is always the result of human mastery of the nonhuman. It can only be investigated scientifically by looking at the modal differences that are present in both nature and culture and that are the same in both.

203. The result

The result consists of scientific statements (propositions) whose content is neither only analytic nor only nonanalytic. The proposition "2 times 2 is 4" is not only analytic nor only arithmetic but a biunity; it is arithmetical.

204. The connection of statements

A person who thinks diachronically can often perceive an interrelation between the analytic functions of two (or more) propositions found earlier. Such a person is, then, standing in an analytically perceptive interrelation with the analytic functions of those propositions and yet now sees the analytic interrelation between the analytic functions of these two propositions. This analytic activity is called a "scientific inference," the two propositions in this context "scientific premises," and the proposition gained, a "scientific conclusion."

Such a conclusion always presupposes two propositions. These, in turn, could have been inferred from others. With these inferences, the nonanalytic element of these propositions may not be lost sight of. That is something gotten not through inference but through special scientific labor.

In addition, an inferred proposition can also be found through special scientific research. Inferences, then, are nothing more than a shortcut and stimulus for the work.

205. Cooperation in science

The complex of propositions a special science finds through research and inference is represented in sentences, didactically ordered and communicated to others. These others, in turn, offer their considerations or continue the work on the basis given.

Chapter 2
NONSPECIAL-SCIENTIFIC SCIENTIFIC KNOWING

206. Summary

What falls under this heading can only have justice done to it with a broader discussion than is now possible. Pedagogy, among other things, fits in this bracket. It is much more than a special science.

PART II

THE THEORY ABOUT KNOW-HOW AND TECHNOLOGY

207. Introduction

The theory about expertise can be dealt with much more briefly than the theory about knowledge. Know-how belongs under the historic function and, hence, presupposes the analytic function.

We will first discuss know-how and then its relationship to science.

DIVISION I

Know-How

208. Introduction

We will discuss the following: the relationship between the historic function and know-how, technical mastery, the basis of what is being worked and the working of it, and the combination of mastery and assimilation in a higher interrelation.

209. The historic and know-how

The historic function includes more than expertise. Even the subject–object relationship in the historic cannot adequately clarify what know-how (*technè*) is. There is also a practical understanding of products of skill. Know-how can itself only be circumscribed as a practical effort in the relationship of subject to object within, in the historic sphere, whose goal is to satisfy practical-historic needs.

210. Technical mastery

The subject–object relation in the historic law-sphere stands in the foreground here, connected with the schema active–passive. An example can elucidate this.

From physical things, from pieces of metal, we make machines, among other things. Before that happened, the economic object function of the metal was not lacking; it already had an economic value. But it was not yet a machine. Before it could become that, two things were needed. Here, too, it is first the subject function that has something to say. If metal was less resistant to fire, it would not be used for machines. You can only get out of it what's "in it." On the other hand, a thing does not become a machine without "extracting" what's in it, that is, without the often diligent industry of humans.

> Comment 1: This example also has the advantage that those who take the time to investigate it carefully will be cured once and for all of the theory that claims that all of the subeconomic spheres function like machines. Neither the organic nor the physical (and therewith, the mechanical) spheres are machinelike.

Here, too, we meet the active–passive correlation. In this case, it is connected to a state of affairs that is somewhat more involved than what we have found previously. The "mastery" here is that human activity, taking the makeup of the "material" to be mastered into consideration, changes a thing's already present object function according to a more or less articulated plan in compliance with an observed need that someone wants to satisfy.

> Comment 2: "To master"—broader than "to form"—is not, on the side of the subject, "to create," for it presumes the presence of the individual created material and of the working person. Neither is it, on the side of the object, a matter of connecting functions it does have with those it doesn't. It is only a change within the context of the functions already present in the material.
>
> Comment 3: The "material" need not always be a physical thing. Plants and animals, limiting ourselves for the moment to nonhuman things, can also be used. Think of the part played by flora and fauna in a botanical garden and in a zoo.

Why can this mastery only occur through human beings? The grounds for this are not found in the active–passive schema, which we find already in the physical sphere, particularly in the relationship between corpuscles. The answer to this question first becomes clear after investigating what mastery presupposes modally: not only a psychic desire but also an analytic distinguishing, particularly, of means and ends as technical correlates. That is why mastery is first present in the historic law-sphere, in which only human beings possess a subject function. The more complicated the sphere in which the complex change lies is, the more mastery it also presupposes. Art, for example, as aesthetic mastery of material, presupposes more than just know-how.

211. The basis of know-how
Distinguish between the basis of the mastering and of what is mastered.

a. The basis of the mastering varies but is never lower than the historic function.

b. The basis of what is mastered varies as well. It always lies in the highest of the law-spheres in which the object involved still possesses a subject function. For metal, that is the physical, for plants and animals, respectively, the biotic and psychic law-spheres.

212. The combination of mastery and its appropriation in higher interrelation
A new combination in which the schema of active–passive twice plays a part occurs when what has been made is taken up into another interrelation. Putting a machine into operation following its fabrication and putting coins into circulation once they have been minted are two examples.

The modality of this combination is always that of want, in service of which the mastery took place.

DIVISION II

Know-How and Science

213. Introduction
Distinguish two things here: the relationship of know-how to special science and to philosophy.

214. Relationship of know-how and special science
Know-how is present in every culture but never without technical thinking and knowing in the categories of means and end.

All the same, practical thinking and knowing is something other than doing and having science. Likewise, know-how in its primitive forms is not attached to the special sciences.

The relationship is very different, however, in cultures with highly developed special sciences. There, know-how banks on the special sciences. Surgery builds on organology, chemistry on physics and organology, and experiments on various special sciences.

That, however, is also the reason for the confusion in terminology between *technè* (know-how) and technology. These should be distinguished. *Technè* is the praxis, while technology is the science about this practical know-how. Technology, then, is a subdiscipline of the science called history.

215. Know-how and philosophy

Philosophy, being science, also presupposes practical expertise as part of nonscientific life.

On the other hand, philosophy has to reflect on the place, on the limits, and on the religious sense of practical know-how—something that happens more and more nowadays.

PART III

THE THEORY ABOUT ART AND AESTHETICS

216. Introduction

Art falls under the aesthetic law-sphere and, hence, presupposes much more than the analytic function, namely, the historic function and know-how.

We have to discuss here first art and then its relationship to science.

DIVISION I

Art

217. Introduction

Once again, our attention turns to the relationship between aesthetics and art, then to artistic mastery, to the basis of what is mastered and of the mastering, and finally to the combination of mastery and appropriation in a higher interrelation.

218. The aesthetic and art

The aesthetic law-sphere includes more than art. Here, too, even the subject–object relationship in the aesthetic is not sufficient to make clear what art is. The subjective enjoyment of objective natural beauty is aesthetic but not artistic. Art, then, can be circumscribed as being practically busy in the relationship of subject to object in the aesthetic sphere, with an eye to satisfying aesthetic needs.

Comment: It is best not to replace "needs" with "taste," which is too rational and, hence, one-sided.

219. Artistic mastery
Here is the analogy with know-how. But with art, everything is at a higher plane—not historic, but aesthetic.

220. The basis of what is mastered and of the mastery
What holds for the basis of what is mastered technically, holds here as well.
The basis of the mastery is, in this case, other than before, never lower than the aesthetic function.

221. The combination of mastery and its appropriation in higher interrelation
Artworks can be taken up into jural life as property, into ethical life as gifts, and into the pistic life as symbol.

DIVISION II

Art and Science

222. Introduction
Here, too, given the differences in science, distinguish the relationship between art and special science and the relationship between art and philosophy.

223. Art and special science
Art presupposes the aesthetic function, that is, practical knowledge, not science.
In turn, the science about art presupposes artistic life. This science of art is a subdiscipline of aesthetics, which is broader.

224. Art and philosophy
Art does not need philosophy, but philosophy does presuppose art as part of nonscientific living.
Philosophy about art runs parallel to the philosophy about know-how.

References (1945)
    Editors' note: These references are found at the end of the *Isagoge*.

A. Regarding the philosophy of the law-idea:
    Philosophia Reformata, 1 Kampen: J.H. Kok, 1936 ff.
    Prof. dr. H. Dooyeweerd, [*The New Critique of Theoretical Thought*, I–IV. Philadelphia: Presbyterian and Reformed, 1953.]
    Rev. J.M. Spier, [*An Introduction Christian Philosophy*. Philadelphia: Presbyterian and Reformed, 1954.]

B. Regarding other conceptions.
    The reader is referred (i) to the works indicated in paragraph 2 above,[*] and (ii) to the literature referenced in the newest revision of my *Conspectus Historiae*.

----

[*] *Editors' note*: Strictly speaking, paragraph 2 only refers to authors. The works implied are:
    Andel, H.A. van. [probably]: *Godsdienst en wetenschap. Een boek voor denkende menschen. Bewerkt naar geschriften van Dr. H. Bavinck*, 1921.
    Becher, Erich, *Einführung in die Philosophie*, München 1926.
    Drews, Arthur Christian Heinrich, *Eduard von Hartmanns philosophisches System im Grundriss*. Heidelberg: Carl Winter's Universitäts-buchhandlung, 1902.

Fichte, Johann Gottlieb. [probably]: "Erste Einleitung in die Wissenschafslehre" and "Zweite Einleitung in die Wissenschafslehre" both in *Philosophische Journal* 1797; and *Darstellung der Wissenschafslehre*, Tübingen 1801.

Fullerton, George Stuart, *Introduction to Philosophy*, 1906.

Herbart, Johann Friedrich, *Lehrbuch zur Einleitung in die Philosophie*, 1813, herausgegeben von K. Häntsch, mit Einleitung, 1912.

Külpe, Oswald, *Einleitung in die Philosophie*, 1895, 12th printing 1929.

Land, Jan Pieter Nicolaas, *Inleiding in de wijsbegeerte*, 's-Gravenhage, 1889, 2nd ed. 1900.

Paulsen, Friedrich, *Einleitung in die Philosophie*, 1892, 39th en 40th printing 1924.

Raeymacker, Louis de, *Introduction a la Philosophie*. Brussels: Editions Universitaires Les Presses de Belgique, 1938, 2nd ed. 1944.

Renouvier, Charles. [probably] *Essais de critique générale* (1854-1864), 2nd edition 1875-1896, [as well as] IV: *Introduction à la philosophie analytique de l'histoire*, 1896/1897.

Reyer, W., *Einführung in die Phänomenologie*, Leipzig: F. Meiner, 1926.

Russell, Bertrand, *Problems of Philosophy*. London: Williams and Norgate, 1912, 3rd printing 1918.

Walch, Johann Georg, *Einleitung in die Philosophie*, Leipzig 1727.

Wattjes, J.G., *Practische wijsbegeerte*, Delft, 1924 [possibly a second printing in 1926].

Windelband, Wilhelm, *Einleitung in die Philosophie*, Tübingen 1914, 3rd printing 1923.

Wundt, Wilhelm, *Einleitung in die Philosophie* 1911 [1901?] 8th printing 1920.

Further:

> D.H.Th. Vollenoven, *Conspectus Historiae [Philosophiae]* ("Survey of the History of Philosophy"); this title supported Vollenhoven's lectures on the history of philosophy. A variety of course syllabi under this same title were used between 1926 and 1948 (and are now available in the Vollenhoven-archives). Vollenhoven's last complete survey of the history of philosophy dates from 1956 (*Kort overzicht van de geschiedenis der wijsbegeerte voor de cursus Paedagogiek M.O.A.*, stencil-uitgave Theja, Amsterdam) and has recently been translated in D. H. Th. Vollenhoven, *The Problem-Historical Method and the History of Philosophy*, ed. Kornelis A. Bril (Amsterdam: De Zaak Haes, 2005).

In paragraph 3, the reference is:

Fritz Heinemann, *Neue Wege der Philosophie Geist-Leben-Existenz*, 1929.

Index of Terms

N.B. The numbers listed refer to the numbered paragraphs in the text.

a posteriori 202
a priori 171, 189, 202
a priorism, partial 88
absolutizing 117
abstract 171, 185
abstraction 49, 70, 72, 117, 177
act 40
active 82, 159, 160
active–passive 81, 82, 103, 105, 163, 164, 168, 201, 210, 212
 -in supraspatial interrelations 81
 -in the analytic law-sphere 159–61, 163, 164, 168
 -in the historic law-sphere 210
activity 25, 48, 73, 77, 81, 88, 103, 105, 106, 111, 113, 117, 136, 160, 167, 174, 201, 204, 210
 -analytic 40, 55, 82, 183
 -energetic 40
 -divine 13, 117
 -of coming to know 152–54, 156, 174, 176
aesthetic (law)sphere 218, 220
 -subject–object-relation here 218
aesthetic 31, 48, 217
aesthetic function 112, 216
 -list of object functions 66
 -place as subject function 55
aesthetic needs 218
aesthetics 223
affinity among subjects from different realms 104, 105
affirmative 189
altruism 114
analogy 59, 63
analysis/analyzing 23, 70
 -special-scientific 201
analytic (subject)function 155, 160, 161, 164, 171, 172, 204
analytic 31, 48, 51, 146, 203
 -place as subject function 55
analytic activity 40, 55, 82, 183
analytic coming to know 155
 -connection with the knowable 174

 -vertical connection here 170
analytic interrelation 156, 157
 -and perception 83, 146, 162, 172
analytic laws 152
analytic law-sphere 108, 154, 158–61, 163, 164, 168, 172
 -subject–object-relation here 107, 108, 160
 -subject–subject-relation here 108, 160
analytic object 172
 -list of object functions 66
analytic retrocipation 172
analytic space 65
analytics 201
anarchy 14
ancestors 122, 124
angels 20, 21, 121, 138, 139, 146
 -their knowledge 146
anhypostatos 124
animal meat 130
animal(s) 31, 46, 47, 55, 62, 65, 66, 83, 97, 101, 102, 105, 106, 121, 130, 146, 159, 171, 178, 211
 -their knowing 146
animism 130, 132
anthropology 124, 182
anthropomorphic 105
anti-Christian 125
anticipation 61–63, 68, 88, 98, 172, 201
 -examples of 61
antinomies 33, 201
antithesis 21, 125, 129
antithetic duality of good–evil 88, 92, 121
antithetic structure of love in the love command 114
antithetical 86, 88
 -dualism 21
apodictic 190
apperception 168
apprehending 160
apriorists 155
archè 14, 25
argument 194

arithmetic 61, 200, 201
arithmetic function 57, 202
   -change in 102
   -place as subject function 55
arithmetic laws 35, 36, 46, 54, 55
arithmetic law-sphere 40, 51, 65
arithmetic(-being) 31, 35–37, 43, 45, 48, 54–56, 61
   -arith. retrocipation in the analytic 172
arithmetic/supra-arithmetic 88
arithmetical 203
art 142, 210, 216–224
artist's guild 112
artistic mastery 217, 220
ascending 88
ascension 138
ascetic 92
ascetism 88, 139
associations 63, 112, 136
astrology 21
atom 43, 47, 101, 178
autarky 88, 112
authority 3, 194
   -those who bear authority 111–13
autonomous/-omy 14, 112
Autonomy (vs. Heteronomy) 112, 122
Babylonian world picture 21
baptism 125
Baptists 124
basic connections 27, 28, 88
basic structure of the earthly-subject 115, 182
basis and consequence 78, 172
bees 105
beholding 117
being 8, 13, 147
   -creature/created being 20, 31, 117, 121, 180
   -earthly 20, 22, 23, 30, 35
believing 11, 12
bilateral 118
blessing 118, 125
blood 55, 61
blood revenge 130, 133
blushing 61
bodily 88
body 93, 102, 113, 134, 139
   -defined in its direction 93
   -and soul 93, 122
body of the Lord 65
brain 55, 61, 62

breath of life 117
breeders 105
built in goal 139
business (enterprise) 112, 113, 159
bylaws 113
"by the grace of God" 111
Calvinism 112, 196
Calvinistic philosophy 125
carnal 135
categories 170
causal connection 79, 172
cause 68
cause and effect 78, 172
center of gravity 61
center, religious 139
certainty 11, 190
   -of statements made 188, 190
change in all functions 102
characteristics (Hobbes) 182
chemical connection 102
chemist 102
chemistry 214
Christendom 125
Christian 11, 12
   -action 125
   -faith 12, 15, 125, 134, 136
   -philosophical conception 12
   -religion 140
   -science 125, 173
Christianity 125
Christians 11, 12, 88, 134–36, 139
Church 125, 136, 140
church 47, 124, 125, 136, 182
   -art 136
   -as Christian pistic institution 125
   -as institution 125, 136
   -as organism 125
circle 46, 47, 51, 54, 60, 72, 73, 77, 79
circumcision 125, 132
classes 185
clouding the mind 180
cogito 7, 8
cognitive element 60
cognitive interrelation 154, 163
coincidentia oppositorum 13
color 65, 81, 160
commerce 60
compatibility 61, 191
competence 113
composite statements 1, 186, 187, 189, 190, 192

concept formation 180
concept(s) 13, 175, 176, 183, 185
  -extension of 176, 182
  -ordering of 181, 182
  -perceptual and abstracted 176
  -primary 176
  -secondary 176
  -simple and composite 176
conception 5, 12, 13, 21, 43, 88, 112, 124, 125, 144, 185
  -Christian philosophical 12
  -main 15
conclusion 51, 190, 193, 204
concrete, that which (more) 25, 53, 64, 70, 95, 115
connection (relation) 10, 13, 19, 23, 50, 51
  -between heaven and earth 137–140
  -between subject functions 54, 64, 65, 88
  -causal 79, 172
  -cosmic 201
  -genetic 95, 97, 99, 100, 104, 121, 139
  -horizontal (between individuals) 50, 52, 53, 157, 170
  -marriage- 20, 88, 121
  -religious 130
  -vertical 98, 156, 170
connection, total and not-total 102
connections, vertical and horizontal 67–69, 88, 155
consciousness 170
Conspectus historiae 2
constituent 78, 93, 100, 103, 155
consultation 111
contemplative 174
contemporary 78–80, 82, 88, 157–59, 163, 165 (*see also* interrelation)
continuity 65, 66
contradictory 13
conviction(s) 88, 111, 125
convince 111, 194
cooperation 79, 81, 84, 105, 108, 111, 159
  -of the sexes 121
copy theory 174
corpuscles 210
correlation active–passive 81–84 (*see also* active–passive)
correlation authority–respect 111
cosmic 140, 180, 201

cosmism, pan-/partial 13
cosmos 5, 13, 15, 16, 18, 20, 33, 65, 66, 81, 84, 93, 94, 111, 124, 125, 136, 139, 140, 152, 159, 162, 173, 174, 182, 202
  -genesis 178
  -place of what one perceives in 180
  -as threefold 139
Counsel of God 13, 129
counting 55, 61
course of affairs 168, 173
course of an occurrence 60
covenant of creation (=1st covenant) 119–122, 124, 130
covenant of favor 121
covenant of grace 130, 134
covenant of works 121
covenant, religious 22, 117, 118, 122, 125, 130, 135, 136
  -its institution and structure 118 (*see also* covenant of creation, covenant of re-creation, God of the Covenant)
  -and law 118
created being 13, 19, 20, 31, 182 (*see* being)
creating, activity and result 117
creation 20, 21, 85, 99
  -and societal connections 113
  -of Adam 102
creation ordinance 111
creator 13
creature 31
creatures, earthly and heavenly 139, 173
critical 3, 160
critique 3, 4, 125
cultic connection 112, 113
  -pagan 113
cultivation 130
cultural 202
culture/nature 202
curse 118, 122, 133
  -of the law 134
death 121, 122, 133, 134, 139
  -first and second 134
  -fascination with 133
deceit 136
decentralization 112
decision-making and activity 111
deify 182
demonic 21, 139
denote 1, 13, 18, 36–38, 43, 47, 52, 68, 70, 160, 200

desire 12, 121, 134
destination (function) 111–13, 125
determinant(s) 17, 22, 23, 25, 27–29, 31, 37
  -good–evil 85
  -of law 34, 35
  -this–that 36–38, 47
  -their not being separate 45
  -their irreducibility 41, 42, 67, 89
  -thus–so 30, 33, 37, 42
detour 25, 61
development 48, 60
  -of nonscientific knowing 149
diachronic 157, 168, 204
diagram of good–evil 88, 89, 91
diagram of this–that 88
dichotomous groups of functions 202
dichotomy 57, 88, 139
difference(s) 10, 13, 17, 87, 112, 170
  -intra-cosmic 180
  -left-right 91
  -this–that 39, 40, 42, 43, 48, 50–52, 54, 68, 87, 88, 112, 162
  -thus–so 32, 42, 43, 48, 68, 87, 88, 112, 202
dimension 60, 65
direction 26, 27, 85, 95
  -and genesis 102
  -and soul 93
  -and the church 125
  -between subject and object 88
  -created in a specific 124
  -in the function 60n, 91
  -in the interrelation (of relation) 72, 73, 78, 79, 88
  -of a line 65, 66
  -of a societal connection 114
  -of human life 92
  -of investigation 23, 25
  -of the heart 114
  -time direction 169
  -within a field of investigation 201
directional principle (=spirit) 139
discontinuity 65
  -of points 65
disobedience 86, 121, 125
dissent 189
distance 65
distinguish, ability to 113
distinguishing/distinctions 152, 155, 159, 210

  -subanalytic 196
  -supralingual 196
diversities 19, 20, 22, 23, 43, 68, 88, 115
  -their irreducibility 41, 42, 67, 89
  -within a determinant 28, 29, 31, 32, 35, 37–39, 41
divine 13, 117
dogma, 124, 125
domain (arenas) 51, 136, 182, 196
doubt 88
dualism 21
dualistic trichotomistic 139
duality 88
duration, aesthetic 48
duty, doing one's 60
dying 88, 121, 122, 124, 134, 135
  -and the wrath of God 124
dynamic character, of the supraphysical 60
  -of the subject of a statement 188
earth 19, 20, 22, 23, 117, 122, 137, 173
earthly being (*see* being)
earthly part of the cosmos 139
earthly subject (*see* subject, earthly)
eclecticism 3
economic 31, 48, 111
economic function 111, 112, 210
  -list of object functions 66
  -place as subject function 55
education 113
effect, and cause 78, 172
egoism 114
eidetic 164, 167, 171
elect, the 125
election 124, 129
electron 101
element(s) 101
  -of thinking and knowing 60
emotional perception 83, 146
energetic 31
energetic activity 40
energetic law-sphere 51
energetics 201
energy (forms) 51, 53, 55
environment 31, 121
epiphenomenalism 100
epistemological assumptions 187, 188, 190
epochè 189
equivalent 53
erring 11, 13, 182

error 33, 155 (*see also* knowledge of error)
eschatology 139
eternal life 125
ethical 31, 48
ethical act 40
ethical function 112
   -list of object functions 66
   -place as subject function 55
ethics 200
Euclidean space 31, 65
evil 85, 86, 88, 121, 138
evolution 22
evolution, theory of 100
evolving 22, 100, 178
exist(ence) 11, 15, 114, 117
   -conceivable 189
   -of God 117
expect-able 168
expectation 15, 163, 171, 173, 180
   -expecting expectations 168
   -subject and object here 168
expectation interrelation 168
   -inter-individual 168
   -intra-individual 168
experiment 214
extension 8, 31
   -of a statement's subject 188, 189, 192
   -of concepts 176, 182
faith (sacred) 11, 12, 20, 31, 121, 130, 132, 133
   -assurance of 60
   -Christian 12, 15, 125, 136
   -joy of 63
   -norm of the faith 125
faithfulness of God 21
Fall 85, 120–22, 125, 130, 180
family 112, 113, 136, 182
   -first 129
   -life 125
fatherly factor with the Mediator 102, 124
fauna 210
favor (of God) 121, 124
feeling 63
feel/sensitivity 55, 65
   -as sorts of anticipations 61
field of investigation 16, 25, 201
figure, spatial 40, 43
figures 31, 51, 53, 55, 61, 70, 73, 88, 89
finite 13, 66
flesh 134, 135
Flood 128, 130
flora 210
flower 65
fluids (plant, animal and human) 61
forgiveness 120, 121
form 210
foundation 7, 140
freedom, constitutional 112
friendship 31
fruitfulness, command of 121
function 55–57, 91–93, 98, 130 (*see also* destination function, leading function and prevailing function; *also* analytic, arithmetic, economic, aesthetic, ethical, physical, historical, juridic, lingual, organic, pistical, psychic, spatial, social)
   -change in all 102
   -line 91
   -of societal connections 112
   -of thinking 55
functional body 93
functional decentralization (in socialistic circles) 112
functional exist(ence) 114, 117
functional structure 92, 98
functionalism 92
functionalistic a prioristic 189
functionalistic-dichotomistic 139
functioning of the subject unit 49
functions (modally different) 102, 196, 202
functions, cloak of 93, 139
functions, group of 57, 93, 100, 117, 202
functions, view of human 88, 112
future 108, 113, 121, 133, 136, 163, 168, 173, 177, 178, 193
Garden of Eden 121
gemina 129
genesis 31, 99, 101
   -and the human heart 114
   -of human life and societal-connections 113
genesis of knowledge 180
genesis, statements about 185, 191
genetic 31, 95, 96, 101–03, 171, 173 (*see also* connection, genetic)
   -character of the subject of a statement 188, 189
   -interrelation 99
   -series 99
   -within nonscientific knowing 177

genotypical 99
geometry 200
gesture 63
gift of grace 124
gifts of the spirits 134
glorified Christ 139
glory (of God) 117
gnosticism 124
goal 88
  -built-in 139
  -and means (*see* means-end)
God 12–15, 21, 22, 99, 109, 112, 114, 115, 117, 118, 121, 122, 124, 125, 129, 130, 132–36, 139, 146, 173, 174, 185
  -and cosmos 13, 15, 159
  -his knowledge 143, 145
  -of the covenant 116, 118, 121, 124, 129, 133
  -of the nations 133
good and evil 85–89, 92, 114, 121, 122, 124, 173, 180
  -as third determinant 85
good 117, 121, 124, 129, 135, 138
goods, economic 111
Gospel 125
grace 120, 121, 124, 129
gravitational line 61
growers 105
guilt 125
harmonizing of interests 60
harmony 31
hate 114
heart 12, 92, 102, 113, 114, 125, 132, 134, 135, 139
  -functionalistic view 139
heaven 19–22, 117, 137, 138
  -longing for 139
  -worship of 20
heavenly subject (*see* subject, heavenly)
hell 21, 139
heteronomy 112
Heteronomy 112
historia revelationis 178
historic 31, 48, 55, 111
historic subject 108
historical law-sphere/function 107, 108, 171, 209–11
  -subject–object-relation here 107, 108, 209, 210
  -subject-subject-relation here 108
  -and *technè* 207, 211

historical needs 209, 210
historically determined, being 31
  -list of object functions 66
  -place as subject function 55
history 121 (*see also* meaning of history)
  -of philosophy 3, 4, 65
  -of religion 118, 119 (*see also* covenant of creation and of re-creation)
  -the discipline 214
hold (for) 13, 182
Holy Scripture 13, 20–22, 92, 121, 122, 124, 125, 134, 139, 178, 180
Holy Spirit 124, 125, 134 (*see also* spirit of God)
honey 105
horizontal 50, 52, 53, 157, 170, 201
human being (a unity) 146
human body and societal connections 113
human knowing 146, 147
human language 145
human nature 117, 122, 124
human nature of Christ 88, 102, 124, 134
  -fatherly factor of the Mediator 124
human race 109, 117, 118, 121, 124
humanistic 134
humanities 202
humankind 22, 94, 109, 122, 129, 179
  -and knowing 179
humans(s) 31, 46, 47, 55, 60, 62, 66, 73, 92, 93, 95–97, 99, 102, 105, 106, 114, 117, 122, 178
  -original goodness 117
  -unity 121, 146
hypostasis 139
I/not-I 88
idea, regulative 13
idealism 132
identity of the predicate or subject of a statement 191
identity, statement of 65
idolatry 88
image of God 114, 117, 121, 122
  -as being related to God 117
immorality 132
immortality 134
implications 187–89
incarnation of the Word 124, 126
individual 43, 45, 47, 182
  -creatures 95
  -determinant 47

-difference(s) 48, 50–52, 54, 87, 112
-/environment 121
-existence of the soul 139
-subject unit 49, 60, 139
-thing 102
"this" 46, 47, 64, 68
individuality 20, 81, 85, 101, 102, 124
indivisibility 101
infinite 13, 63
infinity of God 13
inherence 185
injustice (due to out of date laws) 111
innate understanding 117
inner interrelation 76, 88, 160–62
inner perception 162
inner world 11
innocence, state of 122
institutions, human 112–14, 125, 136, 173 (*see also* societal connection)
intellectualististic rigor 12
interaction 31
interest 48
interests 60
inter-individual interrelations 74, 76, 77, 79–83, 88, 100, 102, 105, 159, 160, 161, 168
interrelation(s) 52, 53, 55, 68, 71–73, 75, 77, 88, 91, 122, 130, 134, 164, 165, 212, 217
    -active–passive in the supraspatial 81
    -analytic 156, 157
    -cognitive-interrelation 154, 163
    -contemporary 157–59
    -direction in 72, 73, 78, 79, 88
    -earthly 122
    -expectation. 168
    -genetic 99
    -inner and outer 76, 160–62
    -inter- and intra-individual 74, 98, 158, 160–62 (*see also* inter-ind.; intra-ind.)
    -of recollection 164, 165
    -successive 157
    -supra-analytic 195
    -supraspatial 68
    -perceptive 160, 161, 204
    -with works of art 221
intersecting (figures) 51, 53
intra-cosmic 140, 180
intra-individual interrelations 74, 76, 77, 79–83, 88, 93, 100, 102, 103, 105, 139, 160, 161, 164, 168

intra-mental 66
intuition 31
    mode of 48
invention 193
investigation, field of 16, 25, 201
investigation, route of 23, 25
irreducibility of determinants 41, 42, 67
is 184
Isagoge 1, 4, 24, 141, 185
isolation, vertical and horizontal 201
Jewish law 134
Jews 11, 134
joy of faith 63
judgment of God 12, 21, 133, 135
juridic 31, 48, 125
juridic bylaws in state, family, and cultic connection 113
juridic function 112
    -list of object functions 66
    -place as subject function 55
justification 125
kinematic 31
king 121, 133
kingdom connection 97 (*see also* connection, genotypical)
kingdom(s) 22, 23, 84, 94, 96–99, 102, 104–07, 109, 122, 180, 185
"kingship of God's grace" 111
knowable (what is) 11, 65, 145, 152, 153, 170, 173, 174
    -genetic in the 177, 178, 180
know-how 31, 108, 142, 171, 207–215, 219, 224
knowing 6–12, 23, 25, 108, 150, 171
    -and being 8
    -coming to know 151–156, 163, 174, 176
    -human 146, 147, 179
    -ideals for 174
    -and law-sphere 154
    -means for 173
    -nonscientific 148, 149, 182, 196, 198
    -philosophical 7, 9–12, 14
    -scientific 9, 148, 198
    -special-scientific 9, 10, 199, 200
    -structure of 177
    -technical 214
    -what is genetic in 177
knowledge 7, 11, 76, 150, 155, 173, 185
    -a priori and a posteriori 202
    -of error 173, 174, 176

-of good and evil 121, 180
-knowledge of and about 144
-nonscientific 108, 194, 195, 197
-results 152, 153
-sequence of coming to 180
-sources of 173
-with Adam 180
-with angels 146
-with creatures 143, 145, 146
-with God 143, 145
labor organizations 63
language 31, 55, 145, 160
  -sorts of 60
  -use 60, 196
later, as higher 88
law 33–5, 40, 44, 48, 49, 51, 73, 88, 125, 133, 134, 185 (see also arithmetic, organic, psychic, spatial)
  -and covenant 118
  -curse of the 134
  -determinant of 34, 35
  -of God 13, 14, 17, 112, 114, 117, 121, 122, 133, 152, 173, 174, 180, 182
  -positive 48, 111
  -for the subject 88
  -supralingual 111
laws (see analytic, arithmetic, physical, spatial)
  -normative 13
  -of Mendel 102
  -positivizing of 111, 112
  -supra-analytic 152
laws, modality 44
law-sphere 40, 42, 53, 54, 65, 66, 68, 88, 113, 154, 172, 200, 211 (see also analytic, arithmetic, economic, aesthetic, ethical, physical/ energetic, historical, juridical, lingual, organic, pistic, psychic, spatial, social)
  -and knowing 154
  -good in all 88
  -its universality 65
  -non-analytic 201
leading (of God) 13, 14
leading function 61, 62, 65, 80, 98, 111, 185, 196
left-right 91
length 63
life 11, 15, 113
  -and art 224
  -and *technè* 215

-division of 12
-practical 65, 139, 197
-psychic 130
-unity of 134
life space 65
limit/line 13–15, 25, 143, 174
lines 31, 53, 55, 66
lingual 31
  -list of object functions 66
  -place as subject function 55
lingual 31, 48, 65, 111, 171, 183
  -formulating statements 181, 184
living soul(s) 102, 117, 122, 135
logic 195
logical 31
Logos 117, 121, 124, 133, 134, 136
  -incarnation of the Logos 124, 126
Logos revelation 118, 120–22, 124, 127–34
  -national phase 133
  -patriarchal phase 132
  -its promise of blessing and threat of curse 118
Lord's Supper 125
love 114
love command 114, 116, 135
love of God 129
lupines 105
machine theory 31, 210
machinelike 31
machines 210, 212
management associations
marriage 31, 121, 124
marriage bond 20, 88, 121
mastery 111, 210
  -artistic 217, 220
  -of object by historic subject 108
  -technical 208, 210–212
material (see substance)
mathematical 171
  -character of the subject of a statement 188
  -figure 55
mathematicians 102
mathematics 200
matter 101, 117
meaning 13, 43
meaning of history 121
means 173
means-end 60, 210, 214
meat 130

mechanical 31
Mediator 102, 124, 125, 129
memory 146
metal 210, 211
metaphysics 100
method of the special sciences 201, 202
method, thetical-critical 3
method-pluralism 202
micro-cosmos 121
military service 111
modal 43, 49
modal difference 48, 87, 112, 202
modal diversity 68
modal-being 45
modalities 44, 46–51, 63, 85, 98, 157, 200, 212
-of the subject unit 48, 49
modality of the interrelation 53
moment(s) 78, 79, 93, 160, 204
-perseverance of previous moments in following moments 146
monogenic 121
moral law 114
morphology 31
mortality 134
movement 31, 55, 65
multiplicity 60
mysticism 174
national church 125
natural philosophy 31
natural sciences 202
naturalism, epistemological 160
nature 124, 173
nature–grace-scheme 130
need 111, 212
-aesthetic 218
-historical 209, 210
neighbor 108, 114, 173, 174, 180
neighborly love 114
nihilism, philosophical 3
Noachian covenant 130, 132
noetic 201
non-Euclidean space 65
norm of faith 125
norm of the *principium contradictionis* 176
norm, two-sided character 125
number series 61
number(s) 31, 36–38, 43, 45, 47, 51, 53, 55, 60, 66
-differential and integral 61
-irrational 61

-natural 61
-rational 37
-this number 36–38, 45
-world of 52
nurture 113
nutrition theory 105
obedience, obedient 86, 91, 114, 116, 118, 121, 124, 125, 134, 135, 139, 174, 182
object function 65, 66, 81, 98, 106, 111
-and nonscientific knowledge 108
-by virtue of the structure of thing, plant and animal 111
-in the economic 111, 210
-technical-historical 101
object side 58, 65
object(s) 65, 88, 125, 160, 161, 172 (*see also* subject–object-relation)
-as repetition of substrate in superstrate 65
-examples of 65
objectivism 13, 65, 88
occurrence 60
office 111, 117, 118, 120, 122, 124, 130, 139 (*see* prefunctional office)
office bearer 112, 117, 118, 120, 124, 130, 194 (*see* authority)
-church 125
old-German 111
ontic order 185
order of subject functions (*see* subject functions)
ordering of concepts 181, 182
ordering of statements 181 (*see also* social-didactic)
organic 31, 46, 48, 55, 56, 60, 61, 63, 65, 66, 92, 105, 107
-as retrocipation in the analytic 172
-list of object functions 66
-place as subject function 55
organic law 63
organic law-sphere 107
organism(s) 47, 51, 53, 65, 66, 101, 102, 105, 125
organizations 136
organology 214
orientation point 17, 25
outer interrelation 76, 88, 160–62
outer perception 162
outer world 11
pagan 20, 88

paganism 88, 113
paganistic view of salvation 139
pagans 11, 133, 134
pan-cosmism 13
pantheism 13
paradise 129, 130
parallel between Adam and Christ 102
parallel, within psychic and organic law spheres 107
Parsiism 21
partial apriorism 88
partial cosmism 13
partial theism 13
particular extension of the subject of a statement 188, 189
parties in the covenant 118
passive 82 (*see also* active–passive)
Passover 125, 133
past 7, 12, 108, 122, 125, 136, 163, 164, 173, 177, 178, 180
pedagogy 206
perceptible 65, 81, 136, 160, 161
perception(s) 81, 159, 160, 165–67, 173, 180, 195
 -analytic 83, 146, 162, 172
 -emotional 83, 146
 -inner 162
 -inter-individual 160, 161
 -interrelation of 160, 162, 204
 -intra-individual 160, 161
 -of recollection 167
 -outer 162
 -subject and object here 160, 161
perceptual concepts 176
perceptual space 65
period 48
periods, liturgically festive and ordinary 48
person 124
Person of the Son 124
persuade 125, 194
phenotypical 99
philosophizing 2, 7, 197
philosophy 1, 2, 9–11, 43, 139, 142, 147, 185
 -and art 224
 -and *technè* 215
 -as activity and result 1, 2, 15, 147
 -as complex of statements 1
 -Calvinistic 125
 -current 68, 81, 139

-field of investigation 16
-history of 3, 4, 65
-its orientation point and route 17
-its tradition 43
-limits 2
-place (in cosmos) 5, 10, 11, 14
-task 5, 10, 11, 15
physical 31, 48, 56, 162
 -element 66
 -laws 46
 -material 55
 -matter 101
 -movement 65
 -space 65
 -things 66, 97, 101, 102
physical function
 -change in 102
 -list of object functions 66
 -place as subject function 55
 -retrocipation in the analytic 172
physicists 102
physics 201, 214
physiology 31
pisteology 200
pistic function 57, 88, 112, 125, 135
 -place as subject function 55
 -retrocipations in the pistic 60
pistic law-sphere 65
pistic object 65, 125
 -list of object functions 66
pistic office bearers 113
pistic/subpistic 88
pistical 31, 48, 61, 125
plan of God 121
planes 31
plant(s) 31, 46, 55, 60, 65, 97, 102, 106, 121, 125, 159, 178, 211
point(s) 31, 65, 66
political strikes 196
polyhedron 55
positive law 48, 111
positive-negative (*see* statement's relation)
possessed 138
possibilities 189
 -realm of 182
power 31, 88, 113, 125, 134, 136, 140
power, connections of 111
practical life 65, 139, 197
practical reason 125
prayer 136
preaching 125

predestination 13, 124, 129
predicate 176, 183, 184, 188, 189, 191
prefunctional 92, 93, 113, 114, 121
  -character of love in the love command 114
prefunctional office 117, 118, 121, 122, 133, 136
  -of the Christ/Messiah 133, 136, 140
premise(s) 51, 193
presupposed, being 55, 56
prevailing function (of a connection) 111–13, 136, 196
price 111
priest 121, 133
primary concepts 176
primary statements 185
primary states of affairs 173
principium contradictionis 176
principium exclusae antinomiae 201
principium exclusi tertii 192
priority, social 48
prius and *posterius* 48
problematic 2, 3, 4
process 13
promise of blessing 118, 125
promise of God 118, 124, 125, 129, 130, 132–34, 136
proof 176, 188, 190, 193, 194
prophet 121, 133
propitiate 124
pseudo-religion 92
psychic law 34, 35
psychic law-sphere 107
  -parallel here 107
  -subject–object-relation here 107
psychic life 130
psychic suffering 62
psychic(function) 30, 31, 35, 46, 48, 51, 55–57, 63, 146, 160, 162, 171
  -as retrocipation in the analytic 172
  -as substrate 146, 155, 160
  -list of object functions 66
  -place as subject function 55
  -suprapsychic distinguishing 155
psychology 31, 171, 201
  -of thinking 171
psycho-somatic 146
punishment (of death) 121, 122, 124, 125
qualitative 43
qualities, secondary 65, 66
quantitative 43

quantity 31
rainbow 130
rationalistic 2, 8
realism 13, 185
reason, practical 125
recognition/denial 61
recollectable, what is 164
recollection(s) 73, 77, 81, 82, 160, 163, 166, 171, 173, 180, 195
  -recalling perception 167
  -subject and object here 164
recollection, interrelation of 164, 165
  -intra-individual 164
reconstruction 108
re-creation 120, 124
re-creation, covenant of (=2nd covenant) 119, 123–26
reflect God's glory 117
Reformation 122
regeneration 125
regressus ad infinitum 63
regularity 13
regulative idea 13
relata 72, 73, 77, 78, 93
relation 13, 65, 66, 72, 104, 109, 111, 117, 122, 185 (*see also* subject–object-r.; subject-subject-r.)
  -between things from different realms 104
  -in societal connections 113
  -of simple statements 191
  -of specific composite statements 192
  -of subject and object 66, 196
relational 117
religion 20, 22, 25, 31, 95, 109, 110, 113–16, 118–21, 124, 129, 130, 132–34, 139, 140, 185 (*see also* history of religion; covenant, religious)
  -of the heart 125
  -pagan 88, 92
religious center 139
religious task 121
remembered, assimilating what is 181
Remonstrants 125
repetition (with objects) 65, 68, 172
representation space 65
reproduction 31
  -asexual 101
  -human 102
  -sexual 102, 113
res cogitans 57

resolution 23
respect, those who pay 111, 112
result 117
   -positive/negative 1, 3, 4, 14, 15
resurrection (from the dead) 125
   -revival of the body 139
resurrection 133
retribution 31
retrocipation 60–63, 65, 66, 68, 88, 98, 171, 201
   -in the analytic 172
   -in the pistical 60
   -[in the supraesthetic to the aesth.:] harmonizing interests 60
   -in the supra-analytic to the anal.: elements of thinking and knowing 60, 155
   -in the supra-arithmetic to the arith.: inherent multiplicity 60
   -in the supraeconomic to the econ.: the thrift principle 60
   -in the supraethical to the eth.: the assurance of faith 60
   -in the suprahistorical to the hist.: roll of means-end-scheme 60
   -in the suprajuridical to the jurid.: [doing one's duty] 60
   -in the supralingual to the ling.: sorts of language usage 60
   -in the supraorganic to the organ.: development 60
   -in the supraphysical to the phys.: their dynamic character 60
   -in the suprapsychic to the psych.: the "feel" of things 60
   -in the suprasocial to the social.: commerce 60
   -in the supraspatial to the spat.: occurrences can be tracked 60
return of Christ 134
revelation 12, 135 (*see also*: word revelation)
   -history of 178
righteous, being declared 124, 125
righteousness 117, 122, 139
"right" time 48
river 60
Roman Catholicism 122
rooms 112, 117
route of investigation 17, 23, 25
sacraments 65, 125, 136

sacrifice 60
salts 105
salvation, pagan 139
Satan 122, 124, 129, 136
Saumur, school of 125
scheme of means-end 60
scheme of nature–grace 130
scheme of substrate and superstrate 88
schisms 125
scholasticism 12
school 113, 182
schools of thought 4
science(s) 9, 11–13, 15, 16, 200, 202
   -Christian 125, 173
   -division of faculties 201
   -ecclesiastical 196
   -history as 214
   -humanities 202
   -nature/culture 202
scientific and nonscientific 139, 148, 193
scientific knowing 148, 198
   -nonspecial-scientific 206
scientific language 43
Scriptural belief 13
Scripture/al 2, 12, 173
seasons 130
secondary concepts 176
secondary qualities 65, 66
secondary statements 185
secondary states of affairs 173
seed 125
   -of the serpent 122, 129
   -of the woman 122, 124, 129
self-objectification 66, 88
self-sufficiency 88, 112, 139
senses 62, 65
series 61, 99
sexes 121
similarity 51
simultaneous 48, 77, 82
sin 21, 88, 124, 130, 132–34
skepticism 174
social 31, 48, 55, 111, 194
   -function 112
   -graces 61
   -intercourse 31, 60, 70
social-didactic ordering of statements 181, 185, 205
socialist 112
societal/social connections 107, 109–11, 113

-competence 113
-decision-making and activity in connection with 111
-distinguishing their destination 113
-diversity 112
-functions of (between historical and destination function) 112
-(functional) character 111
-given in virtue of creation 113
-nonChristian pistical 125
-reciprocal relation of 113
-relation to the religion 114
-unique task 113, 114
sociology 201
Son of God 124, 134
-and the human nature 140
sort(s) 22, 23, 99
soul 92, 93, 102, 117, 122, 130, 134, 135, 139
-and body 93, 122
-as setting the direction 93
-prefunctional 93 (*see also* living soul)
sovereign 13, 140
sovereignty 112
space 45, 60, 61, 65
-Euclidean 31, 65
-non-Euclidean 65
-technical 65
space and time 48
spatial 13, 31, 35, 37, 48, 54–57
-as retrocipation in the analytic 172
-figure 40, 43, 66
-laws 35, 46, 54, 55, 63
-law-sphere 65
spatial function
-change in 102
-list of object functions 66
-place as subject function 55
speaking 55
special science(s) 9, 15, 65, 139
-and art 223
-and *technè* 214
-method of 201, 202
special-scientific analysis 201
special-scientific knowing 9, 10, 199–205
speculation 13, 15, 139, 182
sphere sovereignty 112, 113
spirit 92, 134, 135, 139
-and higher functions 139
spirit of Christ 135
spirit of God 22, 117, 125

spirits 20
-world of the 121, 173
spiritual 88 (*see also* substance)
-body 134
spiritualism 139
splitting (of stars) 31
standpoint 2
-one's own 3
starry heaven 20
stars 31, 178
state 47, 111–13, 125, 159, 182
state of affairs 2, 61, 160, 175, 176, 183, 210
-primary 173
-secondary 173
state of innocence 122
state, as connection 113
state, life of 88, 113, 133
statement(s) 171, 172, 175, 176, 181, 183, 185
-complex of 1
-composite 186, 187, 189, 190, 192
-genetic 185, 191
-had immediately and mediately 176, 188
-primary and secondary 185
-simple 183, 185-191
-subject of 183, 184, 188, 189, 191, 192
statement's relation 176, 183, 184, 188, 189
-positive and negative 176, 188, 189
stimulus 65
stone 46
storm 160
strata-theory 63
strikes, political 196
striving (activity) 1, 7, 14
structure 22, 27, 43, 88, 92, 98
-and direction 27, 60n, 95
-and object functions 111
-and the human heart 114
-of a pistic object 125
-of the cosmos 65, 111, 136
-of the covenant 118, 124
-of the functions 98
-of the human 92, 117, 122
-of the human body 113
-of the kingdom and of the humankind 94, 122
-of the knowing 177
-of the work of creation 124

-of nonscientific knowing 149
structure, statements of 185
struggle between Church and world 136
struggle of a Christian 135
subject and object 65, 66, 79, 83, 88, 196
  -with expectation 168
  -with perception 160, 161
  -with recollection 164
  -with the same subject unit 66
súbject function 59–66, 81, 98, 155, 160, 161, 164, 171, 172, 204, 210
subjèct function(s) 49–51, 54, 58, 59, 65, 73, 79
subjèct functions, natural order of 54, 55, 57, 60
subjèct modality 44, 46, 50
súbject side 58
subjèct unit(s) 47, 52, 55, 60–62, 64–66, 68, 70, 74, 80, 81, 88, 139
  -named according to highest function 60
  -their unity 62
subjèct/being-subjèct 17–19, 30, 31, 33–35, 44, 49, 66, 125, 140, 185
  -earthly subject 18, 22, 30, 31, 35, 37, 85, 95–97, 115, 185
  -heavenly subject 18, 19, 85, 185
subjectivism 13, 65, 88
subjectivity 17
subject–object-relation 111, 164, 196
  -and kingdoms 104, 106
  -in analytic law-sphere 107, 108, 160
  -in historical law-sphere 107, 108, 209, 210
  -in organic law-sphere 107
  -in psychic law-sphere 107
subject-subject-relation 111, 108
  -in analytic law-sphere 108, 160
  -in historical law-sphere 108
subsidiarity principle (Roman Catholic) 112
substance, spiritual and material 139, 146
substrate 56, 57, 59–62, 65, 66, 88, 146, 171, 182
  -psychic function as 146, 155, 160
substrate function 56, 57, 60, 65
substrate spheres 100
subsume 8
succession 48, 157, 163 (*see also* interrelation)
successive 78–80, 88, 164, 165, 168

suffering, psychic 62
suggest 51, 82
sun 105
superstrate 56, 57, 59–62, 65, 88
superstrate function 57, 100
surgery 214
symbiosis 51, 53
symbols 160
synagogue 125
synchronic 157, 159, 160
synthetic 201
system 3, 7, 15
task of humankind 109, 129
  -of institutions 113, 114
task, religious 121
taste 218
technè 105, 171, 209, 214
  -difference with technology 214
technical knowing 214
technical space 65
technical-historic 101
teleological pseudo-religion 92
tellurian themes 88
temptation 124, 138
Ten Commandments 114, 133
tension 48
testimony of the Holy Spirit 125
theism, partial 13
theology 200
theory about knowledge 142–44, 147, 197, 198
  -formulating statements 181
  -ordering concepts 181, 182
theory of categories 185
theory of knowledge 6, 10, 76, 147, 160, 179, 196, 197, 201
theses 51, 203, 204
thetical-critical 3
thing 47, 57, 66, 70, 71, 73, 75, 80, 88, 89, 91, 92, 95–97, 99, 101–03, 130
thinking 1, 3, 7–11, 14, 60, 61, 63, 65, 98, 112, 130, 170–72, 178, 196, 214
thinking subject 57, 174, 176, 204
thoughts 160
threat of the curse 118 (*see also* vengeance of the covenant)
thrift principle 60
time 48, 93, 124, 125, 163
  -direction 169
  -of movement 48
today 12, 122, 136, 173, 177

totalitarian 113
totality 114
tradition 31
transition, genetic 100–03
transmigration of the soul 130
triangle 61
trichotomies 57, 139
Triune God 117, 121
troth 31, 65, 113
trusting 60
truth 21, 121, 176, 185
truth claim 188, 189
unbelief 12, 130, 132, 133
understand 108, 117, 172, 180, 183, 185
unilateral 118
unity of humankind 121
unity of the subject unit 62
universal extension of the subject of a statement 188, 189
universality of the law-sphere 65
uranic 88
value 182, 185
-economic 31, 65, 210
vegetation gods 130
vengeance of the covenant 125
verb, time of the 48

verification 193
vertical 98, 156, 170, 201
vinculum substantiale 124
vitamins 105
whole (and part) 13, 23
will of God 134
will(ing) 63, 125
-historical w. to order 181
wisdom 1
word of God 115, 118, 122, 124, 125, 136, 138, 173, 178
word revelation (of God) 11–15, 20, 25, 121, 145, 146, 180, 182
word, the preached 125
words 13
work of God 99
work of the Holy Spirit 121, 125
works of art in higher interrelation 221
world 13, 121, 122, 136, 139 (*see also* angels, spirits, Church and w.)
-inner and outer 11
-of numbers 52
-picture 21
-subject 66, 88
wrath of God 121, 122, 124, 134

Index of Names

N.B. The numbers after the names refer to the numbered paragraphs in the text.

Archimedes (287-212 B.C.) 61
Aristotle (384-322 B.C.) 174
Avenarius, R. (1843-1896) 43
Barth, K. (1886-1968) 13
Bavinck, H. (1854-1921) 2
Becher, E. (1882-1929) 2
Boethius (480-524) 189
Calvin, J. (1509-1564) 13
Descartes, R. (1596-1650) 7, 8, 57
Drews, A. (1865-1935) 2
Fichte, J.G. (1762-1814) 2
Fullerton, G.S. (1859-1925) 2
Galileo Galilei (1564-1642) 160
Hartmann, Ed. von (1842-1906) 2
Hegel, G.W.F. (1770-1831) 13, 15
Heinemann, F. (1889-1969) 3
Herbart, J.F. (1776-1841) 2
Hobbes, Th. (1588-1679) 182
Husserl, E. (1859-1938) 2
Kant, I. (1724-1804) 31
Kepler, J. (1571-1630) 160
Kohnstamm, P.A. (1875-1951) 124
Külpe, O. (1862-1915) 2
Kuyper, A. (1837-1920) 12, 112, 125
Land, J.P.N. (1834-1897) 2
Leibniz, G.W. (1646-1716) 182
Luther, M. (1483-1546) 65
Mendel, G.J. (1822-1884) 102
Nestorius (c.375-c.450) 124
Nicholas of Cusa (1401-1464) 13
Parmenides (c.540-c.475 B.C.) 121
Paulsen, F. (1846-1908) 2
Plato (427-347 B.C.) 174
Pythagoras (c.575-c.497 B.C.) 1
Raeymacker, L. de (1895-1970) 2
Renouvier, Ch. (1815-1903) 2
Reyer, W. (..-..) 2
Russell, B. (1872-1970) 2

Ursinus, Z. (1534-1583) 122
Van Andel, H.A. (1875-1945) 2
Walch, J.G. (1693-1775) 2
Wattjes, J.G. (1879-1944) 2
Windelband, W. (1848-1915) 2
Wundt, W. (1832-1920) 2

Names from the Bible

Aaron 133
Abraham 130-134
Adam (the first) 102, 117, 121, 122, 124, 134, 135, 136, 139, 180
Adam (the second) 117, 124, 126, 127, 140 (*see also* Christ; Jesus Christ)
Cain 129
Christ (the) 12, 31, 88, 102, 114, 116, 124, 125, 134–36, 138–40 (*see also* Adam, the second; Jesus Christ)
David 133
Eve 102, 121, 122, 124, 129, 180
Isaac 132
Jacob 132
Jesus Christ 140 (*see also* Adam, the second; Christ)
Judah 132, 133
Melchizedek 132, 133
Messiah 133, 134
Moses 133
Nathanael 134
Noah 130, 131, 132
Paul 88, 134, 135
Sarah 132
Shem 130

www.ingramcontent.com/pod-product-compliance
Lightning Source LLC
Chambersburg PA
CBHW032113090426
42743CB00007B/337